Street Z...

Street Zen

The Life and Work of Issan Dorsey

TENSHO DAVID SCHNEIDER

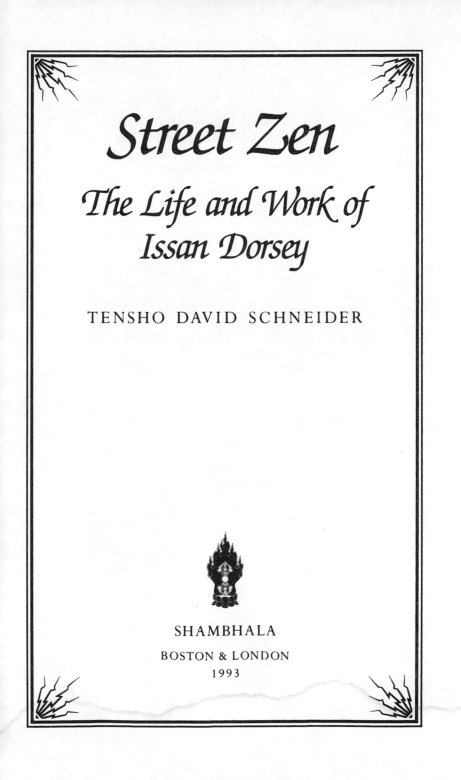

SHAMBHALA

BOSTON & LONDON

1993

Shambhala Publications, Inc.
Horticultural Hall
300 Massachusetts Avenue
Boston, Massachusetts 02115

© 1993 by David Schneider

9   8   7   6   5   4   3   2

Printed in the United States of America on acid-free paper ∞
Distributed in the United States by Random House, Inc.,
and in Canada by Random House of Canada Ltd

Library of Congress Cataloging-in-Publication Data

Schneider, David, 1951–
Street Zen: the life and work of Issan Dorsey/David Schneider.
        p.   cm.
        ISBN 0-87773-914-5
    1. Dorsey, Issan, d. 1990.   2. Gay men—Religious life.
3. Priests, Zen—United States—Biography.   4. Gay men—United
        States—Biography.   I. Title.
        BQ950.O77S25   1993   93-22186
        294.3'927'092—dc20   CIP
        [B]

Dedicated respectfully to
Shunryu Suzuki-roshi,
Tamer of Untamable Beings,

and to Mark Foster Ethridge
and Willie Snow Ethridge

Contents

Preface

From 1972 until his death in 1990, Issan Tommy Dorsey was my best friend, both in the usual sense of the word and in a spiritual sense. He conquered difficulties presented by the Zen path one after another; he was kind and welcoming, and I've often thought that just by being who he was, he made it possible for me to practice Buddhism.

That I feel this way isn't particularly remarkable. In fact, it's an odd admission for someone proposing to write an evenhanded biography. The truth is that, with slight adjustments in dates, there are a hundred people who could have written that first paragraph and who would subscribe to it today: "Issan Tommy Dorsey was my best friend."

Issan's life, painted in broad strokes, seems a kind of salvation story: a person begins in a middling station of life, slides rapidly and pleasurably into a hell, pulls himself out of it, then dedicates the rest of that life to working for the benefit of others. Because Issan used Zen meditation and Zen community to extricate himself from a destructive path, his biography can be read as a kind of Buddhist success story.

On a more intimate level, the story of Issan's daily life, and his "good" and "bad" sides—or at least his socially acceptable and socially reprehensible sides—takes a complicated shape.

While he practiced Buddhism at the San Francisco Zen Center or in Santa Fe, or even as he operated the Maitri Hospice, Issan never acted much like an angel, nor like a particularly "pure" person. Similarly, when he ran the streets as a drug-addicted, alcoholic, female impersonator hooker, he never acted much like a devil. Associates from those days always describe how special he seemed: patient, accepting, compassionate. Zen students, on the other hand, might tell you about his pettiness. He could be a dictatorial, fussy, bitchy pain in the ass.

People from all periods of his life will readily use the word *outrageous* in talking about Issan. Outrageous. Far out. Applied to Issan, the word means he actually outraged people, which in fact he did all his life. Some of his caregivers, it's safe to say, felt moments of outrage about his relationship to pain-killing drugs and the amounts of these drugs he asked for right up to his death.

The point I would like to make here is that Issan Dorsey's difficult and benevolent instincts were present and operative in him throughout his life. His acceptance of all sides of himself—in fact his celebration of them—distinguishes him from most of his Buddhist contemporaries.

Though I'd been thinking of writing Issan's biography for a few weeks and had discussed the idea with him, I actually began to work on the project the day of his installation as abbot of the Hartford Street Zen Center on November 4, 1989. Issan died ten months later, in early September 1990. In this interim, we did a dozen interviews, which I recorded on audiotape. We took two trips to Southern California together, one for vacation and rest, and one during which Issan taught a weekend seminar at the Ojai Foundation, near Santa Barbara. Throughout this period, and until all the major ceremonies surrounding Issan's death were complete, I kept a journal. Here I wrote down significant conversations that we had away from a tape machine, and I also tried to record his physical decline and death. I introduce some of this material toward the end of the book.

Issan was very much in favor of my undertaking this biography, though he never saw anything of it other than an outline. He was flattered personally by the attention, but also he seemed to want the story told for the encouragement it might provide to others. Issan gave me introductions to his relatives and to friends from every period of his life, including several people whom he thought I should see because they held a low opinion of him. With all these associates I also recorded dozens of interviews. When the time came to write the book, I could not see how my labors at composition would improve the direct speech of these colorful people. Much of the text then is drawn from these interviews. To protect their privacy, I've changed the names of several people. There are not, however, any composite characters here; everyone is a real person.

In telling Issan's story, I tried to steer clear of both sensationalism and cover-up. I aimed to reflect in my account the level of detail Issan himself used about each of the periods of his life. Wherever possible, his own words speak directly.

It may offend some readers to read about the actual life of a female impersonator, or to hear details of initiation into a gay lifestyle. Aspects of Issan's life often shocked me as well. But as a biographer, I envisioned my job as being simply to tell the story, not to edit out difficult episodes. Issan's was, by any standard, a remarkable life; I can't presume to know which parts made it so and which parts were ordinary. I've imitated Issan's own spirit of frankness then, and included, with as little judgment as possible, everything I could discover.

Acknowledgments

Readers of this book will see that most of the words in it come from other people; it would have been impossible to construct it without their help. The following people submitted to interviews, and I am very grateful to them: Steve Allen, Reb Anderson, Richard Baker, David Bullock, Howard Cassassa, Jan Clark, Peter Coyote, Ann Dee, David and Sharon Dorsey, Ed Kenzan Levin, Richard Levine, Mickey Martin, Reggie Mason, Barbara Nichols, Joel Roberts, Paul Rosenbloom, Angie Runyon, Marlene Sorum, Frances Thompson, Eddie Troia, Phyllis Vittel, and Carolyn Ware. In addition, Sharon Kehoe generously made available to me transcripts of interviews she conducted for a film about Issan and the Maitri Hospice.

A number of people, hearing about the project, wrote to me or called with stories. For these kindnesses, I thank: Steve Abbott, Elisa Atkinson, Joanna Bull, Bruce Jewell, Iva Jones, Robert Lytle, Dennis Marshall, Marilyn Montgomery, Bob Roberts, John Steiner, Teah Strozer. I am particularly indebted to Joanna Bull, who came up with the book's title, over long-distance telephone, with no warning whatsoever.

Many people contributed material and logistical help, without which the book would have remained just another good idea. In this regard, I am particularly grateful to: Tim Brackett, Del Carlson, Tyrone Cashman, Joseph Jacobs, Michael Jamvold, Joan Halifax, the Hartford Street Zen Center, James Hormel, Ken Ireland, Michael Katz, Pamela Krasney, Robert Levering, Amy Lyman, Gaetano and Ayelet Maida, Connie Packard, Vanja Palmers, Hilary Parsons, Ted and Amita Preisser, Hanelor Rossett, Marc and Georgia Schneider, and Larry Watson.

Issan Dorsey was extremely photogenic, and something of a ham. Watching him with photographers afforded me valuable insights. I shared their aim, obviously—of recording a remarkable person—and I thank them, regardless of whether or not their work appears here: Morgan Alexander, Lise Kraal, Rob Lee, Barbara Lubanski-Wenger, Eileen O'Leary, Judi Russell, and Gigi Carroll Sims.

The book concentrates rather narrowly on Issan Dorsey. This focus was possible because remarkable writing has already been done about the founding of Buddhism in America generally, and about San Francisco Zen Center specifically. Readers who care to know more about these things should enjoy Rick Fields's *How the Swans Came to the Lake* and Helen Tworkov's *Zen in America*. For reports on the Zen Center troubles of 1983, see Katy Butler's article in *CoEvolution Quarterly 40* (Winter, 1983) and a later piece by Lewis MacAdams in *California* magazine ("Love Conquers Zen," March, 1988). Thanks to Arnold Kotler and Parallax Press for permission to reprint "Please Call Me by My True Names."

Many people read portions of the manuscript and contributed helpful corrections and criticism. Some of these readers have been mentioned above in other contexts; in addition, I want to thank: Keith Abbott, Rachel and Douglas Anderson, Frank and Helen Berliner, Christine Brand, Casey Conroy, Dana Dantine, Susan Edmiston, Charles Galatis, Carol Gallup, Barbara Grob, Amy Hertz, John Iammarino, Tracy Johnston, Denis Kelly, Marty Krasney, A. Pesci, Alix Pitcher, Britton Pyland, Dean Rolston, Gabrielle Roth, Jack Shoemaker, Andrew Zoldan. In particular, this book owes a great deal to the suggestions of Peter Matthiessen.

I had illuminating discussions about the full text with Martha Casselman, Art Moore, Amanda and Fred Stimson, and especially with my editor, Emily Sell. I am very grateful for their time and attention. Despite all this help, inaccuracies, mistakes, or oversights that remain are solely my responsibility.

Finally I want to thank my wife Melissa Moore, who first saw that this book must be written and that I had to do it. Her unfailing support, provocative criticism, and pride in me were invaluable.

Issan gave inspiration, courage, and humor to companions all his life. I can only hope his life's story will continue to do that.

1

The Mountain Seat

For a follower of Zen Buddhist life, the Mountain Seat Ceremony is aptly named because it marks a peak of Zen training. In this ceremony, a new abbot is installed in a temple. The person honored at the ceremony is usually installed by their teacher; thus they have approval from above. A proper Mountain Seat Ceremony draws local Zen and Buddhist peers, who question and confirm the new abbot as worthy. The abbot will have worked deeply and for years with his or her own students, so that to them, the new title changes little. It formalizes the relationship somewhat—an important shift because it makes their practice together more public and honorable. The ceremony crystallizes daily life and puts all mundane actions into the context of a lineage of ancestors. It is graduation, birthday, marriage, anniversary, bar mitzvah, and cor-onation rolled into one. Proclamation. Celebration. A big deal.

This morning though—November 4, 1989—things haven't quite come together yet at the Hartford Street Zen Center in San Francisco. Zen students busily unfold chairs to fill the dining room and living room, each twelve by fifteen feet and carpeted with a faint purple rug worn by age and traffic to an indistinct gray. The chairs face a bay of windows, with a stage rigged in front of it. *Stage* is perhaps too grand a word; more accurately, the chairs face a big plywood box with a tatami mat on top. Three rickety stairs lead up to this platform, and the whole contraption is nestled as far back as possible in the bay of windows. A black mat and a black pillow complete the pile, providing a focal point. Were a person to sit on the pillow, they would seem to be floating in space against a backdrop of trees. This is the Mountain Seat.

Issan Dorsey, who will soon climb the shaky stairs—ascend the Mountain and take his seat as abbot—prepares himself upstairs in his room. Because he hates to rush, he got up earlier than usual—not at 4:00 A.M., as he has done for the past twenty years (those days are gone, done in by the medicines), but early. He's had a cup of coffee, eaten a light breakfast, and taken the first round of medications. Issan then bathed and shaved his head. His skin, flaky from years of drug abuse, has already drunk several applications of lotion and thirsts for more. As he dresses, he pauses to work more balm into his face and head and hands.

Dressing takes a while. He pads stiffly around his room, going from closet to dresser to miror to desk, back and forth, getting the layers of his robes to fall just right, drinking lots of water as his doctor told him he must, working the cloth, keeping himself calm. Naturally he's nervous. He puts on lip balm, checks his notes, keeps steady.

All over the San Francisco Bay Area, people are preparing to come to Issan's Mountain Seat Ceremony. His old partner and manager, Mickey Martin, puts on a white shirt and leaves his house in Sonoma. Eugene, a crony from the psychedelic Haight Street days, makes last-minute arrangements, dons a sport coat, and heads across town. Zen students and Zen teachers cinch robes, pack up religious implements, and converge. None of the travel is easy. San Francisco's most recent earthquake struck just a month ago, knocking out a section of the Bay Bridge and snarling traffic patterns. People have now learned to allow hours of extra travel time.

Consequently at 2:00 P.M., a half-hour before the ceremony is scheduled to begin, a crowd throngs 57 Hartford Street, milling not only in the two main rooms but in the kitchen and hallways and spilling onto both front and back porches. Everyone wears their fanciest robes, their most dignified suits; the happy chatter of reunion floats in the air.

Issan sits next door—as is traditional—receiving visitors. As the abbot-designee, he must come from another building, stop first at the main gate and recite a verse, something he's written. He'll do the same at each important room in the temple until he gets to the Mountain Seat, where the most public parts of the ceremony will occur. Technically, he's already sitting on the temple grounds, even though he's next door; he's seeing guests in the Maitri Hospice. A few months ago Issan fulfilled a passion by obtaining a long-term lease on this adjacent building. He now has a whole house he can fill with homeless people with AIDS. Carpenters have just knocked out walls between the two buildings so that temple and hospice are now literally indivisible. Their functions flow back and forth through the blown-open walls.

Time to go. The musicians line up: first the high bell, leader of the procession, then Issan and attendants, then a low-bell ringer, and a person to strike sharp wooden clackers. The big *taiko* drum is stationary, but it booms an echo to the other instruments. Issan himself carries a ceremonial wooden staff with three iron rings affixed to the top. It rattles and thuds with each step. The crowd, jammed and jostling in the two rooms, follows the procession by its music: *Bing . . . bong . . . rattle-thud . . . clack . . . boom . . . rattle-thud . . . bing . . .* Members of the procession walk like elephants, very slowly.

A new ring, a trilling bell—at first no one notices. Hearing it, Issan suddenly detours the procession from its prescribed route, taking it to the room of one of the very sickest men in the hospice. The man has fallen from his bed. Too weak to pull himself back on, he had managed to reach his attendant bell and ring it. Issan hands his things to an attendant, stoops over, and helps the man back into bed. "We came here just to see you," he says, then straightens his robes and continues. The crowd downstairs knows nothing.

The procession leaves the hospice through the front door and congregates on the porch of 57 Hartford. Issan turns and says, "The doors of Hartford Street Zen Center, Issan-ji, One Mountain Temple, stand wide open. While I remain within this place, the doors shall never be closed to any living thing." Speaking then for all the residents and practitioners, David Senseri welcomes Issan with a few sentences.

The group clomps into the temple, following Issan past the waiting crowd and upstairs to his bedroom. Here he addresses his Zen teacher Zentatsu Richard Baker-roshi, who had been waiting there: "Settled in closeness, I am always with you."

They snake back to the first floor, then down to the meditation hall in the basement. A little section of the room has been set aside with a shrine for Shunryu Suzuki-roshi, Issan's first Zen teacher, dead since 1971. "Roshi, at your disciple Zentatsu Myoyu's Mountain Seat Ceremony, you gave us a teacher and told us to call him 'roshi.' I heard you. Thank you for this practice, my name, my teacher. Your continuing presence is the form of our practice."

Issan then offers incense and silent prostrations to images of Tibetan Buddhist teacher Chögyam Trungpa, Rinpoche, and to Shakyamuni Buddha.

On the main floor, the procession troops into view at last. The musicians play their final notes as Issan arrives at the Mountain Seat. He speaks facing the seat, his back to the assembled hundreds. It looks as if he's just talking to a pillow in front of a window: "This incense is offered for the Buddha of no-marks, the Buddha who is all things, for Shakyamuni Buddha, for all buddhas who do not know they are buddhas, for the protectors of Buddhism, for the ancestors who with unceasing effort crossed the ocean of one-point, bringing us this immense Dharma, and especially our first teacher in America, Shogaku Shunryu-daiosho. For this fruit of many *kalpas,* all the world pays homage."

Then in an unscheduled speech, Issan turns and faces the audience. "This Mountain Seat, climbed many times before, is the everywhere-*bodhimandala.* With the help of Baker-roshi and everyone here, and in the ten directions and the three times, I will climb this mind-seal altar. Do not wonder about it at all."

Before he actually climbs up to the Mountain Seat, Issan doffs one robe, dons another, and stands while statements of support for his work and teaching are read. Jerry Berg speaks for the gay community: "It became clear to me that your intentions were to establish a Buddhist practice engaged in unity. . . . It has happened, and it's something that makes all of us feel very happy. It seems so appropriate and connected that this center is also a hospice because that is what is going on in the community now. I want to thank you, Issan, for sharing with the gay community your heart, your practice, and who you are. We are all so enriched by it."

Next, Dr. Richard Levine, medical director of the hospice, says: "I'd like to convey to you, Issan, the affection and the support of the community of people working with AIDS in this area, and more particularly my own love and deepest wish that you continue for a long time to come."

Speaking on behalf of Buddhists near and far, Blanche Hartman says, "Today, as One Mountain prepares to ascend One Mountain, all the beings in the Dharma realm rejoice." The name *Issan* means "One Mountain." "This Bodhisattva brings his big wide heart to stand on the mountaintop and shine the light of wisdom and compassion for us all. May your Dharma live long and prosper, and may your descendants be many."

Once in his seat, Issan gives a very short teaching on the theme of "settling in closeness." He summarizes: "I'd like to recite a poem my teacher and I both like, from the koan 'Where to Meet After Death':"

> True friendship transcends intimacy or alienation.
> Between meeting and not meeting, no difference.
> On the old, fully blossomed plum tree
> South branch owns the whole spring.
> North branch owns the whole spring.

In the Zen tradition, Issan adds his own verse:

> We have bonds with each other that are more
>   important than life or death.
> Ah! the original face has no birth or death.
> Spring is in the plum flower
> Entering a painted picture.

Next, questions. The only real challenge comes as Philip Whalen—also a Baker-roshi Dharma heir, resident at Hartford Street, poet, and Zen man in his own right—rises to speak: "Hojo-sama. The One Mountain has two peaks; which one is real?" Silence covers the room for a few moments. Issan beams at Philip and says softly, "Neither one of them."

Baker-roshi makes his closing remarks in a voice crackling with emotion: "Life and death, appearance and mind, one breath tastes awareness. The Dharmakaya throne has been realized. *The Dharmakaya throne has been realized.* Issan is here, at home at Issan-ji, One Mountain Temple."

A final bell rings, the musicians retrieve their instruments, and Issan threads the procession out, past practitioners, admirers, and friends. But then something stops him. "Uh, just one more thing. There's a saying that I always like to use. I first heard it from my friend Eugene. It's by Meher Baba:

" 'It's a divine art to be cheerful. Do your best. Don't worry. Be happy.' "

The crowd rises and cheers, breaking into applause and tears.

A few weeks later, Issan claims his new post is "nothing special. It's good for Buddhism that there is a seat here now, that will stay here and be passed on. It's also good for the gay community. For me, it's the same as before. Just daily life, you know, one thing after another—with a little more hassle maybe."

2
A Little Bit Different

When Issan Dorsey climbed the Mountain Seat to Zen abbotship, he'd trod one of the most unusual paths in history to such an honor. It began however, in the usual way. Born March 7, 1933, in Santa Barbara, the first issue of Thomas James Dorsey, Sr., and his wife, Marjorie McBride, the boy was christened Thomas Junior and called Tommy.

His father was descended from Irish and Scottish stock; most of this side of the family lived in New York. Marjorie's family—her mother and maternal grandparents, particularly—was from Italy and had adapted their native lifestyle to the Mediterranean climate of Santa Barbara. Tommy: "There was an Italian feeling in the early years, when Great-grandpa was alive. We'd go to their home, and they had homemade wine and fresh bread, and every day you'd sit down and have bread, and wine, and minestrone on the front porch. A rocking chair on the front porch.

"My Italian family all got along very well with the Mexicans. Most of my Italian family spoke Spanish. My great-grandfather bought land—the Italian side of the family was all rich, but you would never know it to look at them. They were just ordinary people.

"Being young in California was fascinating: the fiestas in Santa Barbara, the Mexican people around my family that I knew growing up, watching my grandmother work and cook and scrub clothes in the sink, digging and cooking—I just thought it was wonderful."

Tommy loved his grandmother very much. She was a sharp, successful real-estate speculator, yet she lived frugally and close to the earth. Most important for Tommy, she was gentler with him than were his young parents. "When I stayed at home, if I peed the bed, I got spanked. When I stayed at Grandma's house, she woke me up in the middle of the night and took me to pee, so I didn't wet the bed.

"Grandmother was always buying houses, and she and my mother would fix them up and sell them. My grandmother had more houses than she knew what to do with. She didn't even know how many houses she had. She was a real-estate mogul. They had money, but they all worked. Grandma left quite a bit of money to her grandchildren."

Her investments notwithstanding, the woman labored vigorously all her life, according to Tommy's sister Carolyn: "She always did heavy, hard, manual work. She was a saver—she wouldn't spend money for any frivolities. She walked everywhere. Occasionally she'd take a bus, but she almost always walked. She did her laundry by hand. She would wash the sheets in the sink with a scrub board. She'd get out there with a saw and an ax and trim her own trees, chop up the firewood. She was very sturdy. . . . She even worked for other people, did the laundry, housework, cooking. She did it all her life."

While relations were pleasant in the extended clan ruled by this hard-working matriarch, young Tommy found it tougher at home. Thomas Senior had a temper that could get out of hand at times, and the boy felt, even early on, an odd distance from his family.

"I think I was a neurotic child, a problem child—a confused or strange child. I don't think I ever related to my family quite in the way I would have liked to because they didn't know what they were doing, or what to do with me. I wasn't exactly what they expected, I think. They were twenty-one or twenty-two, and I was the first one, so they're having a boy, and all of a sudden their boy is a sissy. I think they loved me, but they didn't really know what to do with me. I don't remember ever being very close to them. It was sort of, they are the mother and father, and you're supposed to be close. But there was no real bond."

If the young Dorseys didn't know much about raising children, they certainly knew how to produce them. Three years after Tommy was born, Marjorie gave birth to Phyllis; then, in rapid succession to Carolyn, Mary Ann, David, Teresa, Claudia, Patsy, Louie, and Margie. The Dorseys moved to a seventeen-room house just a few blocks from the old Santa Barbara Mission. As one of his wedding promises, Mr. Dorsey had agreed to a Catholic upbringing for his children, and he was the kind of man who kept his word. Consequently, the children marched off to church each Sunday, to parochial grade school during the week, and to parochial high school when they came of age—unless they went into the seminary, of course. Tommy's younger brother David did attend the seminary, and Tommy was on a path there himself: "When I was in school, I felt very strongly that I wanted to be a Catholic priest. I loved one of the Franciscan priests, and when the nuns found out that I—about me and my *vocation* to be a priest—they really were at me. They wanted me to be in the church praying for my vocation on recess time, instead of going to recess. It was a real *thing*: 'Tommy Dorsey is going to be a *priest*.' That was just all there was to it.

"Came time to go to the seminary—you either go to seminary or to high school—I was still wetting the bed all those years. That's why I didn't go into the seminary, because I was afraid to, wetting the bed."

He went instead to Santa Barbara Catholic High School, the

first of a long string of siblings to attend. The family scraped by in the early days, largely because Mr. Dorsey worked indefatigably. Mrs. Dorsey retreated to her house and garden, overwhelmed by her brood, "but Daddy worked. If he got money from Grandma, helping with the big house that we lived in, *if* he got it, he paid it back. He used to *work*.

"He worked in a restaurant, and then he sold coffee beans; then finally he worked his way up. He was a contract analyst, and then he was the highest-paid civilian at Point Wianimi, a navy base. So Daddy made good money and took good care of us."

Like many children in big families, the younger Dorseys also learned to take care of themselves. If someone wanted to wear a particular garment, they cleaned and pressed it themselves; they each fixed their own breakfast and packed their own lunch. The ten children competed for the two bathrooms, for the single telephone, and sometimes for the food at the table. Everyone was expected to be at dinner, a more or less formal gathering, but no conversation took place. Mr. Dorsey cooked and portioned out servings, and the siblings soon realized that any lapse in attention or any delay in eating meant their share might turn up missing. Dessert was served only on birthdays, which meant once a month; each member of the family had their birthday in a different month (and different from Christmas, too), except Tommy and his father.

Mr. Dorsey liked things to be orderly, and he expected the children to keep their rooms straight. Though he never, in the memory of any of the children, fought or argued with his wife, he was a fairly strict disciplinarian. Corporal punishment was common practice in those days, and Mr. Dorsey meted out his share, sometimes with a belt. Tommy even caught it once from his mother, who was usually slow to anger. Carolyn: "I only saw my mother lose her temper once, and it was at Tommy. She chased him up the stairs with a broom. The final outcome was that she had him downstairs on the kitchen floor, sitting on him, yelling at him. He was in high school, and he had come home late. He snuck out and had come home late."

Tommy had been provoking her for a while, however, with scampish behavior. David: "She'd give him money to go get a haircut, and he wouldn't get the haircut, and he'd come home, and of course there'd be hell to pay. He'd claim he got a haircut, but it was pretty obvious that he hadn't, even then, when hair wasn't very long anyway."

Tommy hated to study. He despised even the idea of homework, and it showed; he became a very mediocre student. In the arts, however, he excelled. He drew beautifully, played piano, acted, sang, and danced. Carolyn and Phyllis: "There were musical instruments around the house, but none of us were any good at playing them. Tommy was the talented one. Our grandmother bought him a baby grand. He had lessons at school. They'd hit your fingers with a stick—if you hit a wrong note, they'd hit your fingers. They were strict."

The high school also mounted an operetta each year as a fundraiser. Tommy worked on the shows and several times played leading roles. He began performing regularly with a young classmate named Marlene Shapro: "In high school Tommy Dorsey walked into my life. He was about five feet tall, a redhead, with freckles, and we just became fast, fast friends. He's the closest thing I ever had to a brother.

"We danced together for the next four years, and those four years were absolutely terrific. He was such a good friend. It seems like he was involved in everything I did—we were in each other's heads. We spent hours, hours practicing.

"Their house was a big old house, and we practiced in the ballroom. There was nothing in there; I don't know what they used it for. It was a huge, wonderful room, I don't remember there even being a chair in there. I very seldom saw any of the Dorseys. We didn't spend time in each other's homes, except for practice. We both sort of escaped from our homes. . . .

"We did a lot of tap, we did a lot of shows, we went to army and navy bases and entertained, and we did revues for the college. Sometimes we got paid, for a club or something. We did a cakewalk for a revue—an exhausting kind of thing, but fun. We choreographed most of our own things. We performed at the Fox Theater in a contest, and we won—we won a cigarette lighter and holder, and he gave it to me because he didn't smoke.

"He loved to dance. He loved to entertain, but he didn't really know what he wanted to do. He never gave any indication of being a particularly original thinker—he was much more a follower than a leader. *Much* more a follower, and comfortable with it. But as a dancer, he was wonderful.

"We both took lessons—and had to struggle to support it—from a couple named the DeCottas, Jack and Evelyn. They'd come to Santa Barbara and taken us on as students. Jack DeCotta had all of Bill Robinson's routines, and he wanted to give them to us, but Tommy was really the only one who was capable of doing them. He was a much better dancer than I was. He could have learned them if I had hung in there and pushed him.

"Jack DeCotta was really interested in Tommy going on with it, but he didn't. He didn't have the drive. And he had other things he wanted to do. But he was delightful, and he was really *cute*. Freckles and red hair, and he just looked good. It worked."

Tommy kept up a good front, socially. He made friends, he dated girls, and he even professed serious crushes from time to time. But in terms of sexuality—a subject typically much on the minds of high schoolers—Tommy felt a little removed from the behavior of the students around him: "I was making an effort to be normal, but it just didn't work. There were three or four girls along the way that I liked. I used to kiss them and muster up all my energy to play with their boobs—not really like I couldn't help doing it, but this is what you were *supposed* to do. I never had sex with any of them—it just didn't happen. Some of those girls liked me so they were kind of encouraging me to get it on, but I was very shy. I never had sex with a woman until after I was already quite gay."

At the same time, he was going through the usual adolescent exploration of male sexuality: "It's what boys do. Most of the guys I was fooling around with are married and have kids now. I was just more into it than they were, and I didn't even know it. We were mostly just jacking each other off. I was sort of scared of all of it, because of my religious background. I don't know, it just wasn't an option then. It was sort of like it accidentally happened with other guys. You'd stay over their house—they used to like to invite *me* to stay over at their house at night, because they knew it was probably going to accidentally happen. That used to happen with quite a few other guys, as a matter of fact. There was nothing said about it, before or after; there was no lovemaking, absolutely not. It was just sort of mechanical."

Then he met Leland. "We were working in the Children's Theater Group together, a number of us. We were studying not only how to be in the plays but how to build sets, do the lights and all that. A number of us were buddies—maybe five of us, a clique. This young man was a very fine actor, and he was going with this girl whose father was the director of the museum, and we went to the movies—Leland, her, and myself.

"I hadn't come out of the closet exactly, yet. I had only done the fooling around you do when it's not gay, it's just fooling around.

"So we went to the Fox Theater. I always thought Leland was kind of cute, and all of a sudden his knee was rubbing against mine. I thought, oh my god, he likes me. So then he kind of put his hand on my knee, so I put my hand on his. That really was a *tremendous* experience for me. I mean, it really wiped me out—

not the movie, I can't even remember what the movie was—but this man, who I liked, who was with his girlfriend.

"We took his girlfriend home, and he and I walked off to the park and made love in the park. We made love in that park a lot, back behind the old Mission. It wasn't really much of a public park; it was kept sort of wild, and not many people went there. That's why we went there. It was kind of on the way to his house.

"He and I had quite a few encounters. I would say that it was my first real homosexual encounter, when I made *love* to somebody. I made love, and had sex also. I was in high school, in my teens. See, I actually made love to him. We held each other in each other's arms, and kissed, and made love, what you call making love.

"But nobody knew, because he was with the girl, so I always kind of felt like—well, he's with her, but I'm kind of seeing him on the side.

"Back then, being gay wasn't a thing that anybody talked about, at all, period. At least not anybody I was around or talking with. The word *homosexual* we knew, but *gay,* I didn't even know that word.

"I read *The City and the Pillar,* and to read this book and see that there were bars where people met—I didn't know that life, because I had never been introduced to it. I read that book and it was all kind of a spark in my mind: 'Oh, I'm a homosexual, there are other homosexuals in the world, they actually meet and have conversations and have friends.' I mean it was nothing like it is now.

"I never talked about it with my family. *Never.*"

While Tommy was becoming acquainted with the problems and pleasures of homosexuality, he also continued his performing life. After graduating from high school, he worked with a new partner in the nascent form of record pantomime. "Sally Grafton and I would pantomime records, and we'd do comedy pantomimes sometimes. We had this one number where I was the man, and between records—we had some way where we'd run quick and change, or we had it on underneath—and all of a sudden, I'd become the woman and she'd become the man. We'd turn our backs fast, and I'd take off my pants, and I had a dress on under; she'd put on a hat. So that was my first attempt at any kind of drag. Comedy drag. 'Wait Till the Sun Shines, Nellie' we used to pantomime, with Bing Crosby."

Tommy drifted along, idly taking classes in a junior college and working in a small way as an entertainer. Then suddenly he made a move: "I hated that junior college worse than regular school—I just never brought a book home and studied with it, period. So I was walking home, carrying these books I was never going to study, by the post office, and I saw 'Uncle Sam Wants You.' I realized in my mind, 'The Korean war is happening, the army is going to get me in a few years.' So I went in and joined the navy—I just walked in and joined.

"I went home and told my parents afterward that I had joined the navy, because I could get in on a kiddy cruise, which meant you just go for three years. That was if I got in, because I was seventeen when I went in to sign up in 1950. They didn't take me until I was eighteen. So then I was supposed to do four years.

"I wanted to get away from home. I wanted to get away from Santa Barbara. I wanted to get away from school. I just wanted out. I wanted to get out there, where there was possibly some gay activity, though I didn't even know the word *gay*."

It didn't take Tommy long to find what he was looking for. "The navy was like a big coming-out party. Immediately after getting out of boot camp, I began meeting the gay men, quite a few of them. They'd take you under their wing.

"I was very young and cute. I had freckles and a cute little ass and that naval uniform, and I was just going along with whatever they wanted to do. We used to go to the bars and drink and cruise, go to cruise Laguna Beach on weekends. Laguna Beach was the big first gay area operating in America, at least in 1950. It was openly gay on the beach, openly gay in the bars. People used to come there from Los Angeles, from all over. They'd rent little rooms, and have parties, and be there for three or four days. They were really experimenting with gay life. It was being allowed in Laguna Beach. There were no raids. . . .

"But I was stationed at Camp Eliot, which was stuck out in the desert, just outside San Diego, and I was in special services. Special services takes care of movies and shows and the library. Sometimes I'd work in the library. I was in a navy show once, called *Sailing Rhythm*. Sally Grafton came and joined me, and we toured whatever navy bases were around.

"They liked me. I was in a lot of navy shows, and a television show once—I was on Ginny Simms. We did shows that were like USOs. They took entertainers and put them in special services.

"We'd also book in other bands, big bands like Stan Kenton, and Bob Hope came. We would organize all this out of special services department, and people in the department who were also entertainers would put on shows. It seems like we did them quite often—once a month."

Being stationed a couple hundred miles from home worked well for Tommy. He'd escaped the familial clutches of Santa Barbara but could visit whenever he wanted. David: "Tommy used to hitchhike and come home. That was big with servicemen back then. I can still picture him in his service uniform, with his duffel bag, and it was always kind of sad to see him leave, go hitchhike back. My dad would give him a ride as far as he could, then he'd hitchhike back to San Diego."

Tommy, on the other hand, found the hitchhiking to be anything but sad. He saw it as an adventure, one that often didn't take him home at all. "Sometimes I'd have a weekend leave. I'd just go outside, walk out of the gate, put my thumb out, and say, 'I wonder where this is going to take me.' I'd just wait for the first car to pick me up. They'd say 'Where you going, sailor? Oh, why don't you come with me.' and I'd go. They'd get me back to the base, and I didn't need any money."

Tommy also became very much involved in the gay world rooted at the base, but extending beyond it: "In special services, I met my 'gay guru,' one of the young men who'd been in the gay world a lot. He took me under his wing and showed me around. He wasn't my lover, but he liked me because I was young and cute. So he used to practice on me, to show me how to do stuff (*laughing*). 'You can suck my dick, then I'll suck your dick.' Then we'd go out and party. We weren't lovers—it was just practice.

"We went out on leave once and came all the way up here to San Francisco and met all his friends. Of course, they were thrilled with me, and I was just passed around from bedroom to bedroom. I loved it. I was happy. See, I didn't realize at the time how cute I was in this little sailor uniform, with these freckles. But I was really mopping! I was really having a good time. Also, I liked to drink, so I was getting drunk and having sex with all these people. . . . Coming up here to San Francisco on leave and going to gay parties—why, I was just the belle of the ball, in my little uniform."

Tommy was in the armed forces, however, and the Korean war was on, so soon he shipped out. "I went to New York first, and we shipped out from there. We were going on a shakedown cruise to Guantanamo Bay, Cuba. A shakedown—how to run the ship, a big rehearsal. The ship went around to Florida, and aboard ship came Mack, out of the brig. He'd been in the brig for some scene—gambling, fighting—and he was cutting hair aboard ship.

"I had been eyeing him because he was a tough. He had scars on his knuckles from fighting, and a tattoo on his arm, a beautiful body because he was a bodybuilder, curls all up in his hair. One day he was coming down a ladder and I was going up. So we were passing each other going up and down the ladder, and I looked over at him. He looked at me, and I leaned over and kissed him. And he kissed me back. Then we started seeing each other every day—we started a relationship that lasted a few years. He was my first real lover, where we said, 'We're lovers. I love you, and we're going to stay with each other forever,' and all that stuff.

"We thought we were being cool, but you can imagine, there was really no way we could be very cool, with three thousand guys on the ship. All the other gay men started hanging around us, of course. We became the nucleus of this gay scene. I had an office where I worked, the Information and Education Office. I had a desk with a record player on it, and we used to tie down the hatches and all these gay guys would come down and dance. We'd smuggle booze aboard ship, and we'd have little parties down there. Mack and I would meet down there and have sex.

"Later, when we were going through the Suez Canal on our way to Korea, we were sleeping up on the deck because it was too hot below. He and I found a place we thought was safe, the captain's quarterdeck or something. No one goes there. You're not even supposed to walk on it. Anyway, we were sleeping there at night because it was a hundred and forty degrees below.

"One night, a light suddenly shined on us, and we were sitting up, trying to get our clothes on. This master-at-arms, this chief petty officer, starts yelling, 'Hey, you guys aren't supposed to be here! Get off here!' But he thought he saw something phony going on there, so he started an investigation. They got next to one of the people who was a friend of ours, and they told him, 'Okay, we know everything about all you gay guys,' or whatever they called us then, probably not *gay guys*—we know all about you guys, and we know about Mack and Tommy and all you guys that hang around them.'

"So he broke down and told them everything. Told them about

times we spent together in my room, everything. And we denied it. They came to us, and we denied it, but we did accept an Undesirable Discharge Under Honorable Conditions. I admitted to having had a sexual relationship with a man sometime while I was in the navy. So they let us have an Undesirable Discharge Under Honorable Conditions, because we accepted the discharge and got out rather than going to a captain's court martial and all that. They threw us off the ship together, Mack and me.

"We were put on an aircraft carrier, and they flew us off to Korea. We went drinking in some beer bar there, away from all the firing going on. Then they flew us from there to Japan. We always had liberty every night; we were in restricted barracks but never behind bars, because we were under Honorable Conditions. It was like a honeymoon. They flew us from there to Guam and from there to Hawaii—we had liberty every place. See, Mack had a lot of money, because he used to gamble, so he had plenty of money."

3

Descent into Heaven

The navy discharged Mack and Tommy on Treasure Island, in the middle of San Francisco Bay. In a long tradition of "blue discharges"—the paper color of the document—the two young men found themselves feeling cut off from their families and past histories, and like thousands before them they wandered into the gay life of San Francisco. Tommy renewed his contacts from his earlier wild partying days, and initially he and Mack stayed with this circle of friends. "We used to live around them, dress in our Brooks Brothers suits, go to the cocktail parties, and do that whole number. I was very chicly dressed, in suits and ties, and I had Mack all dressed up too."

Eventually they set up house together. Ninety dollars a month got them a picturesque flat on Telegraph Hill, with front and backyards, and though neither of them had the temperament for it, they sought straight jobs in downtown San Francisco. They ended up taking a disastrous string of what Tommy called "diddle jobs": "First I worked at the offices, weighing things. Then we both worked at J. C. Penny's. They caught Mack stealing and fired us both, because they knew we were living together. Then I worked for the insurance companies, as a fire underwriter trainee.

"I hated it. Sometimes I didn't make it to work, or else I'd get drunk at work, go out during the breaks and drink too much. I'd always get fired.

"They liked me at all my jobs, and I did good work, but I always got fired.

"I didn't take it seriously. I never took anything very seriously. I never cared about losing a job, or not having a job, or where money would come from. That never entered my mind."

What then did Tommy Dorsey think about?

"My boyfriend. I was taking it kind of loose and getting into other things, too. I went into this club—there was another good-looking guy singing, and I picked him up, brought him home, and stuffed him between Mack and me."

Tommy was just twenty years old; he was healthy, handsome, and very much in love. At the same time, he felt at loose ends. On a quick visit home, probably at Christmas, he told his parents that he'd been discharged from the navy for medical reasons. But he confided in his old dance partner Marlene: "He told me what happened: he told me he'd been kicked out of the navy. . . . He was really upset and didn't know what to do with his life. I gave him the wonderful counseling to go see Father Ryan, this Jesuit priest who was a wonderful human being, but I mean . . . there were no Catholic priests who understood that in that day at all. I don't think there was one anywhere who could counsel anything except 'Stop it right now!' Tommy did go to see Father Ryan, but it was not real successful."

Back in San Francisco and probably for the first time in his life, Tommy lived free from authority figures, parental, religious, or military. The bowstring of his life had been pulled as taut as it would go, and now it was released.

Given his surroundings, Tommy's "loose" approach was not entirely out of line. San Francisco's North Beach scene smoldered with passionate energy all through the 1950s, bursting regularly into brilliant flame. The Purple Onion, the Black Cat, the hungry i, the Jazz Workshop, the Beige Room, and Finnochio's were just a few of the clubs that thrived up and down Broadway, nurturing musical and satirical talent—talent that would later blossom and mark American arts indelibly.

In a recent reminiscence, author Herb Gold describes North Beach in the 1950s as a "concentration so dense that one strategic bomb could have wiped out most of the nation's resources of unrhymed verse." The Beats had just begun their ascension; jazz players rolled in and out of town like the tides; and alcohol and drugs were fashionable. To a young man like Tommy, with aspirations in the entertainment world, North Beach must have seemed like heaven, and a day job writing insurance policies must have felt like an unendurable purgatory.

Mack didn't drink; he worked off whatever dissatisfactions he felt in a gym on Market Street, lifting weights. Tommy traipsed along a few times and even hoisted bars himself, but after work he much preferred to walk in the general direction of home, stopping in not-yet-famous North Beach bars for drinks.

In these clubs, Tommy made two pivotal lifelong friendships: one with an extremely energetic man named Mickey Martin, and one with Ann Dee, the co-owner of a bar called Ann's 440. Their descriptions of Tommy from those days sound nearly identical. Ann: "He was very, very young, in a gray suit with a tie, very straight looking, and he was working as an insurance person, down on Montgomery."

Mickey: "He'd come in after his little insurance thing, with his little Brooks Brothers suit, his shirt and tie, looking very much like he belonged down there." Ann added that she found him *dead charismatic* and that she was attracted to him.

Mickey Martin worked as the maître d' of the Beige Room, also known as the Club of Beautiful Men because of the female impersonator shows there. Oddly, Mickey—a short, sunny man with a gravelly and charming voice—was the only male who actually worked the floor; all the other waitresses were female, hookers or ex-hookers. After closing the Beige Room at two Mickey would work in an after-hours club he'd opened across town, next to Jimbo's Bop City. Here customers would bring their own booze and pay a dollar for a glass with ice. They could hear jazz, buy drugs, and mingle with prostitutes and criminals in a loose, friendly, illegal environment.

Mickey made a name for himself. He was written up by *San Francisco Chronicle* columnist Herb Caen as "The Barefoot Waiter," for obvious reasons. Together with the crowd of Beige Room performers who also lived in his house, Mickey was the focus of a stylish milieu. The group gained a reputation with the throng of entertainers working North Beach. In a world where "cool" and "hip" counted, they were the coolest, the hippest.

Reggie Mason, a young man who later associated professionally with both Mickey and Tommy, describes the scene: "I was the newest member of this whole social organization that was going on here. All the other people had known each other for some time, so I was the newest one in the clique or whatever you want to call it, the whole social scene. . . .

"All sorts of strange people were in and out of this very tight clique. They were the run of Broadway, I mean people who came by: Pearl Bailey, Lenny Bruce, and the whole scene—all knew of this group. If they were in town, they'd go visit them. . . .

"Mickey had an overpowering personality at that time. He was just go, go, go, party all night. . . . Mickey would do anything for you in the world, but he expected total—the word *obedience* is wrong, but that's what he expected. Loyalty. As long as you went along with what Mickey wanted, you were in the inner circle. If you didn't agree with him or if he didn't care for you, then you didn't have a chance to crash into any of this. It was a unique situation. . . . He was a very strong person; he glued the social group together."

Years later, Tommy remarked that he and Mack made "quite a dashing couple" at the time. Ann Dee thought so too, and she quickly hired them—Tommy to work as the host of her club, and Mack as a waiter. A talented singer and enterprising business-woman, Ann had been working herself ragged at the club. She'd acted as maître d', the emcee, occasional waitress, and per-former—everything but bartender, which she left to her imper-turbable partner, Sarah Stanyan. In addition to running her own club, Ann managed several other stage acts, grooming them, connecting them to agents and to other cabaret owners. She hired Tommy and Mack to bring fresh energy to her scene and to ease her daily worries about running the club, but it didn't work out that way. At just this same time, Mickey left his post at the Beige Room and came to work for Ann too, bringing with him his lover, Don Miles, as a piano player. Fresh energy did indeed come flooding into Ann's 440, but with it came wildness and unpredict-ability.

The floor crew drank constantly as they worked through an evening, cutting into profits and making internal disputes more likely and more explosive. As lines of customers stretched down the block, Tommy fought with Mickey and Mack about where to seat them. Everyone wanted to boost their tips by having more customers in *their* station.

Ann: "It was a fun era. I was the only one not having fun. I didn't drink much, and I was determined to be successful as an entrepreneur of clubs and theaters, and a manager of acts. I was terribly ambitious . . . and I'd be frustrated. They called me Simone Legree. 'Simone Legree is coming, duck.' I wanted to run it like my dad would have run it.

"By the time two o'clock came around, they were drunk, and it made me crazy."

Bumptious or not, the crew at Ann's coalesced into an insepa-rable team, working Mickey's after-hours joint as well. Mickey:

"We'd go up there after we closed at two, and work there till six in the morning. We'd eat bennies and just keep working. We made so much money at that time—and spent it just like we made it. It was coming in too fast. All of a sudden it was high times. But we all got together then, and as a clique we sort of stuck together. One little crowd, you know.

"We were all very entertaining. If we finished at two o'clock in the morning, we'd all gather someplace, mostly my place, and make sandwiches and smoke joints and tell each other our whatevers. 'Cause we worked all night, we'd gather and sleep until eleven or twelve the next day. That was our social life."

Social life, however, did not run smoothly. Squalls and jealousies rose with the shifting passions in this high-strung group. At one point, Mack and Ann Dee took up with each other. Even though Tommy had had a tempestuous relationship with Mack all along— one that survived several separations—the affair with Ann split them irreparably. Mack lived briefly with Ann, and Tommy, brokenhearted, moved into Mickey's household. The joke went that Tommy came for a Thanksgiving dinner, and left three years later.

Drugs also exacted their toll. After drinking through a long night of work, the group would "get loaded." According to Tommy, "Smoking pot was not considered being high. That was just smoking some pot." The really exciting drugs came in hypodermic needles, and Tommy took his first hit early: "The man who played guitar and sang with Lenny Bruce when he was on the road gave me my first intravenous shot. I had already had a muscular shot from Lenny, in a hotel in the Tenderloin.

"I went in there with him and said I didn't just want a snort of that heroin, I wanted a hit. He said, 'Well, I know you're just going to go get it from somebody. I shouldn't do this, but—' and he gave me an intramuscular hit of heroin. Then I got ready to go home, but I couldn't. I came back to his door and I said, 'Lenny, I can't go out like this.'

"So I called up Ann, and said, 'Ann, I'm with a trick, I'll be out all night.' So I stayed with Lenny Bruce all night. I think Lenny did whatever he wanted. But we weren't lovers. I just kissed him.

"Intramuscular's in a muscle, intravenous is in a vein. When the drug goes into your vein, it goes to your heart and you get a rush. We used to call it a flash. Intramuscular comes on slower; you end up getting just as high, but you don't get the flash.

"Usually if you would shoot a hit of heroin, if you had a good hit of good strong heroin, then you would flash. You would flash as you threw up."

As he made clear, Tommy began turning tricks, mostly out of the after-hours club: "I started quite early. It was too tempting not to make that simple money. There was also, I don't know, the whole idea was kind of exciting. See, the club scene in North Beach had this underlying kind of hustling theme, because whores were everywhere. There weren't just whores on the street.

"I always had a great respect for whores. I like them a lot. Later, when I was in Chicago, some of my best girlfriends were whores. I had affairs with them, and I lived with some of them."

This carousing life—which ran for at least five years, according to the understandably inexact memories of the survivors—did not make the best employees of Tommy, Mack, Mickey, or any of the crowd. Consequently, with Ann's 440 as a homing beacon, they floated in different jobs around the club scene. Mickey particularly had an entrepreneurial knack. He started up several bars, and in each one he found a way to employ Tommy, usually as the barkeep. Mickey thought Tommy made a good bartender, and Tommy thought so too, "but I'd get a little wild sometimes. If things got too quiet, I'd just pick up a glass, throw it against the wall, break it, and yell. Just to get things going."

The central residence of the gang moved too, from the Victorian house Mickey had occupied, to a big, ugly gray building of prefab apartments built during World War II. "After we left Shrader

Street we all went to live on Octavia. They used to call the place Vaseline Flats, because it was forty units and all gay people rented it. You'd get three small rooms and a little shower, and I think we were paying something like seventy-five dollars a month. We lived there for a number of years, and each one had his own apartment. We were always attached to each other somehow. Wherever one went, the others went."

In a nameless club one evening, Tommy heard a woman singing with utter abandon. "Aggie Dukes—she was this beautiful, black, black lesbian who would sing so hard her veins would pop out. . . . Hound Dog. She was always stoned and always late. Wherever she was playing, she would arrive an hour late, but she was just cool— 'Hey, baby, what's happening?' Then she'd play straight through. Really she was very good. I was just always hung up on Aggie Dukes.

"I had a guy hire her at that club where I was working, the Beaded Bag, because I was in love with her. I was just her little white boy. I had to go out and get her money and dope and whatever. She just had me. She had my ass out on the streets.

"I can't remember why the Beaded Bag thing didn't last very long. Probably the same reason: she'd pack the club, but she'd be too outrageous. Too outrageous for everything—the way she talked, everything, and this club owner just couldn't handle it.

"So she quit and moved into my apartment with me, on Octavia and McAllister, at the Vaseline Flats. They also called it the Gray Ghost or the Warehouse. It was mostly gay, but also there were whores.

"Then I went down to Los Angeles with her, because I was in love with her. She had this white girlfriend living down there in a house, and she was strung out on heroin, so we went down and I lived with them. But just briefly."

Briefly, because Tommy soon began to run with a different sort of crowd. He rekindled a friendship with a young man—of European nobility, apparently—who'd grown up in Santa Barbara. "I had never really had an affair with him. I just moved in with them, with the viscountess, into the fancy house in Beverly Hills. They had twelve-course meals, and maids. I wasn't sleeping with him actually, but I *was* sleeping with the uncle, some relation to the viscountess.

"They'd lived a few blocks from my family's house in Santa Barbara, so they had known me as a child. But this was a whole different life. All of a sudden here I had Aggie Dukes, this black girl, swimming in their swimming pool in their garden, and these strange people were coming around. They were, well, royalty, from Belgium."

From there, Tommy bounced around a bit as a favored guest at parties of well-to-do male actors. He passed several happy weeks in a mansion in Bel-Air "being a young pretty thing" until, on a visit from San Francisco, Ann Dee fairly captured him and drove him back to North Beach.

Fresh from contact with Los Angeles and New York actors, their ambition stoked, Ann conspired with her husband, John Barret, and with Sarah Stanyan to mount a Broadway-style show, using profits from Ann's 440. They rented the Encore Theater, refurbished it down to the seat covers, and revived a Broadway play from some years earlier, *Buy Me Blue Ribbons*. They hired an actor named Jay Robinson to play the same lead role he'd had in the original show.

Ann: "Tommy helped my husband and me refurbish it. He was involved with stage sets and with everything that went with it. We got a cable car front, so people could walk down and in through it. We really did it. And we lost a lot of money. Thirty thousand dollars in 1958 was a lot of money, but this young man stood by us the whole time."

Crowds and reviewers packed the Encore on opening night, but the production just didn't click. One review that ran the next day merely quoted the title, *Buy Me Blue Ribbons,* then added a single word in boldface: **WHY??** The show closed next morning.

Ann and Sarah had just seen another of their ventures, 181 Club, fall flat. This second club they'd refurbished at a cost of $70,000, only to have the star, Lynn Carter, wooed away to the Mocombo in Los Angeles. Now, to lick their wounds, Ann, her husband, and Tommy piled into a car and headed to Baja California. "After all these disappointments, we went for a camping trip. The theater thing was a bust, the 181 Club thing was a bust, and we were flat busted."

They rested in the desert, unwound, and found a new perspective. Back in San Francisco, Ann felt that the 440 needed what she called, ironically, "a shot in the arm."

"That club had been running steadily, giving us the money to buy all these other things to fail in. We came back, and I decided to put on a drag show of many boys, because we had Gilda, who came from Paris, and he was one of the most outstanding impersonators of the fifties. He had been at Lou Walters's nightclub in New York and with the Folies Bergère in Paris. He had a wardrobe that probably was a quarter-million dollars in ostrich plumes. Diamonds were his best friends.

"He was *so* masculine when he came offstage, you could hardly believe it. His mannerisms and everything were *so* macho.

"So I started auditioning boys for the chorus. I couldn't get satisfied. We had Eddie Akuna, who was a tremendous force as a hairdresser in town—he passed, as far as I was concerned. Johnny Cornell—he was so beautiful in drag that men went crazy when they came into the club. Who else? Lewis White, yeah, a black man who was singing in the style of today back then. Way ahead of his time—rock and roll, blues, anything you wanted. But the fourth boy I couldn't find, and I wanted a sort of ballsy, hard girl, you know, but beautiful.

"So Tommy came to me and said, 'I can't use my last name—my family would be disgraced. How about if I use your last name, and be Tommy Dee?' I said be my guest. We put him in opera hose, he danced around onstage, and he looked gorgeous. He had a feather here, and a feather here, and a feather here.

"He said, what will I sing? I said why don't we do 'Hard-Hearted Hannah,' so that was his introduction of Tommy Dee to the world, as a performer."

4

Boy So Pretty

Whatever bad habits Tommy Dorsey had, the creature named Tommy Dee had worse. By changing his name, Tommy slipped the last and most binding loop of authority, his family. Tommy Dee came from nowhere, answered to no one. Unmoored, he had permission to go any direction—and he went toward more drugs. His habit "got bigger as I was performing at Ann's," he recalled. "I started shooting more and more heroin all the time. I got strung out. If I didn't have my taste, I'd be sick.

"At one point, I moved in a man who was Lenny's pusher, a black man named Jimmy. I moved him in with me, and I had all the heroin I wanted. He one day told me that it was costing us seventy-five dollars a day for my habit—that meant before we could sell it. In other words, I developed a pretty big burner, because I could get it.

"When I wasn't with Jimmy, I hung around with a couple of lesbians. This black girl used to go out and turn tricks, and the white girl and I used to go out and sell heroin down at this after-hours place on the wharf, so we could have some to shoot. I real quick got a big burner.

"After a while I just pretty much knew how to do it. Get it here, sell it there, be in the right place at the right time."

Along with heroin, Tommy got to know addiction's sibling better too—prostitution. "It came with the job. People would expect it. Men would come with their wives one night, then the next night they'd come alone—people who would be interested in a man in drag. Sometimes, too, I would dress up as a butch young guy, and sometimes I'd go out in drag, depending on what they wanted. I think Ann actually pimped me—it's a little vague. She told me to go looking straight, not to be dressed up.

"But I can remember turning tricks with Desirée, a lesbian and a prostitute who used to be one of George Raft's girls. He was a well-known mobster type. Desirée was beautiful—a white girl who was blond and hung around at Ann's. She and I used to go turn tricks together.

"We'd go out with a married couple, let's say. We'd meet them at their motel and have cocktails. I'd be in drag and she'd be in her clothes. Then we'd go to bed with them, the husband and the wife. We'd get our money and go out and shoot it all."

When pressed about what would happen in such a liaison—how it worked, who did what with whom, Tommy said, "Exactly! Who did what with who. That's exactly what happened."

Throughout this period Tommy relished the low life. He seemed so pleased and so much at ease that companions had trouble censuring him, even if they were inclined to. Reggie Mason: "I feel that all the things we've sort of kidded and laughed about in his behavior, being a hooker and a this and a that—they sound so foul about someone else you might know. But I don't find them that way with him. . . . It was a very natural thing for him to do. But I don't ever recall his instigating it. It was that other people would come to him and say, hey I've got a boyfriend out there, or a couple, or whatever, and you can get twenty-five bucks if you want to join us. So even that he fell into rather than aggressively going after it. That all fits in the whole thing of Tommy Dee. He sort of went along with anything, but he never particularly instigated any of it."

Whatever his personal reactions were to successfully negotiating a dark, dangerous world, Tommy had other reasons to count this as a happy time. He'd finally become an entertainer. He may have been only a small fish in a big pond, but the pond was famous, richly stocked with talent, and he was glad to be swimming there. Tommy and Ann used to quarrel, for instance, about which of them "discovered" Johnny Mathis, then singing as an unknown in a little club across the street from the 440. Regardless of who actually heard him first, Mathis performed the next night at Ann's 440 and eventually asked Ann to manage his act. In what she describes as one of her "many mistakes," Ann sent him to Helen Noga at the Black Hawk; from there, Mathis's career skyrocketed.

Tommy himself never qualified as a singer, although he keenly appreciated musical ability in others. He had a rough, low voice and not much aptitude for carrying a tune. In his entire career as an impersonator, Tommy seems to have sung only a very few songs, primarily "Hard-Hearted Hannah" and "Steam Heat"—and those only after he emerged from the chorus of the act Ann produced called *Larry Winters and the Four Lovely Misters*. He could, however, trot around the stage in time to music, and whatever it was he actually did, he did with pride: "We had a much better show, much better than Finnochio's, because Ann saw to it. I mean it was really good. She had us out there in showgirl opera hose and feathers, marching around and tap-dancing on boxes, a live band up on the side, up high. Good musicians, always.

"Finnochio's was a tourist joint. The impersonators were all backstage, and then they'd come out and fawn over the customers. Their show was much more a cabaret show."

Mickey Martin: "Tommy would do 'Hard-Hearted Hannah,' and he was gorgeous. See, at that time, everybody was wearing wigs. Tommy had let his hair grow because he hated wigs, and he had his own beautiful hair. He would put makeup on, and he was absolutely stunning. He was great. He was just so great."

Reggie Mason: "That's how people saw him, and yet he was not effeminate. He did not look like a woman in drag. There was a male image about him that just never left him, and yet people would say, 'Oh, he's so beautiful, he's so this and he's so that.'

"I remember probably his most endearing song was 'Steam Heat.' That was his big number. He didn't try to do it like a Peggy Lee, he didn't try to be like anyone—he never got affectations that were after being feminine. He was Tommy. So he came out singing this very senuous song, 'Steam Heat,' but he just sort of stood there and sang it. Nothing effeminate about him at all. Suddenly he was in a dress and on the stage, and people loved it."

Mickey: "He was gorgeous, and he'd keep his hair up, like this here [*gesturing to create a kind of flip*]. When Reggie introduced him, he'd come out smoking a cigar. Looking gorgeous. Then in the middle of the show, he'd put the cigar out, and he'd take the ribbon and go like that [*unties with a quick flourish*]. And his hair would cascade down, and my god, the people would be with the ooohs and aaaahs. They just went crazy, see. They'd just go crazy about him."

Ann: "I think men were fascinated with Tommy Dee because he had this gorgeous face and body and long legs, so that he didn't look like a fella. Except when he opened his mouth to sing, because he was never a great singer. He had a gravelly voice— what was that other song he used to sing—'Steam Heat' from *Pajama Game*. He'd go 'I've got steam heat' [*imitating a very gravelly*] *sound].* Every time he'd sing that 'I've got' from way down here in his throat, the guys would all go bananas. They wanted someone to rough them up I guess."

With the shift to a drag revue, Ann succeeded in reviving the 440 but not in making her job any easier. What follows is from a conversation between Ann and Tommy held thirty years after the fact:

Ann: "We were harrassed in those years by the police, for drag or for anything homosexual. You had to be in the closet. The police would come and they'd just walk around. North Beach was very corrupt, and you had to pay off the beat cop—protection. You had to keep everybody happy, that was just protocol. Everybody had to pay protection. We never took a chance, because they'd come in and you'd lose your license for ten days, or something like that."

Tommy: "Or else they'd bring in the health department, because none of us were up to code. The way we had these little stages built, the number of people we used to shove into those dressing rooms *[laughing]*—there is no way they were up to code."

Ann: "They weren't bad. . . ."

Tommy: "There used to be four or six of us in a room about this size" [*a smallish motel room*].

Ann: "That's big enough."

Tommy: "Not for drag queens, I'll tell you."

Ann: "It was so funny, they'd come in at 4:00 in the afternoon for a 10:00 show and start making up."

Tommy: "I'd always come in a little later."

Ann: "Eddie Akuna and Johnny Cornell, they just looked in the mirror for *hours.* Sarah and I would be carrying cases of beer in from the back, and I'd have high heels on, three-inch heels, carrying the beer, and there would be the boys, making up."

Tommy: "They were beautiful, though."

During this period, a man named Eugene became woven into Mickey's clique and established a lifelong friendship with Tommy. Eugene worked for the military as a personal assistant to a commander. This day job and the fact that his well-regarded family lived in San Francisco kept his wilder impulses and his gay identity strictly sub rosa. "My mother was still around. I didn't live with them, but still, you didn't go around and act like a faggot and tell your mother you were gay, because she would drop dead.

"But we were constantly at the bars, popping the pills, smoking the goodie. We used to go out and scandalize the bars. Tommy Dee was this big tall person, looking like the young Ann Baxter when she first hit the screen—can you see that? He would generally be in black, wearing maybe a sequined evening dress. We'd go to Banducci's open-air bar there—Enrico's, under Finnochio's. We'd sit there, and be the eyes of everybody, and have all the Finnochio bartenders come down in their tuxes and sit with us. He'd sit there and hold court.

"I'd be all dressed up in either my very smart tuxedo or an evening suit, because I wore expensive clothes and had money to spend. All with the gloves and the clothes, so we were never told to get out of anywhere. We might not have been appreciated, but we were always served, and we were decorous."

Even with a high-level military job, Eugene worked out ways to spend time with the gang. Mickey: "Eugene was always there. He used to come up to my house, when he was secretary to the commander. One time he comes up to the house, he's in uniform, beautiful, driving a Citroen no less. He comes in and says, 'I'm not going to work today.'

"I say, 'Eugene, you're working for the commander.'

"He says, 'Watch this.'

"So he picks up the phone and calls, and I hear him saying, 'I'm sick and I'm not coming in.' Then after a second he grabs the phone tighter and says, 'Didn't you understand what I just said?'

and he starts like, crying, screaming, *'I'm sick, I'm sick, I can't come in.'* So whoever it was answered must have said like, 'Just calm down, okay?'

"So he hangs up and says, 'Okay. Let's get loaded.' I love Eugene."

But by 1959, Mickey was tiring of North Beach. He itched to take a new direction, and with encouragement from Reggie Mason, he worked up plans for a traveling revue of female impersonators.

Reggie: "We had flyers printed up, and just looked to the Yellow Pages of every major city we could think of, and sent them off to the agents listed here.

"An agent in Spokane got one of them, and he knew of a club in Alaska that was looking for a drag show. So it was sort of a fluke. I mean, everyone else was out there, vastly talented, who couldn't make a dime, couldn't get work anywhere—and next thing you know, we were making money by doing these things that people laughed at."

Mickey: "I was the manager. I had conceived it, I directed it, I did the choreography and wrote it. So I was the one that kept them together. I called them the Party of Four. Yeah, but they were tough, especially in Alaska."

Before considering the numerous reasons Mickey might have had for finding the act "tough," it will be useful to know who comprised the Party of Four and how they functioned together. Everyone in the troupe hailed from Ann's 440, though probably they had not worked together in any extended way before going on the road.

Reggie Mason was the Master of Ceremonies. According to Mickey: "Reggie worked as a fellow, he didn't work in drag. Reggie and Tommy got along beautifully together. He was an awfully good influence on Tommy. He was clean, squeaky clean. He wanted to be an actor, and he was in show biz and that's what he wanted to do. He was a brain, and just a nice human being. A nice young man."

According to Reggie himself, "I guess I was too puritanical—I grew up Presbyterian in Michigan. They all told me it was because I was resisting it psychologically, but I just never got into the drug scene. Even though I was around it and all the people were around me sniffing it and shooting it and whatever, I never did it. Few times I took a tote off a joint if someone passed it, but it wasn't because I wanted it. It was that, well, it passed my way. . . . But it just had no message for me. I did drink, like they all did. Well, maybe not quite as heavily. Well, maybe."

Don Miles and Mickey were a couple—"a marriage made in heaven," Tommy said. They'd been together more than a decade by the late 1950s, and they stayed together another thirty years, till Don's death. Don danced in the troupe and played piano.

Reggie: "Don may have been limited in other respects, but he could play a boogie piano, and I really don't think he had an equal in that. He had a left hand that just was magnificent to hear."

Everyone agreed that Tommy—"The Boy So Pretty You Can't Believe It"—couldn't really do anything very well other than charm people senseless.

Larry Winters, the group's fourth member, was a stripper known as "The Male Lily St. Cyr." Mickey: "Larry was fantastic. What do you mean how did he do it? He stripped! He was fantastic. He stripped down to a G-string. When they knew he was a man was after he took the stole off. He pulled down his rice titties. He used rice, so they moved when he did it to the music."

Reggie: "Larry was sort of a strange person, not particularly likable. He was there for work, but none of us ever got really close to him.

"He thought he was a stripper [*laughing*]. You know, he must have been six feet tall, and he had been trained as a dancer, but he was just out of it. He was from a different social clime. . . .

"He read all the tabloids and religiously believed everything. He would argue for hours about whether Marilyn Monroe did or did not do this, because he read it in this magazine. So in a way he was sort of outclassed by the rest of us. He just didn't fit in; he wasn't a bad person, he wasn't a mean person. He *was* a bitchy person at times."

The Party of Four deplaned in Fairbanks in the late summer of 1959 and went to work in a supper club called the Fireside. Mickey contracted for them to play there for two weeks. During the run, the owner of the Last Chance—a club down in Anchorage—saw the act and booked them next for a two-week stint. The Party of Four ended up playing the Last Chance for more than nine months.

In 1959, Alaska was still a sprawling territory, not one of the United States. Entertainment industries thrived in the rough-and-tumble economic boom surrounding construction of the oil pipeline.

Mickey: "Fur trappers, and oil guys. They'd come in after being out in the field for six months, loaded. There was nothing to do there. No place you could go except to the bar, and the bar was open twenty-four hours. There was a lot of money to be made, and a lot of money to be spent. We were paying a hundred dollars a week at the hotel for each one of us, which at the time was real money. It was expensive up there."

But it soon dawned on the Party of Four that they'd been hired by the Last Chance for reasons other than their song and dance.

Tommy: "We realized that we were B-girls too. This guy hired us because he had seen people flocking around us in the other club, buying us drinks. He had a strip joint, with these B-girls stripping and working at his club. So he hired us there in

Anchorage, and after the first night, he started giving us our money. We said, 'What's this for?' He told us it was our cut on the drinks from the customers.

"So then I went crazy. I was the top B-girl in Anchorage, the first week I was there, because I really got into it. We were in sort of a competition with the real girls. Then the real girls got on the ball. That was what the guy hired us for—to get their asses into shape. We'd come out and do our show, and then mix with the customers."

Mickey: "We'd go to the bar, and Tommy would say, 'Oh, this man wants to buy everybody in the show a drink.' We'd say, 'Okay, we'll have vodka with champagne chaser.' Ridiculous things like that, cause you'd get half back of whatever they spent."

The proprietor of the Last Chance didn't leave the buying of rounds of ridiculous drinks to the mercy of the customers' good mood. He provided another enticement, called either the Dark Room (according to Mickey, who observed the scene) or the Blue Room (according to Tommy, who conducted business there).

Mickey: "They'd go back there, in the Dark Room, and they'd fondle the guys, get them all hot, and then they'd say, 'Hon, I have to have some champagne.' The guy would say okay. So the waiter comes in with the champagne, puts the bucket down, and in the bottom of the bucket is a sponge."

Tommy: "A bottle of champagne for a hundred dollars. If the guy wasn't drinking the champagne or if he was real drunk, they'd just fill the bottle full of ginger ale. They'd bring it out and pop it. You'd sit here in the booth, see, with the guy on your right. The waiter would bring it out and pop it, and there would be the bucket with ice here on the left.

"They'd pop it, and the guy couldn't see anything, so they'd put the bottle back in the bucket upside down, with all the champagne running out of it. Then you were supposed to pull it out and pour it into your glass and his, and you'd slop it all over.

They would take a towel and fold it, or use a sponge and put it in the bottom of the bucket so it would sop up the champagne that ran out. Then you'd take your glass and do like this—spill it all around, and he'd have to buy another bottle. Buying and pouring, and they couldn't get you into the room unless they bought champagne."

Mickey: "The girls would all get half of whatever the guys spent. Most of the hookers loved Tommy. They'd say to the guy sometimes, 'Is it okay if I bring my girlfriend [Tommy] too?' The guys would say sure, and then the three of them would go back there. There's safety in numbers, see. The waiters all used to go around with blackjacks in their back pockets."

Tommy: "You tried not to actually *do* anything, because once the guy comes, he's not going to buy any more booze. So the trick is to get him drunk. Then you see him drunk, and you push the buzzer, and they throw him out.

"See, get them drunk, and they spend all the money. When they're broke and don't have any more money, just push the buzzer, and the guy comes and takes them out."

One would think that as customers learned about this kind of treatment, demand for time in the Dark Blue Room would have diminished. Apparently it did not. Tommy: "They came back. If they were drunk enough, they wouldn't remember, but anyway they'd all come back. I think what happens to men who are in Alaska, working in the bush and making all this money, is that they sort of expect to be taken and misused. It's all part of the trip. It's sort of a masochistic tendency, I think. They expect to be taken—and they are."

Tommy's own self-destructive tendencies survived his relocation to Alaska, despite the fact that Mickey made him clean up his heroin habit before coming on tour. He drank heavily the whole time and took speed to stay up long hours at the bar. The Party of Four found drugs generally more difficult to get in Alaska, but not impossible. Friends from the Bay Area sent them what they lacked, and not even heroin was completely out of their reach.

Tommy: "I had one hit up there. Billie Holiday's ex-accompanist was playing for us, at the first club we were in, which was a nice supper club. There was no B-girl action there.

"I went out with him. I got very close to this piano player. Because he was so wonderful, I started singing good, too, at that time, because we had a real rapport. I started thinking this was really working out.

"So we went back to his house one night, and I OD'd. I was out of it. He had to walk me around and around. If he hadn't been there, I would have been dead."

For the most part, Mickey's Alaskan gamble paid off—the Party of Four was a commercial success. As manager though, Mickey endured minor adventures. Once, at the insistence of high-ranking officers, he had to retrieve Tommy and Don from custody in the barracks of the local military base. They'd been "sneaked in" by some soldiers, they swore. Shortly after Alaska became a state, an event the Party of Four helped celebrate in high style, Mickey taught the now-illegal whores how to be strippers so they could continue working in the bar.

What none of the Party of Four could figure out was, in Tommy's words, "why, when we got to Spokane, we were all broke. I don't know. Because we were all so crazy? We made *lots* of money in Alaska. But we were just like those other guys. We got taken."

The Party of Four continued to work steadily for the next couple years, moving eastward, playing some cities several times, knocking back and forth across the Canadian border: Spokane, Washington; Coeur d'Alene, Idaho; Great Falls, Montana; Detroit; Montreal; Rochester, New York; Niagara Falls; Toronto, Ontario; and finally

New York City. The troupe members jammed themselves and their considerable gear into a 1957 Ford "Woody" station wagon that Reggie bought for seventy-five dollars and rolled from city to city. Working drag queens, they paid extraordinary attention to wardrobe; each member had at least a trunkload of costumes.

As if the logistics of the journey weren't complicated enough, at one point Reggie and/or Mickey purchased a baby golden macaque monkey to bring along. Geneva, as she was promptly dubbed, formed an inseparable connection to Reggie; Reggie, in turn, was the only one of the five humans who could drive. Thus Geneva would sit on his left wrist, half hanging out the window as Reggie tooled down the dreary northern highways of 1960.

Mickey: "Imagine dragging around a chimpanzee. And a cage. Geneva liked to look out the window. The three of them—Donny, Tommy, and Larry, in their fur parkas—would sit in the back, and I would sit up front with Reggie. We had just gotten back from Alaska. The top of our car was piled with all that luggage.

"So one time we're on a big highway, and we're pulled over. The cop comes over to the car, and he looks in there. There are those three, sitting there in their fur parkas. He looks at Reggie with a chimpanzee on his arm, in diapers, and he says, 'Oh, never mind. Go ahead. Just go ahead.' He didn't ask us one question. We just drove off. He said, 'Oh my god. Oh no. Just never mind.' "

Tommy must have looked almost as unusual as Geneva to the general population of the era, because he wore his hair quite long. In 1960 and 1961 no one, not even the Beats, sported shoulder-length hair, and it caused Tommy some trouble. Though he seemed insensible of social criticism in most areas, he kept his hair strictly tucked up under a cap when he wasn't actually in drag. At the shrine of Saint Anne de Beaupré, outside Toronto—a site of miraculous healing and a place a Catholic, even a back-slid Catholic, would want to visit—Tommy waited outside for the other troupe members rather than doff his cap, as the doorkeeper required.

But if his hair and his looks inconvenienced Tommy from time to time, they seriously confused patrons of the clubs featuring the Party of Four. In Toronto, assuming that the gentleman with whom he was dancing knew him to be a performer, one of the Party of Four, recently onstage, Tommy confided proudly, "You know, this is my *own* hair." After a few moments' dizziness, the man realized what Tommy's remarked implied: that in fact he held in his arms something very different from what he'd imagined.

Earlier, in Montana, the same kind of trompe l'oeil occurred, with a more dramatic revelation.

Mickey: "There, they allowed them to dance with customers. They could stay in drag. So it was intermission, and Tommy comes back to dressing room and says, 'You know, that man I'm dancing with, he wants me to go out with him tonight after the show.'

"And I said, 'Does he know you're a man?'

"He said, 'Well . . . well, *sure.*' 'Cause you know, he had his own hair and was beautiful.

"I said, 'I don't think he knows you're a man.'

"He said, 'Oh sure he does.'

"I said okay then. So comes the last show, they all have to change. Can't leave the club in drag. They all change. So Tommy comes out in men's clothing and the guy wants his money back for all the drinks he bought. He thought it was a woman, see. He thought it was a real woman."

The vicissitudes of performing on the road are legendary. The grind of constant travel, heavy performance schedules, disorientation, drugs, drink, and bad cheap food have worn many a star to rubble by the end of a run. The Party of Four fared reasonably well; their unexpected and uncharacteristic commercial success buoyed them. They seemed to know one another well and to have made peace with one another's annoying habits.

According to Reggie, Tommy's equanimity was a linchpin of their emotional survival: "He simply went along with whatever happened and never complained about it. If the outcome was bad, he never bitched about it. He just did it as naturally as I can pick this up. Nothing seemed to bother him.

"You know, when we were traveling on the road as the Party of Four, we were frequently in very close quarters. I mean, some of these clubs didn't even have—you had to change clothes in the toilet. When we were traveling around the country, very seldom did we stay in motel rooms, but we did from time to time. Tommy never cared what his surroundings were. He just went along with them. 'Okay, so this is really a scuddy motel, what do I care? I just need a good night's sleep.' The rest of us would be saying, *'My god, we're paying twenty-five dollars a night* (which was a lot then) for a seedy motel?' But those things never bothered him.

"I don't know what Tommy *wouldn't* put up with, because he accepted whatever came along. He'd bitch once in a while about someone, but it would never last. If he got angry at someone, it was momentary. 'Bitch, get out of that dressing room, so I can get in.' But he didn't hold it against them; he didn't stay mad at them. It was just really healthy for all of us—he let his feelings be known at the moment, and then it was over. He had that.

"Once, though, when we were working in Spokane—I think we went in for two weeks and they held us over for six—we just knew that Tommy was way off. Something was wrong while he was out there performing. The timing was gone—not in the musicianship, but something just wasn't right. We didn't know what it was until he got off. Turns out that all night there was a woman in the front row who all through his set just sat there, giving him the finger. But he went on with the show anyway.

"He just took it, but he didn't like it. He was very angry when he got off. It was a rude thing to do, and Tommy didn't like that."

In New York, after an initial engagement in Brooklyn, the Party of Four hit the wall. Despite Mickey's exhaustive hustling, they couldn't find steady work. They roomed, all five of them, in the tiny apartment of a show-business friend, Sandy Rogers from an a capella group called the Accidentals. They ran out of money, and they ran out of food.

Reggie: "We were literally picking up bottles on the street and cashing them in to get a little food. If anybody brought any money in for any reason, we shared it. We bought food with it."

Don found sporadic work playing accompaniment, and Tommy did a few solo gigs in after-hours clubs in Philadelphia.

Reggie: "One night we heard they wanted someone for one night at a club in Staten Island. They wanted a comedian, and I was the only one in the group who was a comedian. I had never been in drag in my life, but we were really hungry. I mean, we really didn't have anything. We sat around there, days at a time. So they all talked me into it. They said, 'Reggie, you don't have to do anything, just go out there and do your act, and you'll get the money, and who cares what they think?' They threw me into a dress that night, and Tommy went with me to put makeup on. I had no idea how you put makeup on."

Their situation became painfully obvious.

Reggie: "There was a prostitute in the apartment next door to us, and she picked up on the picture fast, that we were down and out. So she used to come over, sometimes with like two big bags of groceries, and say, 'I didn't feel like eating tonight.' Pretty poignant stuff. But Rose never did it as charity—never never, never. She'd just say, 'I didn't want to eat it all.'"

"She started to get tricks for Tommy that he got paid for, and that brought in money. He'd go in drag, but they knew they were getting a guy. That's one of the ways he survived."

It appears that for Tommy two habits—turning tricks and shooting dope—came braided together. In New York he had a second brush with death, again from an overdose. He shot up with a couple of friends, turned blue, and passed out. Frightened that they would have a dead body on their hands, the friends decided to drive around for a while with Tommy in the back of their station wagon; if he failed to come to, they'd dump the body in the water. Tommy awoke as the car approached the East River.

Mickey: "So I had been gone to see some of the agents, and Donny and I are downtown New York, and we meet some people I know. One of the guys says, 'Hey Mick, nice to see you. By the way, let me tell you about that crazy Tommy. . . .' "

Mickey listened with a growing fury to the story of how Tommy had flouted his promise to stay clean at least on the road and had nearly been killed. He stormed back to the apartment, but Tommy greeted him quite casually, as if nothing had happened.

Exasperated with Tommy, and frustrated by the stone wall of rejection he'd been getting from agents, Mickey was at last approached by a man about the possibility of the Party of Four playing to audiences on a luxury pleasure-cruise liner. Mickey told his agent that they'd love it, and he made an appointment to discuss the specific arrangements. Mickey arrived a few days later at the agreed-upon time, only to find that the agent had perished from a heart attack in the interim.

"I was so discouraged, because I had been knocking on so many doors—New York was actually kind of a hard one for us. I said, 'Come on, let's break it up and go home.'

"But Tommy said, 'No, I'm not gonna go home. I'm going to go over here with these other ones, these other queens, and I'm going to still work in drag wherever I can. I can get weekends.' "

The Party of Four dispersed in 1961 or early 1962. Mickey and

Don went back to San Francisco, where Mickey opened more bars, and Don played piano in them. Reggie sought his fortune as an actor in Los Angeles—that lasted a year. No one knows for sure what happened to Larry Winters.

Tommy, however, joined another troupe of drag queens and went on the road for a short time. On a cold night's drive from Binghamton, New York, to Rochester, the car in which Tommy and his new associates were riding veered from the road and flew over an embankment. Everyone else in the car was killed—badly mutilated, then burnt. Tommy was thrown three hundred feet through the air into a ditch, and the car rolled over him. The hospital treated him for a simple concussion, though he also lost his voice completely for a time, and ultimately regained only part of his diction. The doctors told Mickey, via long-distance telephone, that Tommy had survived the accident only because he had been dead drunk and thus quite physically relaxed. For his part, Tommy never remembered even being in the car, though he said later, "I always felt kind of partly responsible for that, because I had just scored this big bag of pills, and we were all so loaded. . . ."

5
Baddest of the Bad
Chicago Queens

Tommy lay in a hospital bed recuperating for nearly six weeks. Although diagnosed and treated for a concussion, he'd actually sustained very serious injuries; the gravity of his condition would only become apparent years later. However, the main concern he expressed to Mickey was that Thomas Senior would disapprove of his long hair when he came to visit.

After he got out of the hospital, Tommy headed for Toronto and a gig he'd contracted to do earlier. To his amazement, he couldn't sing. He could dance, move around, and talk, but he was absolutely unable to sing. So with remarkable buoyancy, he found work in another Toronto club, silently pantomiming records. At the end of that stint, Tommy dropped down to Philadelphia for a short visit with friends, then came west.

When Tommy arrived in San Francisco, Mickey found him an apartment in the Vaseline Flats and furnished its three rooms completely. Mickey kept a close watch on his friend, who was still operating at less than full capacity, and gave him work in a Tenderloin bar, doing more record pantomime. Tommy's wounded condition, however, did nothing to diminish his taste for show life.

While he was working for Mickey one night, Tommy's parents

caught his stage act "by accident." "They came to San Francisco to see me, and they knew Mack's address because he was married and had a wife. They had called him up: 'Mack, how can we find our son, Tommy?'

" 'Well, he's in a bar down in the Tenderloin, on Turk Street, called the 118 Club.'

"By the time I was working there, I had been on the road in drag, I was heavy into drugs and alcohol, and I was a real speed freak and a lush. I was a mess. I had hit the skids by this time, because I was stoned, out of it. Not on a bummer—I was having a good time, or at least I thought I was.

"So one night I'm getting ready to go onstage—this is when they put the stage behind the bar and you pantomimed records—and Mickey came back and said, 'Do a good show, Tommy, your parents are in the audience.' I said, 'Don't be ridiculous! They wouldn't be caught dead in a place like this.' But I looked, and there they were! Sitting there!"

Mickey offered Tom a way out, telling him he didn't have to perform that night, but Tommy said, "They're here. They might as well see me.

"I came out in a solid red, strapless, sequined dress slit all the way up the side and did a record pantomime to Diahann Carroll's 'All or Nothing at All.' Then, between shows, I sat with them. We had to take off our wigs and dresses between shows and put on men's clothes, but your face was still on. You were supposed to mix with people.

"I'm sitting there talking to my mother and father, and they're talking to me, just as though I don't have any makeup on, just as though it's all normal. My mother finally says, 'It's not a very nice club, is it?'

"Well, it was a *toilet*. I mean, it was really a sewer. It was one of the worst gay clubs I've ever been in. A big butch dyke named Bunny, the bouncer, sat with them and growled, 'We all love your son, Mr. and Mrs. Dorsey,' and slapped my father on the back. She's in jail now for murder. The place was full of pimps and whores and junkies . . . all those people I attract. That was the only time they ever saw me in drag. They knew I had been on the road in shows, but I don't think they ever mentioned it to the rest of my family."

Tommy went on performing and eventually forged a partnership with his hairdresser from Mickey's club. "This hairdresser wasn't a boyfriend. He just liked to dress me. He used to enjoy dressing my hair. He'd create this creature, and I'd be the creature, and we'd put it out onstage. I'd put on some makeup, and we'd put on a record of somebody that we liked. The hair, the makeup, the record, no sleep, and I'd appear like that, night after night, doing this trip."

The nameless hairdresser apparently liked drugs and was as much given to reckless spontaneity as Tommy. "One night, I just disappeared. I got stoned, I got a box of methedrine tablet ampules. My hairdresser just sat up, shooting those ampules, and before you know it, we had his car parked and filled with all my drag, and we were driving across the country. He and I and a whore that I knew from Montreal—this was who I ended up with on the streets of Chicago. But the first place I could get work was in Kansas City.

"They fired me from the first club. They said, 'You are *too* high, you are *much* too high to be working here.' So then I worked at the little club down the street for a while, until I got kicked out of Kansas City. The police kind of edged me out town. 'Just keep driving'—that kind of thing. A white drag queen in the black part of town."

Motley, motlier, motliest. This new impromptu gang—hairdresser, whore, and female impersonator—arrived in Chicago, with Tommy somehow in charge doling out money: "I used to give them all enough to pay for their first drink, and then we'd go out and hustle.. We'd show our scrapbooks around in the bars, and that's how I got that first job. So it was lucky for me, because already all the queens in Chicago were bad. They said, 'This is a bad queen. Watch out for this one.' I wasn't really that bad. I was just crazy. I wasn't bad."

Since the Chicago days qualify as Tommy's social nadir, it would be good to get some terms and roles straight. For instance, *queen*: "When I talk about a queen, I mean a man who dresses in drag, who's just a little bit sleazy. Turns tricks. Steals.

"We all stole, stole from each other. If you got stoned and someone stole from you, then it was your fault you got something stolen, not his fault. If someone could make you, why then, you tried to figure out how to make them. . . .

"Lots of these queens were in the chorus lines, because there were these big shows on the road in those days. *Jewel Box Revue* was a big show, and there were lots of far-out queens working in it. Lynn Carter, the star, was very professional. The stars would be extremely professional. But these queens were out there, of course. I mean they were on every kind of dope you could ever imagine. Always, yes. There was just a mad bunch of men, female impersonators, in this country at that time."

Or *bad:* "Chicago queens were bad. They'd kill you. They would. They were BAD: Hustling, running with whores, working for the mafiosi. . . . That's how I got into that number. I knew when I got to that city, there were some tough, bad queens there. I knew it was a bad queen city before I got there. I had heard about them when I was in New York."

In Chicago, Tommy found that as a lower-echelon show person, he could apply to just one agency for employment. "I worked for gangsters all the time I was there, because they owned all the clubs. And then I would go out on dates with them, dress up in drag and walk into a club with some little short thing. He'd be a collection man, which meant—shooting guns. Little short white guy, and me on his arm at six foot four."

But between the bad queens and the mobsters, Tommy decided he needed to project himself as something more, something tougher than a crazy queen from out of town, which is how he felt he was initially perceived. He got his opportunity almost immediately. The first Chicago club he worked in simultaneously let another performer go—not exactly *replacing* his first performer with Tommy, but letting him go and then very shortly after, hiring Tommy. The subtlety of these moves was lost on the club's bartender, who favored the first performer. To test, or haze, or hassle Tommy, he stole his wig.

"This had happened to me before. I usually used my own hair, but this one wig was such a perfect wig. I could just take it and shake it out a little bit and put it on and go like this to it and go right out. It was a fabulous wig. Well, I found out the bartender stole my goddamned wig. Someone told me.

"So that night, I did my shows, went through the night, borrowed a wig. . . . But later, I'm sitting at the bar, and I started getting drunker and drunker and drunker, and finally I just blew it. Before I knew it, I had climbed over the bar, I had the bartender's head on the bar, and I was smashing it there, and they were all pulling me off of him, and I said to him, 'Just—get—that—wig—*back!*' The next day it was back.

"See, by doing that, I became the toughest one. I established myself. I wasn't being bad, I just got pissed off at this dumb queen behind the bar who stole my wig. So I developed the attitude. Nobody fucked with me—I was a bad queen.

"Years later when I was in San Francisco, this old drag queen told Mickey that I had the scuzziest reputation of any queen who ever worked in Chicago."

Working for mobsters brought with it occupational hazards. (Much of what follows here will be graphic, and to most sensibilities, distressing. Readers who want to maintain a particular image, or ideal image of Issan Tommy Dorsey should skip ahead to chapter 7.)

"When I used to work for Father, who was Ralph Verdi, he used to sit in a big chair smoking a cigar, watching TV, with a huge black and white Great Dane by his side. He'd spit in the corner. Ralph. *Big Ralph. Ralph Verdi.* No longer a mafioso, right, but all these old guys were hanging round. . . .

"One night the police came in and started axing down walls. They couldn't find anything, but finally they found barbiturates in my makeup bag. That's the only thing they had against this whole place, the barbiturates in my makeup bag. I was working in drag for them. My first night, opening night, and in come the police. This was what busted the whole club was me with my barbiturates. They hadn't come in looking for barbiturates, axing down walls!

"So I was handcuffed to this little old man who was the biggest numbers man in the racket, and they drove us around to all these police stations to delay things. Sometime later, before the case came up in court, I got busted again. Maybe a few times. I was always getting busted."

According to his own count, the law put Tommy in jail twelve times during his Chicago stay. Once the police held him in a jail cell overnight in drag and forced him to appear that way in court the next morning. Bitterly embarrassed, all he told friends was how terrible his makeup had looked the morning after. Another time, he was investigated by homicide detectives to determine if he had any connection to a murder.

During these busts, he was usually taken to the city of Chicago's holding cells. Because he was heavily drugged with barbiturates a good deal of the time, and because the busts became routine—a kind of cat-and-mouse game between police and mob, with Tommy as bait—he had little idea as to *why* he was in jail most of those times. The first time he stayed in the state penitentiary, though, made a distinct impression on him.

The initial provocation involved one of Tommy's roommates, a young man named Billy. "He had been one of the bad kids, before I came. He worked in drag, he stripped. He was cute, and he had a good personality. He was tough. He stripped down to some sort of flesh-colored thing that made it look like he had boobs. Sometimes he put on rice, just laid it right on there, then put on the tassels. All you could really see was his legs and as much of his ass as he'd show—hips and body. But in those days, women weren't doing much more than that anyway."

Billy also "dated" mobsters, even going with them on collection runs and posing as a messenger boy, to gain entry to a building. One day Billy ran afoul of one of his gangster boyfriends, Moose: "Moose kicked down our door, then kicked in Billy's teeth. Then the police came and took us off to jail. Moose was gone, right, but they took *us* to jail and then to the farm.

"See, the way it works is, I had been busted so many times that now it was time to go to the Farm. At the farm you see these lushes and others; they just put them there for a while. You're supposed to go there and spend some time.

"When I was checked into that place, I got fucked in almost every single place, in every stop that they had. You go to the dental department, the medical department, when you get checked into the state farm. You go through this check-in. Everyone of them tried to fuck me, or did.

"Well, it was *fascinating*—some of them were kind of hot, and I was into being bad. First morning in the state farm, when I was standing in line for breakfast, me and Billy, they pulled me out of line. All of a sudden they just pulled me out of line, and this trustee, or whatever you call them, puts me in a cell, and hangs a blanket up over it, and brings out a bottle of Vaseline hair tonic, and says, 'Come on, baby, I'm going to fuck you.' It was rather interesting, 'cause it was all so exciting to be in jail and everything. First you're on the outside, all of a sudden you're on the inside before you know it. I said to Billy when I got back in line, 'Do we have to get fucked every morning before we get breakfast?'

"So then one of the black queens took me under his wing and started showing me how you don't give away anything. I mean this queen's cell was beautiful: he had a TV and a hi-fi, he had on makeup. He was posing on the bars, hanging on the bars, *posing,* with people whistling at him. He had learned how to make it work, to make the system work for him. How to get sugar.

"You don't get sugar, your sugar comes in Prince Albert cans that you barter for. All these things you have to barter for. Well this guy, he was living in like a condominium apartment in his tiny cell, because he had learned when to say yes.

"He told me, 'Now you have to learn to talk mean to those guys.' Well I didn't talk mean to those guys. I was scared, I tried to be nice. I didn't want them to beat me up. I didn't know what they might do to me, but here this queen is talking mean to them. '*Get away* from me.' Just talking dirty and bitchy to these men and the men are digging it, the guards and the trustees.

"But the mafiosi bought me out that first time, because I was working for them. They took care of you. I had been working down in the laundry with all the faggots. The laundry is where all the queens are. You can see the ones who the queens favor because they're all wearing these starched shirts. . . .

"So one day they called my name and I go downstairs, and this woman at the desk says, 'Some guy with diamonds all over his hands and a big Cadillac came. They're taking you. So go on, get out of here.'

"They picked me up, Father and the others, because in a few days I had to appear in court for when they busted the club for the barbiturates. It didn't look good for me to be coming from the

57

state farm to testify. It was better that I was out for a while. I cleaned up a little bit, tried to look a little decent.

"I went to court, and the lawyer clearly said, 'We found the barbiturates in Tommy Dee's makeup kit.'

"The judge looked at me. 'Was the makeup kit locked?'

" 'No.'

" 'Was the door to the dressing room locked?'

" 'No.'

" 'You have no case. Dismissed.'

"So they didn't mind that I busted their whole club. The police came in to bust them, not to bust me. They didn't care, they liked me. They used to hate to fire me, when I would get in fights and fall off the stage."

His employers did seem to like Tommy. Under trying circumstances, they continued to give him work in a variety of clubs, and when he began to complain of feeling poorly and perhaps of having been misdiagnosed in the New York hospital after his accident, they hired a lawyer to look into it. But they made their demands of him too. In addition to testifying and working onstage, Tommy was expected to perform another function in the clubs: his service was the currency with which protection was paid.

"Ralph would bring the policeman back, maybe a beat cop or whatever he was—and introduce you to the cop, and the cop would stay, and he'd pull his dick out, and you'd suck him off.

"What I'm saying is, there's a more interesting . . . at the point when you're not in drag yet, but you've got on the hose, but you're sitting at the table making up, you don't have your tits on yet—what is the word for something that's not man or woman?—you're just this beautiful creature, that's not a man or a woman. It turns both men and women on."

Years later, Tommy told incredulous Zen students that he had fallen off more stages in Chicago than they even knew existed.

"The Shoreline Seven is one club I remember the name of, but I worked in four or five others. Then I worked in some that were on the outskirts of town, that stayed open late, after the other bars closed. They were sleazy, I have to say sleazy.

"I can remember only once appearing onstage not drunk—one time that I went on sober. It happened through some fluke, and I always remember thinking, 'Oh, this is kind of nice.' But I was always stoned. We drank, and we always smoked pot. All the time. Drinking too much just made you kind of sloppy; shooting heroin made you a bit sluggish.

"We were also out of it on barbiturates. I had a barbiturate habit. We were taking everything else, but they were a steady diet. There was actually a drugstore where I could go in and buy a little bag of barbiturates, 'cause they knew I was working for the mafia.

"Barbiturates are . . . you don't talk. You could just pass out and OD and die. But it was my drug of choice at the time. I loved barbiturates. Tuinols, Seconals, reds . . . I'd take them by mouth, or melt them down and shoot them. If I had tracks, I'd just put makeup on them. That covered the tracks."

As before, habits like these did not advance Tommy's professional career; nor did they stabilize his domestic scene.

"After a while, after I'd been there, I had kind of a little following. My kids—the ones that liked me—my kids and me, we moved from one house to another. I usually had the apartment, so at least there was dope and food. Some of them were performers; sometimes, they'd be working, sometimes they'd be out turning tricks, sometimes they'd be out stealing. Sometimes they'd be living with me in my apartment, sometimes they wouldn't.

"But there were days when I couldn't keep a job because I was too fucked up, too stoned on those barbiturates. That's when I moved in with Bang Bang La Toure. She moved me in with her and kept me for a long time. Bang Bang La Toure was a prostitute;

she was beautiful, and she could dance. She loved me, and I actually liked her a lot. I lived with her a long time.

"She had tits that hung down to here. She said, 'People have been stretching and swinging on my tits since I was thirteen.' She'd been in shows and stag parties, and she said they'd been pulling on them, and she actually had stretch marks on them. When she stripped, she wore a brassiere that fit right up under them, so they sort of layed there. She had a gorgeous body, but if she ever took off that thing, they'd just go *whomp*.

"Billy remembered nights when Bang Bang would come home from work and find me passed out on the front table, OD'd from shooting barbiturates. She'd take that needle out of my arm, drag me to bed, pull me into the bed and lay on top of me, and fuck me. She was my girlfriend. She was a very sweet girl, red hair, but bad. Nobody wanted to fight with Bang Bang. *Bad*. She'd punch you out. Big, too—she was as big as me, bigger. But it was all put together quite beautifully.

"I used to have sex with Bang Bang, but the only reason I fucked her was because she was in love with me. And she was paying the rent. I had that place full of people. She'd come home, and suddenly she'd be supporting—she'd be lucky if she could find someplace to sleep. The place'd be full of people—junkies.

"Bang Bang used to sit in the window of the apartment that she paid for, that we lived in, and look out at the church down below. Whenever there was a wedding, she'd just *cry* and *cry*. 'I always wanted to be married in a white dress.' Here she is this big whore sitting there. . . .

"She drove tricks home, and we robbed them. We used to get their pants and go through them while she was fucking them. Then she'd scream, 'Oh, something's happening!' And the guy'd be out chasing us, but we'd be gone. They could never trace it back to her, because even though we did it at our house, they didn't know it was our house.

Baddest of the Bad Chicago Queens

"Most of the places we lived—Bang Bang's apartment, or any apartment I had or any of these kids had—you never really knew who lived there. There might be one person who saw that the rent was paid and had a bed. That was the rent-payer's bed. People would crash all over everything else and leave that bed open. Since mine was in the middle of the room, and big, there used to be quite a few people in it.

"The second time I was in Bridewell State Farm, Bang Bang fucked me out. It was Bang Bang. Bang Bang slept with somebody, and I got out. She was great; she loved me, just loved me to death.

"It's hard to believe that whole period. I'm just remembering it now. How sleazy and inviting, and tempting. Tempting? I just couldn't wait to get into that. And I did it completely. But I always had my own apartment and some money. Sometimes I didn't, but then I finagled. I did really well.

"There was this continuous game going on. In Chicago, you know, in the weather, the snow was coming, the wind was blowing, and things were slamming around and falling down, I mean, like signs in the streets! It's a rough city. You had to be up to it."

After a few years of this though, suddenly, and for reasons as inconceivable to him as those for how he'd arrived, Tommy split. Just a month before, he'd received a settlement from the hospital that had treated him after his car accident in New York. He had been suing for hundreds of thousands of dollars, but "they called me up on the phone and said we can settle for three thousand dollars out of court. Well, you know, I'm crazy, I wanted the money. If I had held out, I would have been rich. But I took that three thousand, and it was gone in a month. Three thousand dollars in those days was like thirty thousand dollars today."

He'd also taken up with a new companion, a woman named Stormy Reaves: "She was a whore and a bisexual lesbian. She liked

being a lesbian, and she was a whore—she liked doing that too—
and she stripped. There was an article once in the paper when
they raided the strip joint she was in. She bit a cop's leg, and they
had to take him off for tetanus shots.

"Stormy was blonde and bad. We started running around
together, dressing alike: black boots, black jacket, black pants. We
were just *loaded* on barbiturates, I mean, just *days* of taking
barbiturates. We used to shoot dope together too, and drink. She'd
turn a trick and get some money, so it was easy when I was living
with her, because she could always go out and fuck somebody and
get some money. I mean easy.

"It was more difficult for me to turn tricks than it was for her.
I could do it too, but it meant more effort. Sometimes I could get
a job—one-night gigs here and there, working in drag. At that
point, though, most of the jobs I got hired to do for more than
one night, I got fired. I never lasted very long. And everyone sort
of knew that. I was known as somebody you'd hire for the night,
to draw people in for a minute, but they knew I wouldn't be
around very long. Because of who knows—falling off stages, hitting
people with beer bottles, screaming or yelling or fighting, creating
disturbances.

"So I got this money which I blew all of—I just had enough
left for a plane ticket to get Stormy and me to San Francisco. I'm
not sure how it happened. There was that much money left, and
we were stoned, and we threw some stuff in a bag and went.

"How we got on that plane, I'll never know, and the way we
were looking—this is back in the days before people looked
however they did. I had on my black leather boots, and she had on
hers, and our black leather pants, and black jackets, with whatever
we were carrying, just out of our minds. Just drunk and with a
barbiturate bag, and we'd probably shot up, and had our outfits in
the bags we were carrying."

But they made it, and back in San Francisco, Tommy figured to take up right where he left off. Stormy and Tommy arrived from the airport at Mickey's club, and Mickey greeted them with outstretched arms—arms that pointed to the door. *"Out!"* Mickey bellowed. "Just, *out!* I don't need it. Run out on my show, come back three years later, leaning in the door, looking like that, with that woman—*out!"*

So Tommy reached deeper into his bag of connections and pulled out Mack, who by then was married, the father of several children, and living in a suburb south of San Francisco. Mack's wife Jillian: "Mack called me from work saying Tom had got hold of him. They'd ended up in San Francisco with nothing somehow, had lost all their money, and could they come stay.

"So here comes Tommy with Stormy, who looked like your typical . . . hard blonde, you know, that you'd see. She had 'gun-moll' tattooed on her knee. But she was such a sweet, great person when I got to know her. She was wonderful. So Tom and Stormy stayed with us. They had no money, and we had the children. It was sort of a home atmosphere—this house, with three bedrooms upstairs, and one big room downstairs. Everybody got along okay.

"He kicked some drugs he'd been on in Chicago and stayed for quite a while. He stayed there for over a year that time, and we had our little routine: getting up in the morning, having our coffee, and then Tom used to take a nap in the afternoon. That was just one of the things he did. He got me into taking naps. Then we'd get up from our naps and have coffee and something sweet.

"We were like family. We were real close at that time, naturally. Especially when I wasn't working. I mean, here we were, sitting out on this little hill, where there were nothing but tract homes, one after another, and you didn't go anywhere unless you had a car, and we only had one car. So Tommy and I would sit around and gossip, you know, about the papers or whatever. This was a whole different life than anything he'd been used to for a long time. He got his health back, because he was really sick at the time."

This period of cooling out, as Tommy called it—a bizarre kind of marital bliss, with Tommy and Stormy sleeping in the same bed, but not having sex—lasted about a year. Economics forced little gaps in the routine. Tommy: "Stormy would run out every once in a while and do a little strip gig or turn a trick, and I would go in to town every now and then, do a drag show."

But the household took it in stride. Jillian: "The kids used to watch him make up, because he would go and do some performing on the weekends at this one club. He would put on his makeup and get ready at home, because there was no place there for it at the time. He'd get all dressed up and put his makeup on, and the kids used to sit and watch him.

"They sort of knew, because we told them he was going to go and get onstage and act as a woman. They accepted that. I was used to it by then, because I'd been around all these people, and I knew Tom.

"He got better at applying the makeup, so he started looking softer. When he did 'Hard-Hearted Hannah' at first, he looked like 'Hard-Hearted Hannah.' "

Stormy left first, amicably just moving on, and then Tommy moved into the hotel above the club where he'd done his occasional gigs, the Hula Shack. Tommy: "There is no way to project to you the real picture of that place. Queens staying there, peeing out the window . . . It was just gross, sleaze-ola. Stoned, drunk, we'd just go all weekend long. . . . We were getting ten dollars a day, I think, for working there, and rent.

"We didn't eat much. One gay guy and his lover who lived in a room there, and they had a little hot-plate situation set up with a refrigerator. He was kind of our cook. Otherwise, I didn't eat.

There were sandwiches sometimes downstairs. Sometimes I didn't eat for days because of shooting speed.

"Mickey used to tell me that people were scared of me because I was so stoned. I was in another world. By this time, my makeup had gotten really bizarre. I threatened to throw queens out the window and stuff. I was older than most of them—I was thirty-two or something—and most of those queens were little young guys.

"There was a whore there named Nickey who kept a room upstairs. She lived someplace else, but she was fascinated by me and by the whole scene. It was a trip. She used to take me out for dinner and spend money on me. She was the one who took care of me."

In fact Tommy's newest patron prostitute drove him to the hospital when the lack of food, the harsh environment, the endless needle-barrels full of drugs, and the constant tricking (with members of the local roller-derby team, the San Francisco Bay Bombers) finally broke his health.

At San Francisco General, he was put in what he called the junkie ward: "It was a big ward, and everybody in it was a junkie. They didn't put anybody in there who got hepatitis some other way." Three significant things happened to him there: his condition was accurately diagnosed, he was put on the government assistance rolls, and he heard about a new drug.

When the doctors examined Tommy—all 116 yellowing pounds of him—they found that in addition to an advanced case of hepatitis, his internal organs were beaten up and badly out of place, either as a result of damage from the accident or from subsequent wear and tear. One lung had collapsed, his heart had been thrust up under his right shoulder, and his stomach and other entrails had drifted through an internal hernia to unhealthy locations in his thoracic cavity. "They looked at me, and they said, 'Do you realize your heart is on the wrong side?'

"I said, 'No, but it figures.'

"While I was in there, the social workers kept asking me all these questions. I said, 'Why are these people bugging me with all these questions? I didn't do anything wrong.' Someone said, 'Shhhh—I think they're trying to give you money!'

"So I went on ATD, which was pre-SSI. Aid to the Totally Disabled. When I went back to living with Mack and Jillian—they picked me up out of the hospital—they used to joke and call it Aid to Tommy Dorsey. 'Hey, we got our Aid to Tommy Dorsey today.'

"In the junkie ward was also where I first heard about acid, LSD. I heard first of all that there was such a thing, and I heard— what people said was that it was tricky, difficult. It was supposed to be a hard drug to take.

"In my head, you know, I'm thinking, 'Oh, sure, hard drug, right. I can take anything I want to. You don't even shoot it, what is this sissy drug?'"

6

Go Ask Alice

Tommy's curiosity about the new "sissy drug" would soon be satisfied, but not before he went through a harrowing time. The operation his doctors at General performed nearly took his life. He'd moved to South San Francisco again to live with Mack and Jillian because he thought a penisula hospital would do a better job. But according to Mickey, "they didn't think he was going to make it—it was touch and go for him. They did surgery, and they corrected all of it. They got the lung working again, pushed the stomach back where it was supposed to be, and sewed up whatever was torn. He had this big scar on his stomach that went completely around. They had to open it all up, push everything back to where it was supposed to be. It was a tough one."

Tommy did pull through, and he enjoyed another quiet suburban convalescence with Jillian and Mack, altered only by the fact that they had been recreationally sampling LSD. Acid was available in 1964 and 1965 to those who knew where to look for it, and Mack and Jillian tripped about once a week, hiring a babysitter to stay with the children and taking off themselves for a lazy fishing "trip" on the Stockton River. They would decamp from a bar and boathouse on the river, owned by Ann Dee's old partner Sarah; they chose this rural setting for turning Tommy on.

Jillian: "We went there for a weekend, it was in the country, and pretty, and the first time he took acid, I remember that he had a little bit of a bad trip. He went into the bathroom to wash his hands, and he saw blood, coming from the faucet.

"So we told him it wasn't blood—'Come on, Tom, you know that, it's just the drug.' And of course he'd done enough drugs to know that it *was* the drug, so he got over that. But then he got really high. It kind of worried me for a while, and I remember watching him pretty closely. But then he loved it, and there was no keeping him away from it."

Tommy: "They had all been taking it, just as another drug to take: Sarah, Mack, and all those people out there on the Stockton River. They were all scared when I took acid that first time. They all thought I should never take it again because I got so freaked out. I really got *freaked* out. They were scared to death and told me don't take it again. There were stories running around about people jumping off bridges. . . . They said the terror on my face was too much.

"These were fabulous people. Most were lesbians, but some were also whores. They had their clienteles, they got money sometimes just by asking for it. They weren't turning tricks for anything less than a couple hundred dollars back then. But that kind of whore, and that way of life down in North Beach was fading out: The psychedelic scene was coming in."

Having caught the hint of a nascent movement, Tommy quickly joined it. He left Mack and Jillian's, teamed with Mickey again, who was in the Tenderloin again, building a bar again—but this time it was different. Tommy: "This was the first psychedelic bar: it had all the colors, pictures on the wall of all our pasts, pictures of me in drag, purple steps leading to pink doors in the middle of crazy walls—it was just fabulous. Before its time. Nobody knew what to do with it.

"It was a gay psychedelic club, and we had the first go-go boys in San Francisco. We had a black go-go boy, a white go-go boy, and gospel singers on the bill. This was unheard of.

"The go-go boys were wearing little tiny costumes and dancing around on these platforms we had—this had never been done before. Then the black gospel singers would come out and sing beautiful gospel music. Well before the Summer of Love."

While he was working in the Larkin Street bar, the 1721 Club, connections Tommy made earlier in his life began to circle back, this time with significant impact. Grant Dailey, who'd seen Tommy's show at the Hula Shack and begun a friendship with him there, now wandered into the new club to find him.

Tommy: "He came in with long hair. If you came into any gay bar or any bar with long hair, they'd kick you out, period. It was so new, this long hair. Grant had long hair, and was working at the Coffee Cantata on Union, which was the chic place at that time.

"I was kind of frightened by LSD, but Grant came along and took me in hand. He was my psychedelic guru. He said 'Come with me, come with me,' and he moved me in with him. After I recovered from the operation, I moved into Laussat Street with Grant.

"That was the scene of the first real psychedelic parties and the psychedelic scene in the city, at that house in Laussat Street—because Grant was fabulous. With the acid, and the Chinese offerings pasted on the wall, and incense, and just the knowhow—I mean, nobody else had done that yet.

"This was very unusual, especially in the gay world, because the gay world wasn't doing this stuff yet. Some straight people had already gotten into acid, but this was gay, chic intellectual.

"He'd go out into the woods and get pine boughs and put them all over the house. . . ." The pine bough incident stuck in the memory of several people. One person who went to that party recalled that it was Christmas Eve 1964 and that the branches were only part of the effect. Grant had also electrified the punch with a hearty dose of LSD. At one point he told the assembled party, "You are all *in* your Christmas present," in case they hadn't noticed.

Another party Grant gave, a dinner party with an Indian menu—guests seated on the floor, washing their hands between courses in silver bowls brought around by servers—impressed even the hard-boiled Ann Dee so much that she later admitted, "I wanted to be a hippie, for a minute." She'd come up from Los Angeles at Tommy's invitation, and remembered that "there were about twelve of us for dinner. We started out with a drink that Grant had made out of pure boiled hashish and marijuana. It had been boiling for hours and hours, and pushed through cheesecloth, to get the finest oils. . . . It was called Bong. It looked like a Grasshopper, all fluffy and wonderful. *Oooh,* I was high for at least seventy-some hours. But mellow, you know. It wasn't a crazy high, where you feel sleepy, or detached from your body.

"I never had LSD, but that was the most psychedelic thing that ever happened to me. Tommy sat there, right at the right-hand side of Grant, holding court. Grant was doing a very grand number."

But Grant used psychedelics to do more than enliven parties, which he apparently did with some frequency. Joel Roberts, another young gay man who'd caught Tommy's act at the Hula Shack, recalled that "Grant saw things in a spiritual way. Grant was a kind of daemonic saint—not that he did anything bad or evil that I know of—but there was a playfulness in him that could destroy people. He was very much into Krishnamurti. He'd been supported when he was younger by a rich gay man who was into Krishnamurti and knew him personally, so Grant's background was much more Hindu, I think, than Buddhist.

"Grant was in love with Tommy and saw him as a spiritual

being really. He loved Tommy in a very high way. The dramatic connection that happened was that Grant took Tommy on an LSD trip to end all trips.

"If you are ready to use LSD as a spiritual experience, it can work. It's not just like a six-pack of beer. Somehow it worked for Tommy, and he began giving up a lot of the other drugs he'd been taking. Grant was like all those hippies, thinking that there are good drugs and bad drugs: speed is a bad drug, alcohol is a bad drug, tobacco is a bad drug. LSD, pot, mescaline—they were good drugs.

"So suddenly Tommy is really getting into this counterculture and this spiritual thing, and he's meditating. He must have been really ready to make some changes in his life."

Another friend on the scene offered a less charitable view of the couple: that Grant acted like a Chinese prince, with Tommy as faithful manservant. But whatever roles they took with respect to each other, psychedelics played a central part in their house rituals. Eugene, Tommy's friend from North Beach days, also looped back into Grant's group now, and he welcomed a structured approach to LSD. His own first experience with the drug occurred significantly earlier, when it was still called by its numerical surname, LSD-25. And the trip unsettled Eugene: "I had it given to me, a huge horse-capsule of it, in those days. This was before the thing arrived, before Alpert and Leary were known as names.

"I got this tablet from a male nurse at Napa State Hospital. They were giving it to the patients there, the sickest ones, the most manic, the wild people. On my capsule, printed right on it, was the content—a huge thing—it said three hundred seventy-five micrograms of LSD-25 and a hundred fifty micrograms of the chemical symbol for psylocybin, all in one cap. This is such a joke—this is what they were giving these people! I don't know how many they got, I only had one. Neither word meant a thing to me.

"The nurse was proselytizing this stuff. He'd taken many of them at the hospital, so he knew what he was giving me. I could tell by the look in his eye that he thought I had an awful lot of guts, because he'd only taken it in the clinical situation, where there were bars. If anything happened, everything would be under control of the state hospital. But I paid ten dollars and took the tab right then. I just popped it, like I would pop any pill. I was used to popping things.

"I'm at a friend's house, Carole Davis—he was too chicken to take it—and he's on his way to work in a nightclub in the Tenderloin. We left the place to walk him to work, and it was summer and still light, even though it's getting eightish.

"We passed a florist's in the Sir Francis Drake Hotel, and late-afternoon sun was hitting the window, so it was lit by real light. They always filled their windows with a mixture of what they sold—real flowers and vases, and artificial ones, but expensive ceramic stuff. It was hard to tell, when you were normal, which ones were real and which were artificial. That was their object, because these were high-end items. They had them all mixed up.

"Right away, my first hit was that everything started to vibrate like this—real quick. All my life I looked in that window, I always passed by there, so I was looking at a familiar display. But immediately I realized the difference in their vibration, between the natural ones and the artificial. Each object was now vibrating with its own frequency, and I could now witness it. Somehow or another, time was changed, or sight was improved, and I could actually see the spaces between the light pulses. . . .

"I staggered around the streets. I had trouble walking."

Eugene's adventure led him to see vivid caricatures of people he passed on the street, and at a movie he stumbled into, he saw not only the film but the editing numbers written on the filmstrips, the studio labeling on the props, and the actors' faces (not to mention their true natures) through their makeup. After sitting through a double feature, he felt sufficiently in control to attempt the walk home.

When LSD appeared at Grant's, Eugene knew what was what: "So I immediately grabbed the next tablet. It was nice that we could do it in a calm, home situation. We sat around and had these LSD sessions. We had them structured so that we didn't do them out on the street, because so many people that we did it with flipped their lid that way. We structured it all around *The Tibetan Book of the Dead*. Grant did; he'd already investigated it. He'd already read Lama Govinda, *The Tibetan Book of the Dead*. He'd already done Gurdjieff and all these other things. Grant was going down to the library and getting all these books, and we'd read sections of them when we took it."

Because Grant worked hard at creating specific environments, little shrines, or altars began to appear in their new home, a rambling Victorian mansion in the lower Haight. He and Tommy both took pleasure in arranging sacred objects in a corner or alcove of a room; spiritual texts, gifts, crystals, a picture of an ascended master, feathers, special beads—these, and unpredictable other things were fair game as altar objects.

Joel Roberts, a mansion regular, arrived one day bearing a copy of Buddhism's most widely chanted text—*The Heart Sutra*—thinking it would look good adorning one of the shrines. Joel had gotten the scripture in a stunning bit of serendipity:

"One day, Allen Ginsberg, the Beat poet, was walking down Market Street, and we connected. We were walking on Market Street where Powell comes into it—there's a Woolworth's there, a cablecar turnaround—and at that moment he observes two or three soldiers and two or three sailors ready to kill each other. They had just exchanged all the cocksucker, motherfucker insults, so he pulls out his finger cymbals and start chanting MA KA

HANNYA HARAMITA SHIN GYO. . . . I'd never heard this, I didn't know what it was.

"You have to understand the context. I was a young person, experimenting with the whole sixties thing, marijuana, LSD, but this was like magic really. What happened *was* a bit of magic. Instead of them saying, 'Old man, what are you doing?' or slugging him, or continuing with the fight, the fight totally broke up, and not in a way you would predict, with the sailors going off together, and the soldiers doing the same. I'll never forget it. One of the sailors ran toward Woolworth's; one ran the other direction down Market; one of the soldiers ran up Powell and the other crossed Market the other way. So this was like magic.

"I said, 'Old man, what was that you chanted? And where can I get a copy?'

"He told me to go to Sokoji Temple. So I went the very next day. I really wanted to get hold of this, because to me it was magic. Nobody told me what Buddhism was; all I knew was that this was magic, it had prevented a fight. I'm nonviolent, and it was a wonderful thing.

"I went there, and the zendo at that time was upstairs. Downstairs were all these old Japanese and Japanese-American men doing something that appeared to be gambling. They weren't in a hurry to tell me where the Zen Center was, and I was a little bit frightened. Finally, they pointed upstairs, and I went up to this fairly big meditation hall, the zendo. Nobody was there. Totally unattended.

"I looked around, and soon I found a sign that read, 'Say the sutra with your ears,' and below it were a bunch of beautifully made copies of the sutra, printed on beautiful paper.

"There was nobody around, and I waited and waited because, you know, in a Christian church, you always assume that somebody's going to show up because they're afraid you're going to steal something.

"Well, sure enough, I waited long enough to say to myself, 'It's probably okay'—you know how you do when you're getting ready to steal something—'it's probably okay if I take a few of these sutras, because nobody's showing up.' So again it was like magic, because at that very moment, Suzuki comes out from behind the chrysanthemums and says, 'Can I help you?'

"So I don't know what to do, I know nothing about Buddhism, I have no clever questions to ask of this great teacher. All I said, very stutteringly was, 'Uh, uh, can I have one of these?'

"And he said, 'Oh. Yes, take more.' I must have taken like, seven copies, and one of those copies I gave to Tommy.

"I told him the story, and because of the way we were operating, he also saw this as magic. I told him, 'I chant it even on the bus. It said, "Say it with your ears," so I say it out loud. This is really important, I want to tell you that.' And he took it that way, that it wasn't just a little gift, that it was something really important. I myself didn't know how important it would be, but it really was his introduction to Buddhism."

Beyond physical possession of the text, which in Buddhism is considered to be a beneficial circumstance in itself, Tommy and Joel enjoyed puzzling out its meaning.

Joel: "For one thing, for those of us who took drugs, it presented constant paradox that just totally blew the brain apart. 'It doesn't increase, it doesn't decrease, it wasn't born, it doesn't die.' Then while you're chanting you're saying, 'No eyes, no ears, no nose, tongue.' But what? you're reading it with your eyes, you're chanting it with your tongue, you're hearing it with your ears, and it's saying no, no, no.

"Much later, I understood a little more subtly about emptiness, but at the time I took it literally. I'm saying this with my no-tongue, hearing it with my no-ears, seeing it with my no-eyes. I got stoned by it, I really tripped out, and I think Tommy came to see it that way, too, because later he saw it as something worth getting up early in the morning for, obviously. To sit and to chant. Later when he would introduce me to people, he would say, 'This is the guy that turned me on to the *Prajnaparamita Sutra*,' so I guess it became as important to him as it was to me."

As magically powerful as the *Prajnaparamita* texts may be, the seeds sown with Joel's gift took a few years to sprout. Tommy had other business in the Haight-Ashbury, not the least of which was running a local newspaper called *The Haight-Ashbury Tribune* or more frequently, *THAT,* its acronym. A year before, the rag had been a gay nudie tabloid featuring very young men. Now its owner, a friend and supporter of Grant Dailey's, wanted a hipper, more widely readable paper, and put its publication in Tommy's and Grant's hands. Much to their surprise, they succeeded with it as a financial venture, taking in substantial advertising revenue. These newspaper profits contributed about a third of the funding for their psychedelic salon; Tommy's ATD kicked in a second regular monthly share, and to make up the shortfall, they did what all self-respecting San Francisco hippies did—they dealt drugs.

Thus they passed a brief, blithe period as true hippies. Tommy's hair grew long again, and he went without shoes. He and Grant formed the core of a crowd that tripped regularly, partied often, broadcast news of the latest events through their newspaper, and inculcated themselves with a smorgasbord of spiritual teachings.

Tommy: "Grant was one of the main people in my life. He introduced me to everything that even resembled Zen practice. Before that, I just had been a crazy drag-queen junkie, but there was this complete metamorphosis that happened to me when I lived with Grant."

Their lifestyle, however, was not destined for longevity, and they split up over an incident with a street urchin.

"It had to do with this kid who had stolen some grass from Grant and me. This was a kid Grant and I brought up from Los Angeles. We'd gone down there on my ATD check, to Disneyland, with a bag of acid, and we picked up this kid off the street in one of our deals. At some point this kid stole some grass from us. Then he came back, and he had hepatitis. I wanted to take care of him. I was into being a good psychedelic person, and I wanted to take care of this kid. But Grant said he couldn't stay, he had hepatitis, he had stolen grass from us. . . . This is at the same time that the newspaper was becoming a big deal, and this big fabulous hippie scene is happening. . . . So I left."

The *way* they fell apart—with Tommy taking the side of the boy, arguing for compassion and understanding beyond what his housemate could accept—was a pattern that would repeat itself later in Tommy's life.

Tommy landed on his feet though, and hooked up with two men who were lovers and had been living together for about a year, Eddie Troia and Jorges. Eddie owned a large house on California Street and made good money as a hairdresser and dress designer. Jorges, known to his intimates as Jeremiah, was a small-time pot dealer. Tommy: "I had been selling grass, and Jorges, had been selling some grass too. We sort of combined our outfits, and then he *really* got into selling grass, and right away he had a big psychedelic supermarket."

Joel: "Jeremiah was the biggest-time dealer that I ever saw. He'd make international calls about shipments of this and that. But he was almost Christ-like in his compassion and generosity."

Jeremiah's generosity and drugs, Eddie's well-appointed three-story house, and Tommy's gregarious nature mixed, then coa-lesced, through a steady stream of parties, into the rude beginnings of an urban commune.

Jillian: "We'd come in to Jeremiah's, and what his trip was I never really knew. Whenever you would go to his house, there were always so many people there; he was always putting up people, homeless people, and feeding people. Tommy was helping to feed people too. They got into that.

"There would be so many people at Jeremiah's house. I knew Tom and this woman, and I knew Jeremiah and one other person, but the faces kept changing all the time, because the people came and went, came and went."

Joel: "It was an inter-incestuous time. Everybody knew everybody: everybody knew someone who was in the political movement, into the hip movement, the peace movement, the spiritual movement. The barriers had come down, the illusions had broken, and people were really connected. In those days, you let everybody you knew know everybody else you knew.

"They were taking in a lot of kids, which every commune did, every commune took in people. We didn't really have homelessness in those days. Anyone staying on the street was invited home by *somebody*.

"Jeremiah was the leader of that commune, almost too much so. He had too much power. The only thing that saved him was that there seemed to be no evil in him, so he didn't misuse his power. But he had a lot of it, and a lot of charisma."

Perhaps another thing that "saved" the commune leaders was that they had no idea what they were doing. According to Eddie Troia, they didn't conceive of themselves as a commune; they just did things instinctively, just took people in, just cooked dinner for whoever was there at the time. There did tend to be a number of handsome young men and boys around at any given time, but the house had straight residents as well. They weren't a gay commune as such. At the orgies that happened at most of the parties, it wasn't so much a question of having a particular sexual orientation as just having one altogether. Rules of any kind were in notoriously short supply.

Such prejudice as did hold sway focused instead on drug habits. LSD, peyote, mescaline, mushrooms, marijuana—these were spiritual sacraments. People who used speed, particularly people who *shot* speed, were regarded with suspicion by centrist hippies. The

Family, as the commune came to be known, housed both camps in an uneasy truce.

Tommy could have been a general in either one. "I took *tons* of psychedelic drugs. I used to be—I was actually getting a little far out. Jorges actually said, 'Tommy, you are truly becoming a psychedelic person. Maybe you better think about whether you're taking too much.' I was getting—you know how people got kind of shell-shocked on those drugs? I was really getting out of it. I had to make a conscious decision at one point whether I was going to go over the edge. I could have allowed myself to go that route and be a vegetable. I kind of had to have people lead me around. I had a kid who used to lead me around. It was to the point where I was getting too out of it. I took *too* many psychedelics. Then I went back on hard drugs. I only stopped shooting speed briefly."

Tommy passed a few years this way. The Summer of Love in 1967 came and went and the commune grew subtly more defined. Suddenly both the speed consumption at the house, and the Family's stature as a commune rose several notches, when Jorges installed a rock band in the basement. The group called itself Salvation, and they were, in the words of one of the members, "fun-loving, escapist duggies who saw rock as a way to get along, without a real musician in the lot." The band managed nonetheless to play regular gigs, both in the Haight-Ashbury's fertile musical scene and up and down the West Coast, as acid rock took hold. Tommy enjoyed going to the basement to watch them rehearse and getting loaded with them down there.

He and his new coterie, his new kids, helped the band haul equipment and set up for shows; they became the roadies. In 1968, when Salvation went to Los Angeles to record their second album, Tommy went along as cook and general house-mother-manager. The band set up for rehearsals on a ranch in Simi Valley, some sixty miles from L.A., and plunged into a routine of wild times, heavy drugs, and virtually no practice.

"There weren't even any drums on the property," recalls Bo Rizen, a San Francisco drummer who was called to fill in after Salvation's own drummer "freaked out." "The first thing I realized was that these guys were shooting speed, and I was uncomfortable with that.

"They did it right in front of me, and when they saw how it upset me, they promised not to do that, not to do it in front of me. You could always tell when people were on speed and were losing it. There was a certain frazzled look they had and a certain quality of mind salad, very finely minced mind salad."

But Bo stuck it out there for several weeks and found himself looking to Tommy not only for friendship, but for sanity. "Tommy was so sweet and so lovable, and somehow so wholesome, that it was unbelievable. He was a breath of fresh air."

The feeling was mutual. Tommy: "This guy shows up, and of course, he was freaked out. He was already a kind of semispiritual-type person, quiet. He played good drums. He and I sort of took care of them at that time because they were wild, the band." So much so, that Tommy, even as wild as he had been, often hid from them: "I lived in the barn, and I lived behind the chicken coop for a while. I moved behind the chicken coop to be alone; things were getting too crazy. There were actually still chickens in the chicken coop. These kids were crazy—really crazy, speed crazy.

"They just had no boundaries: screaming, yelling, throwing things. We went into this club where we played one night, out on the water, in some beach—a famous club. The band had this rubber stamp: an army hat turned upside down, with pot growing out of it. This was kind of like their emblem. At this club, they stamped it everywhere, on the walls, everywhere, in this beautiful, clean club. They just destroyed it."

When the conservative, ranching community of Simi Valley finally decided to clamp down on this wartish growth in their midst, Tommy took the heat. It had been a quiet day, with most of the band gone. Tommy and Bo split a tablet of purple acid, and passed a convivial afternoon gardening, pausing only to gawk at the afternoon freight-train as it roared over the rails traversing the ranch. Band members wandered home, evening fell, then suddenly the ranch was swarming with police.

Tommy: "The police came, and everyone was stoned. There were sheep all on the property, and my kids had gone out and found these sheep that had run away from the people next door. The police went to the people next door, and the people next door said those are our sheep. Our kids didn't steal them. They went and found the sheep, and they were on our property, waiting to go back next door. But they took me off to jail and booked me for sheep rustling. The police needed something to book me on, so they booked me on *sheep rustling*!

"They took me off to Ventura County jail, miles away. I hardly had anything on, just a loincloth. I had my hands cuffed behind my back. They kept me for three days and then cut me loose, because there really wasn't anything to book me on. Seventy-two hours.

"At first they were just going to cut me loose out on the streets, but I went upstairs and started a ruckus with somebody. I finally found the right name. I said, 'Hey listen, they just picked me up, and I got busted. I've been in jail, but the minute I go out in that street, start hitchhiking back to Simi Valley, I'm going to get busted again. Just look at me.' Long hair, basically no clothes on, being a hippie—in those days they'd bust you for nothing. So I made them drive me back to Simi Valley."

Bo Rizen's journal of that day reads, in part: "The police raided us in the evening but could find no crimes committed. The neighbor complained his sheep were missing, and Tommy, the gentlest, and I thought, the purest person there, was somehow taken to jail. I felt I learned that it is the most vulnerable person who takes the brunt of the karma in a situation."

Salvation finally finished the record, though how much of it they laid down themselves is questionable, since along with the band members' names, the record jacket lists the top seven studio musicians of the day as players. The band played a gig at the Whiskey à Go Go, another at the Shrine Auditorium, and an outdoor concert in Griffith Park, then headed back to the commune headquarters. Here, Eddie Troia's patience had worn thin.

Eddie had disapproved fiercely of speed shooters from the outset, and had complained to Tommy about it on many occasions. He felt that needle use was "way beyond recreational," and he'd only been irked further by Tommy's vague, hippie-esque responses: "Well, whatever," or, "It's perfect." Pressed like this, Tommy could get bitchy; he caused scenes that Eddie viewed as having "no other purpose but to cause trouble." Finally Eddie lost his temper. To cleanse what he saw as the "horrible karma" of the speed habit, he purged his house—owner's prerogative. He threw out Tommy, he threw out Tommy's kids, he threw out everyone. Eddie even tossed Jorges, and told him to "take your fucking band with you!" Then, with poetic flair, he left the house himself—a complete evacuation.

Eddie stayed away for a while, but most of the commune reassembled in a little cottage (which Eddie also owned) around the corner. Tommy's spiritual side began to assert itself more strongly now, although the manifestations it took were bizarre. He'd continued his altar-assembling all through his commune days: "I had like, an altar here with a drawn picture of the Buddha here, and Sri Ramana Maharshi here, and then stuff for the altar here, below it. But then I had all kinds of things: I had like, a branch hanging. . . . I used to sit in front of my altar, and the altar had a champagne glass on it, right in front of the Buddha, with my works laying in it. I used to shoot up, and take acid, and sit in front of that altar."

Tommy felt that the picture of Sri Ramana Maharshi in particular dosed him with spirituality.

"I saw that picture first from Rosalyn Sharphall, an astrologer book lady. She had the book, and I saw it just by accident. But when I saw that face, it blew me away.

"I don't know exactly what I felt. But when I used to look at it—sometimes I would take acid and look at it, and it would change into a thousand faces. I used to sit and stare at that photograph and it would just change, like *choo, choo, choo, choo, choo,* just like that one face right after another. Fabulous. I sort of knew who he was, just from looking at that picture. Eventually I got hold of the book, but I never really read it. I knew that this whole thing was 'Who am I?'

"That's when I first had some sense of practice—I could also see myself in that picture. Not so much that I could see myself in that picture but . . . I knew that was me. Something like that. I never tried to put it in words."

On Christmas Eve in 1967, Tommy's youngest brother Louie was killed in a car accident. A bizarre symmetry hovered over Tommy's and Louie's accidents: Tommy was the only person not killed in his, Louie was the only person who was killed; Tommy had been saved because he wore no seat belt and was thrown clear of the car; Louie also neglected the seat belt and died when his head cracked on the cement.

Louie's death hit the Dorsey family very hard. He'd been the baby, a kind of favorite, the child his parents had had time to watch growing up. Even though Tommy hadn't been home to Santa Barbara in nearly twenty years, he went back for the funeral.

Phyllis: "He was a mess, long hair, things wrapped around his legs—we hadn't seen him because he never came home like that before. I hadn't seen the depth he'd reached, and he had always been so neat and tidy before, so personally clean. It was a shock when I saw him get off that plane—because we were so devastated anyway, with the death—then him on top of it.

"I picked him up at the airport, I took him to my house and I said, 'Get out of those clothes. Sit down—I'm going to give you a haircut. Mom and Dad are going through enough right now without them having to see you like this.' He didn't like it, but he agreed to it. I gave him some of my husband's clothes to put on, but he was much taller than my husband so they didn't fit well."

Having begun to have a first "sense of practice," then absorbing the impact of his brother's sudden death, changes started to rush in on Tommy. For one thing, he quit shooting speed. He just quit, as if the drug had let him go, the monkey fled his back. A day or so later, walking on Haight Street, he stooped to pick up a Popsicle wrapper someone had carelessly tossed on the sidewalk. In the late 1960s a wrapper was one of the lesser evils one might step around on a Haight Street sidewalk, but for some reason this one stopped Tommy. "I bent down and picked it up, and right as I did, I said to myself, 'Does this mean I'm responsible for whatever I see?' I told myself it didn't, but actually I knew that it did.

"Quitting shooting speed wasn't hard physically, because the impetus to quit gave me a lot of energy. Whatever it was—just quitting gave me energy. Next thing I knew, I was running barefoot in the streets, cleaning them up, cleaning up Haight Street.

"It was a big thing for me. In fact, nobody could believe I did it. People who knew me and how heavy I was into drugs couldn't believe that one day I was doing it and the next day I had stopped."

Tommy avoided squandering this new energy or burning out. A kind of mantra began to run through in his mind—"I am going to try to do everything the best way I can." He brought his insights home. "I started cleaning the commune up, to where it was very beautiful, serene, metaphysical, and spiritual. We had incense and music. At that time, the Beatles' music was popular. *Sergeant Pepper* was playing all the time.

"My vision of the house was that it should shine, the glass should shine, the floors should shine. So it was clean, but still patched and hippie-ish. This was my effort; getting out of drugs to start changing my life was by cleaning up, literally cleaning up."

During this exuberant time, Tommy also saw through the lifelong shame he'd felt about his homosexuality: "I think I wore that guilt for years, even after I thought I dropped it. I can remember actually feeling that condition being torn off my shoulders. I could just really feel it, like it was being torn away. 'Now I can let go of this, *finally* let go of this guilt for being homosexual.'"

Shortly afterward, two young runaways, brothers, came to the commune. Tommy lavished David and Jamie with the special attention he reserved for handsome young men, and within a matter of days he found himself in love with Jamie, the younger brother. The relationship would last the rest of Tommy's life.

Purifying energy continued to surge through Tommy, with mixed results. Other commune members did not necessarily appreciate having their dresser drawers emptied out and repacked, with items folded in symmetrical piles. Then one day Mickey Martin called to ask a favor, and Tommy finally had an appropriate outlet for his new passion.

Mickey: "I was into shooting dope—I mean up to the eyeballs. Tommy cleaned up before I did, but I decided to clean up too. Something told me, 'Okay that's it.' I listen when the inner voice tells me, and I called Tommy up and I said, 'I'm ready to quit.' He said, 'If you're really ready, I'll be over.' He came over, locked the doors, worked with me for two weeks, and cleaned me up. I've never gone back."

Tommy: "When I went to live with Mickey, that's when the depression hit. With the depression came the words 'Now that

I'm doing everything right, what's wrong with everybody else?' I was irritated by everybody and by the way they were living their lives. I didn't own the irritation myself. That's when I started having a hard time with my head.

"I talked to my friend Yves about it, who I had talked to about a number of things. Yves, Grant, and Eugene used to get together and talk about Krishnamurti and Madame Blavatsky, things like that. I figured they knew something. I always thought they knew something that I could never get into.

"But I told Yves, 'Listen, I'm having terrible headaches. I feel I might have to put myself in an institution or something. I can't get through this period.' He said, 'Well, I just went to this conference called the LSD Conference.' " (The LSD Conference, sponsored by the University of California, had been organized by an enterprising young man named Richard Baker. Psychedelic and spiritual luminaries of many kinds attended, including Richard Alpert/Ram Dass and Shunryu Suzuki-roshi.) "There, they said that people had something called post-LSD syndrome. People who have taken a lot of drugs, speed, and acid and then stopped taking them are experiencing this thing. You have post-LSD syndrome, and the thing you are supposed to do now, is meditate."

7

Beginner's Mind

Tommy had been to Sokoji Temple once before, accompanying Grant on an inspection of San Francisco's spiritual high spots. He'd heard Joel's tale of Suzuki-roshi and the magical Heart Sutra; he'd done sessions of what he thought of as meditation, and he'd even seen Suzuki-roshi at the famed Haight-Ashbury Human Be-In, but he'd never put it all together.

"So off I went barefoot, patched pants, long hair. We got up an hour before you were supposed to be there: me, Mickey, and James used to come with us sometimes too. We'd get up in the morning, have a cup of coffee, smoke a joint, and go off to the Sokoji Temple to sit. We were living at Mickey's house in the Haight then. It was a long walk, and it was freezing cold, but we'd get up and walk in the cold. It was like we were flagellating ourselves. We probably could have figured it out better."

Mickey recalls that even after arriving, there was more figuring to do: "We went to the temple, and we went in there, and went up along the little balcony. I says, 'Well, what do we do?' I'll never forget this—Tommy says, 'Well, let's do what they're doing.' I said, 'Well, they're just facing the wall,' so he says, 'Well then, let's face the wall.' I said, 'Okay, seems simple enough to me.' That's how we started with Buddhism."

But the reason these two shriven yet unsavory hippies were

whispering at 5:00 A.M. about a practice that neither of them knew—the reason, in fact, that anyone at all was sitting in the balcony of the Sokoji Temple facing the wall—was a quiet, humble, and extraordinarily potent Zen teacher called Suzuki-roshi, who himself rose at that hour to sit with his disciples in the meditation known as zazen.

Shunryu Suzuki was born in Japan in 1904. His father, a strict Zen master, sent the boy to one of his own disciples for early training—an even tougher Zen teacher named Gyakuju So-on, who ran an austere rural temple. Following the traditional pattern of his lineage, young Suzuki studied religion at Komazowa Buddhist University in Kyoto and at an early age developed an interest in coming to America. He pursued a course in English language at the university, spent time with English-speaking visitors, and boarded for a year in the house of an elderly British woman named Mrs. Ransome.

To obtain requisite experience and certifications, Suzuki entered Eiheiji Temple. He thrived at this rigorous training monastery of the Soto Zen school and stayed a number of years practicing intensively. He would have preferred to continue living quietly at Eiheiji, he said later, but his teacher suddenly died. Suzuki, now thirty-one, became saddled with the administrative and religious responsibilities of his teacher's temples. He left the monastery dutifully, entered the ranks of local officialdom, married, and started a family.

Unlike many such temple priests, Suzuki continued a daily practice of meditation and study. Though he took a vocal and extremely unpopular pacifist position against World War II, he slowly gained in stature after the war, devoting himself to physically repairing and rebuilding temples and schools in the area. Warm, mature, brightly handsome, and steeped in Zen teaching, he was an ideal candidate to teach abroad should the call ever come from Soto headquarters.

Finally, in May 1959, Suzuki-roshi flew from Tokyo to San Francisco. Here the local Japanese congregation installed him in the priest quarters of what was called Sokoji Soto Zen Mission, a large, rambling, slightly crumbling structure built in the 1890s as a synagogue. On the corner of Bush and Octavia streets, the building sat squarely in the burgeoning Japantown section of San Francisco, and with daily *go* games in an adjacent parlor, it functioned as a kind of community center. The congregation expected Suzuki-roshi to perform ceremonies—funerals, particularly—and to appear regularly as the Buddhist functionary at festivals and other community events. Suzuki-roshi fulfilled these expectations, but he also went beyond them: he continued his daily zazen practice, letting it be known that anyone who cared to join him at 5:30 A.M. was welcome.

Word of the genuine-article Zen master leaked out to the Beat community, and soon Suzuki-roshi had magnetized a small but devoted sitting group. Among the adventurous types making their way to 1881 Bush Street during the early years were poets Joanne Kyger, Gary Snyder, Allen Ginsberg, and Lew Welch. By 1962, the group had incorporated as the Zen Center. It existed under the good graces of the Japanese community, sharing—sometimes dominating—not only the space of Sokoji but the attentions of Suzuki-roshi.

For his part, Suzuki-roshi found himself more and more engaged by the naive energy of his American students. He never ignored his obligations to the Japanese congregation, but having come through the political, somewhat decadent temple system in Japan, he'd longed for a fresh approach to Buddhist teachings. This he now found with his new students. Crude, certainly, in their understanding, often arrogant, disrespectful by Japanese standards, and frequently operating on questionable premises about food, politics, and spirituality in general, Suzuki-roshi's American students nonetheless exhibited an openness and a hunger for the teachings that he valued. He liked their "beginner's mind," as he called it, and he went so far as to equate beginner's mind with the loftiest goals of Zen meditation.

Not that these people didn't need work. Suzuki-roshi inflicted as much decorum on his students as possible, but he did it primarily through example and simple observation. He made pointed contact with the practitioners every day. Tommy: "After zazen was over, you had to file through his office to get out. I figured that that was what you did everywhere, but no, this was his special thing. Each person had to pass him. Each person would come in front of him, and he'd look you right in the eye, and bow to you, and you'd bow back. He bowed to every single person.

"There weren't really any rules about anything. You should have *seen* the people who arrived at Sokoji Temple—if any of us had arrived at any other practice place in the world, we wouldn't have been allowed in the front door. But Suzuki-roshi used to bow to us."

The gentle, daily, very personal inspection by a Zen master had its effect, often making students notice their own deportment more carefully. Tommy himself rounded a big corner in grooming: "I remember riding a bus to Sokoji—later we figured out how to do it on a bus—and I had my feet crossed, my bare feet. I looked at my feet and I thought, 'My god, am I sitting in the zendo with those filthy feet?' It never occurred to me before, so that's when I bought some *zoris.* I didn't have a pair of shoes because I used to run barefoot. I ran barefoot for years."

But what was it that Tommy and Mickey (and about sixty other people) were converging to do each morning at the antisocial hour of 5:00 A.M.? Exactly nothing. While Zen Buddhism looked exotic, the actual practice of zazen couldn't have been more plain: a person simply sat still for forty minutes at a time, facing a blank wall. Senior students gave newcomers instructions about proper body posture during zazen—back straight, eyes half open, mouth closed, legs folded stably, arms relaxed, and hands forming a kind of circle. They told them to "follow" their breath, or to count their exhalations one to ten, and they told them that should their minds wander, to simply return their attention to posture and breath.

Suzuki-roshi emphasized that this practice—zazen—was the ultimate goal of Zen; there wasn't another enlightenment to attain. He didn't completely dismiss the notions of satori or nirvana—so popular with the Beats and with the hippies after them—but he taught that they were already present in the simple sitting practice. Zazen, he stressed in lecture after lecture, was not a means to enlightenment but was rather the fullest and most complete expression of enlightenment. Like it or not.

Thus the specifics of meditation became significant. What shape Buddha would you be? Students sometimes fixated on tiny distinctions—the hand *mudra* should be held just here, actually a little higher, and closer to the body, and the chin should be tucked slightly more—and the same scrutiny applied to meditation in action. How to move in the zendo, how to take a seat properly, and rise from one after a period of sitting, which foot was used to enter the room, and which was used to cross the threshold on the way out—these things counted, there was a *way* to do them. Suzuki-roshi demonstrated that the Buddha's path was expressed not only in formal zazen but in mindful awareness of the details of daily life. Necessary acts of eating, sleeping, washing, working, and cooking were regarded as sacraments; not holy in the usual sense of the word, but vivid and poignant.

With his Buddhism of simple meditation and direct, clear mindful action, Suzuki-roshi hooked Tommy, who was still cleaning up madly and trying to do everything the best way he could.

Zen Center matched Tommy's needs in another important way:

among most students there, intellectual study was considered secondary, often something to be avoided altogether. Tommy—having never read a book all the way through, and having abandoned traditional studies to learn the invisible sciences of the street—could only have felt scholastically inferior to Grant and Eugene and Yves during their thematic acid trips and the spiritual discussions that followed. But now at Zen Center, where meditation and postmeditation experience were the texts most highly prized, Tommy read as well as the next person—he read a bit better in fact, partly because he was a good decade older than most Zen students. Suzuki-roshi studied Buddhist texts constantly and took them up in his talks, but he told his students that the main purpose of his teaching was to encourage them to practice zazen. As eloquent, persuasive, and magnetic as he was to some, Suzuki-roshi said he wished he could refrain from speaking after zazen.

Whether Suzuki-roshi spoke or not, or what the subject was, mattered little to Tommy. "Suzuki-roshi was a funny little old Japanese man that I couldn't understand. I couldn't understand his English, but I just made myself go anyway. I went to all his lectures. There was something about him that attracted me."

And after that first morning of zazen, Tommy said, "I never stopped. Various people came and sat with us: Yves, Eugene, Grant, but I kept sitting. I never missed a period."

Mickey: "Tommy, of course, had come home. He had come home because he immediately became part of the community there. He belonged.

"We were doing it about two months, and they were having a seven-day *sesshin*. So Tommy says to me, 'You want to try it?' I said, 'Oh I don't think I can do it.' You know, I'm still oooh and aaah when I get up from the pillow. 'I'm aching all over, and you want me to go seven days. . . .'

"He says, 'Let's try it. If we don't like it, we'll quit after two or three days.'

"I said okay—after sitting for just two months. So we're doing it, and our seats are up on the stage. They had like a little podium, and we were sitting up there. Then we'd do the walking meditation. I'd pass Tommy, and I'd go—I'd make a face, like saying *'Let's go'*—and he'd shake his head *'No way.'* Every time he'd pass me he'd do the same face. He made me do seven days. After the fourth or fifth day I started to look forward to it, see. You know, you get that lightheadedness, it's wonderful. That's how we did it."

To make their trek to morning zazen easier, Zen students had invaded the Japantown neighborhood, rooming together in cooperative apartments. The Zen Center itself maintained a flat, and Tommy soon moved in: "It was like a hippie pad that they showed you to. It wasn't really like a dormitory facility, it was just a room. I was sleeping on a tatami, in a sleeping bag I had bummed from somebody. No mat even.

"I started cleaning the place up, and that's where they first saw me. Reb Anderson tried to talk me into painting, and I said, 'No. What you see me doing is what I'm going to do. Don't mess with me.' I could see that he thought I was a live wire, and he thought he was going to get hold of me. All these other guys are lying around, sloughing off. Because I'm cleaning, he wanted to get me to paint too. I said, 'Nope. This is what I do. Cleaning, cooking.' I didn't live very long in the dormitory though. After about six months I went to Tassajara."

Other Zen students liked Tommy, though they thought he was "fuzzy" and they found his speech to be nearly unintelligible. Still, he was responsible—he did what he said he'd do—and he worked calmly and with humor at his tasks. It was clear to everyone that he had a rough time getting to zazen: age and previous habits now cost him in terms of energy and health, but get there he did.

Suzuki-roshi emphasized sincerity and steadiness in meditation practice, and Tommy demonstrated both. It was natural, then, for him to proceed to Zen Center's "baby monastery" at Tassajara.

Suzuki-roshi founded Tassajara with the aim of giving his students an undistracted taste of Zen life: the monastery stood in a remote valley inland ten miles from the Big Sur coast, accessible only by a narrow, serpentine dirt road. Buildings had been built on the land, and a road to the property cut into the steep ravines of the coastal mountain range because sulfur springs bubbled to the surface in and around Tassajara Creek. The restorative properties of the springs were legendary. Indians made their way there for dozens of centuries and visitations by white folks began in the 1860s. By the time Zen Center obtained the property in 1967, a big hotel had been erected and burned to the ground, and a saloon had thrived (complete with free-flowing liquor, gambling, loose women, murders), then fallen into disuse (except for the ghosts). Electric lines had been strung to some of the redwood shacks dotting the property, but no power ran through the wires. The baths still gave access to the sulfury waters of the hot springs, but the plunges were grimy and old, and the bathhouse itself was in a dangerously decayed state. Zen Center obtained the property with the surging support of San Francisco's artistic, literary, and spiritual communities, including the waning psychedelic scene. A Zenefit, as it was advertised, featured the Grateful Dead, Jefferson Airplane, and Big Brother and the Holding Company, playing for "the first Zen monastery in America."

Zen Center had run just a few "practice periods"—three-month intensives—at Tassajara when Tommy ventured there, in the fall of 1969. Physical conditions alone at Tassajara wearied a practitioner: the temperature often fluctuated fifty degrees in a day, from icy mornings in the thirties or lower to sweltering afternoons in the eighties. The cabins offered no hot water or electric power, and as aged, undermaintained resort shacks, they barely provided shelter from the elements. Students used plastic stretched across wood frames for windows, kerosene lamps for light and minimal heat, and a couple of communal sinks and rope lines for a laundry.

If survival didn't sufficiently test one's Zen ardor, then the daily schedule did. A wake-up bell circulated through camp each morning at 3:40 A.M., and the first period of zazen began at 4:05. Forty minutes of sitting were followed by ten minutes of walking meditation on the cold, polished linoleum floor of the zendo. Socks were not permitted. Forty more minutes of zazen followed; then students rose and reoriented their scats for a half-hour of bowing and chanting. An hour of study came next—Buddhist texts only. The old dining room where study hall convened was heated by a wood stove, and students clustered around it for warmth, and around the teapots set out on a nearby table.

Breakfast was served very formally back in the zendo, to practitioners who dragged their aching legs and backs into meditation posture once more. They ate from a set of nested bowls, following a highly prescribed ritual for using the bowls, the cloths they were wrapped in, and the eating utensils. After saying the proper chants, and eating the food, and rinsing and drying and rewrapping the bowls—this while still sitting in zazen posture—and after waiting for the most senior practitioners to leave the hall, students were released for a short break. The bell convening work-meeting rang about thirty minutes later, giving people enough time to change from robes (required at all times in the zendo) into work clothes.

Renovating the old resort and keeping the monastery going required lots of physical work: carpentry, masonry, gardening, "general labor," and kitchen work. The morning work period ran close to three hours. Then it was back to the cabins for a change into robes, to go back into the zendo for another forty-minute sit, more bowing and chanting and another formal meal. A tea break divided the long afternoon work period, and at the end of the day, students trooped out for a bath in the hot springs. On cold days, this might be the only time a person felt completely warm. Another service of chanting followed, then dinner in the zendo, a short break, and two more forty-minute periods of zazen. Lights were to be out around 9:00 P.M.

Tommy: "It was the hardest thing I ever did in my life. I was on a bummer from the minute I got up every morning until the sunlight started coming over the hill. I hated it. I was on a big bummer the whole time. Getting up at three o'clock in the morning, in the freezing cold, living in a cabin with no heat, going to that zendo. If it hadn't been for Suzuki-roshi, I wouldn't have made it through that first practice period. Suzuki-roshi's presence—and there is no way I can tell you how—but because he was there.

"I was on a bummer, but if they hadn't had me in the kitchen, I would have been dead. The kitchen was warm at least, but it was crazy in there—all the macrobiotic people were running the show."

Tommy recalled that he "hid" in the sink, washing an endless stream of dishes and letting the bummer rinse out of his mind. "I had all kinds of negative thinking going on. 'This isn't right, that isn't right.' But even I knew enough at that point to just keep my mouth shut. That that was just my trip going on in my head."

Angie Runyon was Tassajara's head cook at the time: "He washed every dish in the place, he washed every pot. I'd say to him, 'Wouldn't you like to do something a little more fun? Something a little more creative?' 'Oh, no, I'm happy doing this.'

"When he first came in, he was so discombobulated I thought, this guy isn't going to make it three days. But his way was just to take care of whatever was right in front of him. He washed dishes, swept the grounds, he planted little things around his cabin. He kept that kitchen clean. He'd just come in and take care of whatever needed to be taken care of. He was completely unpretentious, completely unassuming."

Frances Thompson, another early cook at Tassajara, recalls the relief of working with someone easygoing: "At that time, there was a lot of complaining in the kitchen. Some people didn't like to be told what to do, other people had strong ideas about what the right food to serve was. Some people would pout and stay in bed. I mean opinions were *raging,* and there were always people arguing. Tommy was the only one who was always just there, always cool, who always took care of things, took over if he needed to. Working with him was divine. Absolutely. He never got freaked out, he never got ruffled. He was a saint."

Not everyone felt exactly that way. In order to get meals to the zendo on time, kitchen workers followed a schedule syncopated from the main one. Tommy's breaks came during work time, and even though he was putting in a full day in the kitchen, Frances remembers: "He used to spend a lot of time raking and sweeping, particularly in the central area, making it look really nice. This was his idea of a job. Someone in the administration didn't like it; they didn't think it looked good for people who were just arriving at Tassajara to see Tommy first thing. He was much more swishy in those days than he was later. Fortunately, wisdom prevailed, and no one ever said anything to him. No one told him not to sweep there, but somebody in the administration didn't like it.

"See, no one knew for sure what he was going to do next. Some people had heard about his history, and they thought he might suddenly do something weird, but of course he never did."

Tommy had come to Tassajara just six months after leaving the psychedelic life of the Haight. He'd made an impressive effort in the midst of somber surroundings, but at the end of the practice period he "flew out of there." Zen Center had in the meantime moved its urban operation from Sokoji Temple in Japantown to a large, handsome brick building designed by Julia Morgan. Page

Street, or the City Center, as it was called, sat in a fairly rough low-income district. Rent was low, and Zen students again teamed up to live in apartments. But the City Center building itself was large enough to house fifty permanent residents, and Tommy, using his ATD money for rent, moved in.

A great deal of work needed to be done in this location as well, to convert what had been Emanuel Residence Hall into the San Francisco Zen Center. With time on his hands, Tommy found that this approach to an environment was helpful to the community and pleasing to Suzuki-roshi. "I used to clean the halls at Page Street after my first practice period. I just used to busy myself, cleaning halls, working in the office, working in the kitchen, and Suzuki-roshi liked that."

Tommy's favorite project, though, was the long red front hall and entryway of the building. Waxed and properly buffed, the floor could be brought to a near-mirror finish. Tommy took it on—perhaps because he still liked to see things shine—and soon he was running the temperamental industrial buffer as smoothly and lovingly as a biker might run his Harley Davidson hog. Word leaked out years later that the Zen name Suzuki-roshi gave Tommy—*Issan Dainei*, meaning "One Mountain, Great Peace"—came from the steadiness and calmness he'd shown buffing the front hall. Tommy himself deduced that his attitude toward this job had an effect on Suzuki-roshi. "One day when I was on my hands and knees fixing the buffer, he came up and jumped on my shoulders. Then the next time, when I was getting ready to go back to Tassajara, Suzuki-roshi came running up to the door and hugged me, and people said they'd never seen him do that to anyone before.

"He didn't say so much to me in the early days. I only had brief meetings with him, but I think we had a strong connection. Moments meant a lot with him. In the courtyard, or in *dokusan*."

Suzuki-roshi now shuttled between his Japanese congregation at Sokoji Temple in Japantown, his Page Street City Center, and several satellite sitting groups around the Bay Area, most notably in Berkeley and Palo Alto. But when practice periods happened at Tassajara, which they did twice a year, Suzuki-roshi spent a good deal of time there. For this reason, and because of the sheer challenge of life there, Tommy went back. He returned during the summer, when non-Zen students—paying guests—filled Tassajara's cabins, enjoyed the hot springs and ate well-made vegetarian meals. (Opening Tassajara to the public as a resort four months each year had been a condition for Zen Center's purchase of the land. Students still meditated every day, but less; they ate outdoors at picnic tables; and they worked longer, harder hours.) Even though he'd drawn inspiration from Suzuki-roshi all along, Tommy suddenly became more conscious of his teacher's power. "I didn't really see who he was before. He came back to Tassajara for part of that summer and gave lectures. I was working in the office, and I used to come and look through the side window at him up there giving lectures. I'd peek at him. That's when I can remember saying to myself, 'Oh my god! Who is this man?' I saw him before, but I didn't know it, and now it started coming through, 'Oh my goodness. This man is far out.' "

When the weather turned, and the practice period began, Tommy stayed on. His feeling for Suzuki-roshi continued to deepen. As anyone who has fallen in love knows, sometimes the most mundane moments can pack a tremendous, inexplicable whallop.

"I was sick for six weeks during the next practice period. Suzuki-roshi was visiting, and he used to come from the baths at the same time every day. One day I looked out the window and I saw him. So then every day I knew what time, I'd look out my window at him. It just thrilled me to see him.

"One day that I particularly remember, I saw him and he was carrying a teacup. That's the story. There's nothing else; just, he was carrying a teacup. For some reason it blew me away, to see that man, walking down the path, carrying a teacup. So I always say that's one of my memorable moments of Suzuki-roshi, and people are usually waiting for some great story. But I just end by saying, 'He was carrying a teacup.' "

Tommy recovered his strength and rejoined the kitchen staff, where he was given more responsibility. He accepted reluctantly. Frances: "He never wanted to be in charge himself—he seemed to enjoy the subordinate role. It seemed he didn't want to be directly responsible, which was strange, because he was actually the best at just getting things done. If you were in charge, then you'd take the heat, but Tommy was really good at getting work done."

Tommy's reticence stemmed from several sources. For one thing, food mattered very much to Zen students. They had to wait three hours each morning to get any, they worked hard physically for hours each day, and they did a meditation built on mindfulness of body. The fact that diets like the macrobiotic, fruitarian, and lacto-ovo-vegetarian were fashionable at the time only accentuated the tendency toward food fixation. There really wasn't much else to think about: radio and television signals couldn't get over the ridges and wouldn't have been permitted in any case; such newspapers and magazines as did arrive came weeks late; drugs and alcohol were forbidden under penalty of expulsion; and there wasn't adequate time for sex. But food—food happened three or four times a day. Students would drift by the kitchen to deliver reviews of a meal, together with their suggestions for improvement. Angie Runyon once noted that when things were going well, students credited their meditation, and when things went poorly, they blamed the food. Whoever had headed the crew for a meal was hero or goat, but rarely neutral.

In addition to maniacal scrutiny of its product, the kitchen set-up itself was inadequate. One of the first big construction projects at Tassajara was a spacious, well-equipped kitchen, but until that got built, the three meals and tea treat each day for thirty to fifty hungry Zen students were produced in a cramped, inefficient kitchen. The pressure was terrific.

Another reason Tommy hesitated to take responsibility was that he was unsure of himself. He knew he hadn't quite recovered from the disorientation visited on him by his drug use, particularly the psychedelics. He had strong ability to focus on a task at hand, and he had the right spirit about work, but he could lose the bigger picture. Angie spent time with working with him, suggesting concrete sequences, and soon, she said, "I relied on him, and he was absolutely reliable."

But if he inherited spaciness from his hippie days, he also brought with him some of that era's best offerings: love and acceptance of others. Angie: "There wasn't a sharp edge on him. I never heard a sharp word out of him. He was kind to everybody, and he encouraged everybody."

Frances: "In the kitchen one time, I freaked out and lost it. I said I just can't take it anymore and I started to cry. Tommy stopped what he was doing and came and put his arms around me. He walked me to my cabin and put me to bed. I don't think anyone had ever done that before. He just put me to bed, and all the way while we were walking, he kept saying, 'I love you. I love you.' He did, too, that was the thing. He really did.

"It was like he was your lover all the time. He was my best friend. I thought I could marry him. I wouldn't even have cared if we never fucked, it would have been great to live with him. Tommy was my best friend; he was a lot of people's best friend.

"He was completely sympathetic. There wasn't anything you

could tell him that would shock him. He had seen so much and done so much himself, that he just completely accepted you."

At one of the next practice periods, Tommy became the head cook, or *tenzo,* and here his warm-hearted style found full expression. He slowly developed a menu that satisfied the students' emotions as well as their bodies. "I kind of extended things a little bit: cream sauces—that had never been done before; I cut down on the brown rice; they used to serve soybeans every other morning—I stopped that. . . ."

He also brought a new atmosphere to the kitchen. Despite the previous cooks' best efforts, problems had arisen: night raids on the kitchen by hungry students took place; food and ingredients turned up missing. . . . One head cook finally spent a few nights by the stove, guarding the next day's gruel, and a visiting Zen master told the assembly to "put locks on the doors and take them off your minds." Tommy made sure they stayed off both places. Creating a warm, open feeling in the kitchen, he managed to defuse the awful tension about food without sacrificing a sense of crispness in the work. He emphasized a kind-hearted approach rather than a rule-oriented one.

Unwittingly, Tommy was following the inner tradition of Zen. Seven hundred years earlier in Japan, a seminal Zen master named Dogen-zenji wrote "Instructions for the Head Cook," a short section of his masterwork, *Treasury of the True Dharma Eye.* In this fascicle Dogen lauded the head cook as one of the six prominent officers in a monastery, a position usually held by senior monks with deep understanding. Dogen-zenji took pains to distinguish the head cook from an ordinary cook, and he told many stories of enlightenment resulting from kitchen work. He ended the treatise with the admonition that the head cook should never forget to rouse a joyful mind, a kind mind, and a vast mind. To test their understanding, the six officers at Tassajara each gave a lecture to the assembly, followed by questions—a kind of Zen ritual resembling combat more than debate.

Tommy was pressed on the point of vegetarianism:

Questioner: "*Tenzo!* We are vegetarians, so we don't kill animals. But we eat carrots and potatoes. What do you think about killing vegetables?"

Tommy: "Well, I definitely think we should kill them before we eat them."

Another questioner probed his unnervingly open way: "Tommy, have you learned to say no yet?"

Tommy: "Nope."

As his warm-hearted kitchen practice matured, so did Tommy's sitting. He watched students slightly senior to him take initiations and ordinations in the Zen lineage of Suzuki-roshi. In this early phase of the Zen Center, distinctions in rank among students were few and were thus significant when they did occur. Going through an initiation ceremony meant, roughly speaking, that a person could consider himself or herself an official member of the Buddhist religion. Someone practicing regularly at Zen Center for a few years would have been eligible for this. Ordinations were given only after further years of study and as a result of a deepening and specific relationship with Suzuki-roshi. Ordained people kept their heads shaved, wore an additional set of robes, and used a more elaborate set of eating bowls. "Priests" or "monks"—the vocabulary was uncertain for ordained people, and inaccurate in either case, given Western connotations—took more responsibility for the atmosphere in the community and for promoting a pervasive sense of practice. They were to act as examples. They were to help Suzuki-roshi very directly in his work of establishing Zen in America.

Because Tommy had experienced such a drastic uplifting of his life with Zen practice and because he felt so personally committed to Suzuki-roshi, he thought of asking for ordination himself: "I went to him and said, 'Roshi, I was going to come here and ask you if I could become your disciple.' Because other people had been ordained by him, you know, but I just had patches on my pants, I was completely green. So I said, 'Now I realize that that was just an ego trip on my part. So I'm going to keep on practicing and just do the best I can.' He said, 'Well, there is no difference between that, and being my disciple.' That made me feel good. It encouraged me to continue practicing."

8

White Bird in Snow

Though he'd concluded that he was unready for Buddhist ordination, Tommy did ask for and receive lay initiation from Suzuki-
roshi in August 1970. In the *Jukai* ceremony, Tommy was given his
Buddhist name and a minature Buddhist robe called a *rakusu,* to
be worn bib-like around the neck. The ceremony began with
confession, and students repeated after Suzuki-roshi: "All the
karma ever created by me since of old, on account of greed, anger,
and self-delusion, which has no beginning, born of body, speech
and thought, I now make full open confession of it."

Next, postulants took refuge in the Three Jewels of Buddhism:
the Buddha, his teachings, and the body of practitioners. They
received the Three Collective Pure Precepts—"to abstain from all
evil behavior, to strive toward righteousness, and to strive for the
benefit of all living beings"—and the Ten Grave Prohibitory
Precepts, which again, they repeated after Suzuki-roshi: A disciple
of the Buddha abstains from willful taking of lives, from committing robbery, from committing unchaste acts, from telling false-
hoods, and from taking harmful intoxicants or drugs, from
speaking ill of others, from extolling the self while slandering
others, from being avaricious in the bestowal of teachings or
materials, from harboring hatred, malice, or ill-will, and from
denouncing the Three Jewels. (Translation of the vows became

subtler over the years, but these were the vows Tommy took in 1970.)

Tradition holds that Zen students are supposed to act from a clear, unobstructed mind, fresh in each moment, rather than being bound by external rules. While it might be impossible, strictly speaking, to live without contravening these precepts, Suzuki-roshi explained that the vows should simply be borne in mind.

Tommy had been practicing diligently for some years, and perhaps he now thought of himself a Buddhist; the *Jukai* ceremony marked acceptance from the other side, from the lineage of Buddhists stretching back to the founder himself. Indeed, the text of the ceremony said that having taken the vows, participants were "seated with the Buddha." But Suzuki-roshi went on to elucidate a deeper message. He described the vows he'd administered as bodhisattva precepts. (Bodhisattvas are those who put off their own enlightenment until all other sentient beings are also enlightened, and bodhisattvas work energetically toward that end.)

Suzuki-roshi: "I decided to have lay ordination for you old students just to help others, not to give some special idea of lay Buddhist, because all of us are Buddhists actually. Every sentient being is a bodhisattva, whether or not he is aware of it. As this is our conviction, I didn't want to give some special idea of lay Buddhist, but the time has come for us to strive more sincerely to help others.

"Our way is like Avalokiteshvara Bodhisattva: when he wants to save ladies, he takes the form of a lady; for boys he takes the form of a boy; for a fisherman he becomes a fisherman. A more sophisticated Chinese expression is to be like a white bird in the snow. When people are like snow, we should be like snow. When people become black, we should be black. And always being with them, without any idea of discrimination, we can help others in its true sense, without giving anything, any special teachings or materials. This is actually the bodhisattva way. Softness of mind is the foundation of our practice to help others. . . . None of us, including various great teachers, find it easy to be like a white bird in the snow. But somehow, we should make our best effort. If you help yourself through practice, you can help others without anything. Just to be with people will be enough."

Suzuki-roshi fell ill in the summer of 1971. His gall bladder was removed, but he continued to decline, and he soon became bedridden, invisible to most of his students. He was diagnosed with inoperable liver cancer. In the fall he roused himself from bed only one final time—for the Mountain Seat Ceremony with Richard Baker. Suzuki-roshi had already recognized Baker as his successor, in a midnight ceremony in Japan the year before, but had not installed him as the abbot of Zen Center.

Students from Tassajara and outlying locations now converged on Page Street for the event. Baker himself has rushed back from a temple in Japan where he'd been studying, and on November 21, 1971, a greenish, thin, and frail Suzuki-roshi led a procession into the Buddha Hall. Literally on his last legs, Suzuki-roshi still evinced an iron will, and completed the hourlong installation ceremony. As he tottered from the hall supported by his son, his students— Tommy among them—wept openly, realizing they would never see their teacher alive again.

Early in the morning of December 4, just as the bells finished ringing open the first period of a seven-day sitting, Mrs. Suzuki walked boldly into the zendo and summoned Richard Baker to her husband's room. Suzuki-roshi died moments later. Baker then stood as the second abbot of Zen Center, Suzuki-roshi's sole American Dharma-heir.

In early summer of 1961 a twenty-five-year-old Richard Baker had arrived in San Francisco. He'd nearly completed his studies at Harvard, but then had done a two-year stint in the merchant marines. After a period of residence among artists and poets in New York, Baker came to San Francisco hoping to meet a Zen master. He imagined such a master in Chinatown, surrounded by hundreds of disciples.

A few evenings later, he stood by the counter in Fields' bookstore with a painter friend, talking and perusing books. Baker began to describe a samurai film to his friend, and as his enthusiasm mounted, he drew an imaginary sword, raised it as if to sunder his opponent, and uttered a cry. Just then the owner, George Fields, leaned across the counter, pointed at Baker and said, "You should go hear Suzuki-sensei talk. He's a Zen master; he lectures every Wednesday night." Stunned, Baker sheathed his imaginary sword, and convinced his friend to accompany him to the talk that very night. With directions from Mr. Fields they set out.

Suzuki-roshi struck Baker as "someone who was exactly what he said he was. . . . I had heard Tillich lecture at Harvard, and other philosophers, and there was such a discrepancy in basic feeling between what they said and their lives. They didn't exemplify what they were talking about. But Suzuki-roshi sounded just like all the Zen books I'd read. He was obviously speaking from his own life and his experience, so I decided to come back."

A few weeks later, walking to his warehouse job after lunch, Baker was thinking about Suzuki-roshi's lecture, and about Zen practice. He decided, "I'm not good enough to practice Zen." He opened a book of D. T. Suzuki's—he was always carrying at least one book—and his eye fell directly on the sentence "It's a form of vanity to think you aren't good enough to practice Zen."

"I thought, 'Oh shit, that's true,' and the next morning I got up at 4:30 and went to sit zazen at Bush Street. I don't think I missed a morning after that for the next five years."

Over those five years Richard Baker became Suzuki-roshi's most prominent disciple. He attended all the meditation periods, all the lectures, took voluminous notes, and badgered Suzuki-roshi with questions. He tried to read every book in English about Buddhism—this was still conceivable in the mid-1960s—and he accompanied Suzuki-roshi whenever he could.

On these outings they were a spectacle. Suzuki-roshi, about five foot five, trim, with a shaven head and usually wearing robes, stood beside Baker, who was six foot two, long of limb, serious—even somber—with dark hair and eyebrows, dressed in the Beatnik style. (In college, a close friend had nicknamed him El Darko.)

But physical, chronological, and cultural differences didn't seem to faze Suzuki-roshi; he took Baker seriously as a student. Baker, in turn, began to assume more and more responsibility for the administration of Zen Center. He recalls working with his teacher: "We developed Zen Center so much together that I never felt I didn't understand him. We would talk about things, and we would always agree, *always* agree." As early as 1966, Suzuki-roshi began talking to the young Baker about becoming his successor. In 1967 he ordained him as a priest and shortly after that sent him to Japan for further training.

Back in the United States, and newly empowered, Baker soon took his first distinct readings of Tommy: "He was having trouble with the cold, he was kind of bundled up, living in the dormitory—he had a little beard at the time I remember, a little beard that followed along his chin line. I had been aware of him before, as someone whose presence catches you, stops you—a good way. But I hadn't distinguished him more than that.

"At Tassajara, I got more of a feeling of him as a specific person: he was a kind of strong sissy. He acted—not effeminate, but like oh, everything was too much for him. Underneath that, you felt that nothing was too much for him. It wasn't that he wasn't a sissy—I think a lot of things bothered him—but it was like the surface of a lake being ruffled. Below that, he was like, I don't know, iron, very still. Clearly he was up for anything, but he was not the least bit hesitant to complain about the surface problems."

In the summer of 1972, Tommy assumed the job of head cook at Green Gulch Farm, Zen Center's newest practice place, a windy, overgrazed valley of six hundred acres, running to the sea at Muir Beach in southern Marin County. Much renovation was needed to make it a habitable Zen temple, and even the concept of what the property should be hadn't focused when the first crew went there to live.

Baker: "I wanted to see what Green Gulch would become. People had had a lot of ideas about living on a farm, romantic ideas, etc. So I let it be, to see if the ideas were real or sustainable. I left it up to the people out there, what the schedule should be. The first year or so, it was pretty miserable. People had a hard time with the cold and damp and the work, people were getting sick. In that initial period, I wanted it to form itself, but I had to depend on a few people to carry it. What I remember is that there were a few people I could call on who could handle it—who wouldn't complain, who'd just do it, and do it with a good spirit of trying to make it work, even if it wasn't very pleasant. I knew that Tommy was such a person, who could be asked, and he would do it and he did."

Tommy enjoyed the job, in fact, and felt his cooking improved at Green Gulch—a result of the produce grown there by famed horticulturalist Alan Chadwick: "I started cooking good food then. I don't know why, I didn't know how to cook. I mean, I had some learning—I knew how to cook zendo food. But I got into cooking my own way, with Alan Chadwick's vegetables coming out of the garden. People always complimented me on it, but it was very simple, using that beautiful food that he grew."

Because the circumstances of life at Green Gulch were some-what grim, humor helped keep people together. For example, students traipsed in from pickaxing before breakfast one morning to a breakfast table set with an unusual centerpiece: a huge watermelon that had been savaged the night before by a raccoon. In the bloody-looking hollow of the rind sat a little sign: ALRIGHT, WHICH ONE OF YOU KIDS DID THIS?!—THE COOK.

Cleaning out the old barn another day, students found some abandoned swallows' nests. They took them to the kitchen and begged Tommy (mockingly) for bird's-nest soup. He accepted the nests and smiled and said nothing. In the middle of the next meal, a silently taken lunch, Tommy announced that he hadn't been able to make bird's-nest soup since he'd been brought such "low-class nests with not *nearly* enough shit in them."

After a couple of long years at Green Gulch, Tommy was transferred again, this time to become head cook in the City Center. While it wasn't unusual for Zen students to move around from one practice center to another, Tommy was the first person to work as *tenzo* in all three locations. In Suzuki-roshi's style of Zen, mindful everyday action was regarded as both fruit and practice of enlightened life, so that the kitchen could be a training ground equal to the meditation hall. But working in the kitchen with Tommy rarely meant solemnity, it meant attention. What he lacked in planning and training skills, he compensated with spontaneity. "Read me that recipe—not the amounts or anything, I just want to get an idea what kind of stuff goes in." He'd meet with the meal prep crew before going to work, smoke a cigarette, drink coffee, maybe pass cookies around, and ask for ideas. Two and a half chaotic hours later, a soul-satisfying meal for ninety people would appear. The rotating crews under his direction worked hard and were frequently put on the spot, but they were always treated with respect, as equals, and were seasoned with his humor: "If it doesn't taste so good, fry the shit out of it. . . ." In the course of five years Tommy basically triumphed, rising from an emaciated, speedy, dirty waif to a much-loved, warm-hearted Zen crazy.

His path hadn't been painless. He suffered after Suzuki-roshi's death, and he felt unsure of the young, endlessly energetic Richard Baker, a man who worked to build and expand and strengthen Zen Center: "I remember thinking to myself, 'I have got to get out of this place. I can't stand this man Richard Baker.' But, of course that turned.

"I saw that other people stood by him, and they encouraged me to stick it out with him. Little by little, I became his disciple and gained his respect. I also remember that Suzuki-roshi said before he died, 'This is my Dharma-heir. Study with him and call him roshi.' I remember that clearly, and I called him roshi right from the beginning because Suzuki-roshi said to. I did what Suzuki-roshi said, but I had my doubts about him.

"Baker-roshi took an interest in me pretty early on. I think he started grooming me, before I realized I was being groomed. I became his disciple before I knew it."

For his part, Baker saw his position with Tommy as flowing from their mutual appreciation of Suzuki-roshi: "My relationship to the community and with Suzuki-roshi was that I tried to make his teaching accessible to people, understandable. This was a kind of cooperative relationship that we had. He'd call me in, and I'd meet with him quite often.

"Being charged to do this by Suzuki-roshi in various ways, I kind of had a general feeling for the students, but I did not interact with them as a teacher. . . . My position was not to interact with people as a teacher, but as Suzuki-roshi's helper. So I did this with Suzuki-roshi, and my feeling was—you know, there is this proprioceptive program, almost like a computer program or a pace of a new interior consciousness, that you begin to pick up with your teacher, that's in a different kind of—it gets in your body.

"I had this feeling with Suzuki-roshi whether I was present

Tommy in high school, 1950s.

Tommy and Marlene.
(Courtesy Marlene Sorum)

Tommy as a "cute young sailor"
with Marlene Shapro, 1953.
(Courtesy Marlene Sorum)

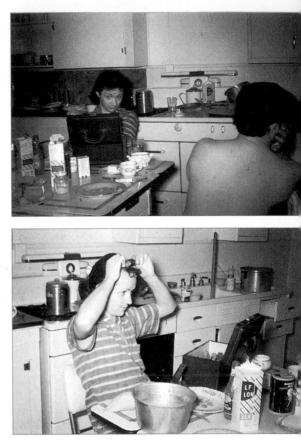

Tommy putting on drag, late 1950s.

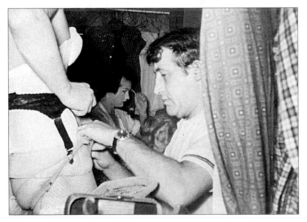

Tommy in the background putting on makeup
while Mickey assists one of the Party of Four.

TOMMY DEE

The finished product.

The Party of Four in Alaska, 1959.

The Party of Four in action, 1960. Tommy is on the
left. (Photo by Syd Torkin)

Tommy with a friend, late 1950s or early 1960s.

Tommy as "Hard-Hearted Hannah."

Tommy (right) with members of the Family, the Haight, 1966. (Photo by Eddie Troia)

Issan with James, Hartford Street 1989.

In the old Tassajara kitchen, 1968.

From left: Kijun Steve Allen, Issan, Zenshin
Philip Whalen, and Zentatsu Richard Baker at
Hartford Street, 1989. (Photo by Barbara
Lubanski-Wenger)

The Mountain Seat ceremony, 1989. (Photo by
Barbara Lubanski-Wenger)

Issan at the Ojai Foundation, 1989. (Photo by Morgan Alexander)

with him or not, a kind of connectedness. I always then noticed when other students had it with Suzuki-roshi, or had it in practice in general. Some did and some didn't; but I was most aware of it when people not only had this interior awareness with Suzuki-roshi, but when it also began to affect the people around them, their friends and their *sangha* relationships.

"Fairly early on, I noticed that Tommy had this feeling that I'm talking about, and that he and I shared it with Suzuki-roshi, and that there was a sharing of it between Tommy and myself. It really wasn't so much that I had a teacher-student relationship with Tommy as that I had a Dharma-brother relationship with him that related to my being Suzuki-roshi's senior disciple. We both had a sense of continuing this, through ourselves and so on, and it wasn't even, after a while, related to Suzuki-roshi. It now became something that *we* felt and did.

"That feeling continued to develop into a more explicit relationship in which I was his teacher. It wasn't so different. It went from being something that we shared together—you could call me the teacher, but really it was just something we shared together and actually helped each other with."

By 1975, Tommy's practice with Baker-roshi had developed to the point that he felt the need to express it formally, with ordination: shaving his head, receiving new robes, new eating bowls and more vows, in a lengthy ceremony known as *Tokudo* (home departure.) The head-shaving symbolized cutting one's attachment to any prior existence and to worldly endeavors generally. Persons who underwent the *Tokudo* ceremony became new people, "monks" in common parlance—male or female— though the actual Zen term for such a person is *unsui,* meaning "cloud-water person." An *unsui* floats like a cloud and reflects like water.

Tommy requested the ceremony, as tradition dictates. "Baker-roshi said to me, 'Well, you are asking me now to ordain you, but your body knew you were a monk long before you did. I'll ordain you this year.' "

Another very heavy implication in the ceremony concerns lineage affiliations: students who have their head shaved this way do not become Buddhist monks at large; they join a particular line of descent, and they publicly acknowledge their teacher as a Buddha. Part of the ceremony runs:

> "This last hair is called the Shura.
> Only a Buddha can cut it!
> Now I will cut it!
> Do you allow me to cut it?"
> Disciple: "Yes."

This potent bit of dialogue is then repeated; ordainees avow it twice, before what is usually several hundred witnesses, that their teacher is a Buddha (or at the very least, his living representative). Though profound, the event was not all solemnity and dirge.

Joel Roberts: "At his ordination, where he had his head shaved, there were all kinds of dignitaries, Lama Govinda and so on. He had invited me because everyone else had their family, so I was Tommy's family. The night before, I'll never forget it, he was very much the drag queen. They'd already shaved most of his head; they were only going to cut the last piece during the ceremony.

"Getting ready, he was just as primmy as any drag queen I ever met. I guess *primmy* is a term for drag queens—it means very meticulous about how you look. Every little thing—this thing had to be tied this way, that one had to go here. Which is great for Zen, right, because Zen is meticulous too.

"I was laughing, and he was too: 'Oh, you've changed from one dress to another!' Part of what made Tommy what he was, was the drag queen, and that never left him. I don't know what you saw when you looked at Tommy, but what I saw was a feminine man.

"During the first part of the ceremony, he kept waving at me I thought, and I would wave back. I'm over here in the first row, and he'd give me a little wave like this, and I'd do one back. Later I realized he was pointing, and I looked down and oh my goodness, I had totally forgotten. You had to take off your shoes to go there and I'd forgotten that I had painted each toenail a different color. He was just laughing at me. You see this row of feet, and suddenly you see these rainbow toenails, and Tommy, even during this very auspicious ceremony, had that playfulness and that ability to combine opposites. I felt it was a very special moment, a very serious moment for Tommy, and yet in the middle of it, he was just as silly, pointing to my painted toes."

Shortly after the ordination ceremony, word leaked down that fellow students should now call Tommy by his Buddhist name, Issan. It was thought in high places that *Tommy* sounded a bit too much like *Mommy*. He'd proved he could take care of students as though they were his own children, and new challenges lay ahead for him. Accordingly, in this book he'll be called Issan from here on. "Rhymes with 'piss on,'" is what he would tell anyone having trouble with pronunciation.

Issan's life was inextricable from Zen Center's during the 1970s. Under the dynamic hand of Richard Baker, Zen Center expanded, acquired property, opened businesses, and generally assumed the shape Baker thought necessary to carry out Suzuki-roshi's vision. When the group bought a bad-luck corner grocery across the street from its city location (several murders had been committed there the year before), Issan worked as assistant manager. Then in an attempt to literally integrate itself more fully in the surrounding, mostly black, mostly impoverished, mostly being-pushed-out-because-the-white-Zen-Center-is-driving-up-rents neighborhood, Baker-roshi created the Neighborhood Foundation, and Issan, together with Baker's wife Virginia and their friend Renee des Tombe, ran that. In both positions, Issan's variegated history proved an asset; there wasn't any kind of person (and certainly no *color* of person) who surprised him. He'd seen violence, death, addiction, and squalor before, and little of it fazed him when he saw it now.

Richard Baker: "If I started something new, or if Zen Center started something new, I could always depend on Issan to be one of the people willing to do this new thing, with intelligence, and awareness, and compassion. And without ego. There were other people willing to do things too, with intelligence, compassion— but usually, with most people, they were involved with their status, their role in Zen Center, how they were seen by other people, and so forth. You had all of the logistics of dealing with their ego. With Issan, you didn't have any of that. He just did it. He never worried about it.

"He had such internal confidence that he didn't care if he was seen as this or that, big or bad or good or high up in Zen Center or low down. He always trusted that if he didn't have this position, he'd have another position, or he'd have no position—it didn't make any difference. So when almost anything new came along, I usually turned to Issan as a possibility. With the Neighborhood Foundation, his experience and sense of the street, because of his own life, was so great, that he was a natural."

During this period, Issan's important friendships shifted radically. First, he ended the carnal side of his relationship with Mack, something that had continued "even after Mack got married and had kids, up until the time I was at Zen Center. Finally I said, 'This is ridiculous. Why I am sucking your dick? Everytime you come to see me, I suck your dick. . . .' We actually had another relationship going besides that; we liked each other. Mack used to keep his eye on me. I think Jillian knew, but she didn't know how much. When I was living with them, I wouldn't do it. Not when I was living at their house. But then, he'd come to visit me in the clubs I was working in, and even when I was living with Grant, he came. He'd always come to visit me regularly, because he was also my friend."

Second, Issan (and everyone else) lost Grant, who was murdered horribly—apparently the result of connecting with the wrong guy in an S&M bar. Police found signs of a violent struggle in Grant's apartment; they also found Grant tied up with telephone cord, stabbed to death. Because Grant had practiced at Zen Center and had even lived in the building for a while as a guest student, and because he was so clearly important to Issan, he was cremated and given a full Buddhist funeral. Issan always kept Grant's ashes with him after that.

Mickey and Don had moved to Sonoma, two hours' drive north of San Francisco, and the closest friend Issan now saw regularly was young James from the commune days. James alternated short stays at Zen Center with long disappearances into the streets of the city where he lived, as Issan once had, hustling, nicking, drugging, and dodging.

Finally, Issan moved to Jamesburg, a rustic, two-bedroom house off the main road in the upper Carmel Valley. The house (with refreshment stand) marked the end of paved road and served as the last stop before the fourteen miles of treacherous, mountainous, dirt road emptying into Tassajara. Zen Center obtained the property as an emergency stop because harsh winter weather often made getting to Tassajara difficult or impossible. Jamesburg quickly became essential to facilitating mail, phone, and transfer of materials to the monastery.

Issan relished this assignment. He appointed the house exactly as he pleased, he ran the refreshment stand with savoir-faire, and he took care of the resident dogs like a scolding schoolmarm. There was always a pot of strong coffee available and always a big vat of chili beans. Zen students coming or going to Tassajara looked forward to their time there—they knew they'd be fed, fussed over, patched up if necessary, gossiped with, and sent on their way.

Gradually the neighbors, mostly upper-middle-class dropouts living in self-constructed houses in the surrounding woods, began coming down from their cabins to hang out with Issan. Baker-roshi: "He was one of the first people to create a real homey atmosphere there. Other people may have created a kind of Zen tightness. He created an atmosphere where everyone felt like joining in."

As Pauline Baez (Joan's older sister) put it, "I never had any interest in meditation before, but then there was this nice priest living there, and you could drink sherry with him in the evening, and it somehow all seemed possible."

They came for sherry, they came for coffee and for the big Sunday breakfast Issan cooked each week, and eventually they came for meditation. Issan had become a parish priest, or, drawing from Zen traditions, one of the mystic "tea ladies" from whom travelers took unexpected spiritual instruction along with food, drink, and lodging.

The relative calm of Issan's two years at Jamesburg evaporated in the late summer of 1977. Two good-size fires in the Los Padres National Forest burned toward each other, circling in remote valleys and draws, eventually becoming indistinguishable and consuming 250,000 acres between them. The fight to control the Ventana Wilderness–Marble Cone fire was headquartered intermittently at Jamesburg, and Issan found himself suddenly feeding and attending to droves of exhausted Forest Service workers. Zen students too crowded the property, lining up for meals, sleeping on the floor, and stretching the limits of the facilities to their utmost. (Zen Center initially obeyed the Forest Service's order to evacuate Tassajara. Having done so, Baker-roshi and ten others then reversed themselves, ignored the government, and went back over the road to defend the monastery as best they could. Faced with this irrational determination, Forest Service officials relented and sent a crew chief along to help. For eleven days, Zen students fought back the fire and Tassajara was saved.) Throughout the fall, Forest Service crews and equipment rumbled through Jamesburg, working on mop-up flood control. Equally unsettling for Issan was the news that he was to return to Tassajara himself in the winter, this time as *shuso* (head monk). More than an administrative job, this is a religious training position, considered a second-level ordination. The head monk rises earlier than anyone else, and wakes other students by sprinting through the monastery ringing a bell. The head monk leads all the meditation periods and ceremonies when the abbot is absent. In Suzuki-roshi's tradition practitioners usually sit facing the wall, but the head monk faces out, looking over the assembly. The underlying theme is that this person is taking his or her first steps toward becoming an official Zen teacher. They must give their first formal Zen talks and must also begin to counsel other students—not in the hugely strict style of the abbot—but in casual chats over tea and cookies.

Appointment to the post marks endurance in practice, and a depth of understanding. The *shuso* tends to feel celebratory throughout the three-month training period, but there is work involved as well. Consistent with the Zen notion that the higher you go up the religious ladder, the lower your work can be, the head monk carries out the garbage and empties the compost toilets. (The term *shuso* literally means "toilet-cleaning monk.") Because Issan's body couldn't support such heavy work, he accomplished the job, as was quite usual, with lots of help.

Midway through the practice period comes the first talk for the *shuso,* traditionally cast in the mold of "How I came to be here." Issan walked into the zendo carrying a little slip of paper on which he had written sparse notes, things like: Navy couple — road — Chicago — Haight Ashbury — Suzuki-roshi. Ten years after he'd first come to Zen Center, a new crowd populated Tassajara, and most of them hadn't known him as anything other than an eccentric, loving Zen student. He soon had his audience howling and reeling with his stories. "People talk about being in the gutter," he said. "When I say I was in the gutter, I mean this body here—this one—was actually in the gutter. Laying down in it."

The culmination of the *shuso*'s training comes toward the end of the practice period, when he or she must go through a Dharma combat ceremony. In this confrontation the head monk fields questions aimed at him like arrows from every person in the monastery and from any past head monks who can attend. (When Zen Center students were first learning the ceremony a decade before, they had been instructed to try to kill the *shuso* with their question.) The head monk must parry each question nearly instantly, certainly before he succumbs to the taint of thought, and in a way that draws forth the Dharma, the truth of Buddhist teachings and of a person's actual life.

"Shuso, why are you so nice to people?"

Issan: "Greed."

This day he was utterly in command, basking in being onstage again. He answered the sixty-odd questions with ease and confidence, and he endured no more trouble than would a sharp comedian dealing with hecklers.

"Shuso, as buddhists, we vow to save all sentient beings. Why do we do that?"

Issan: "We save them for later."

Baker-roshi recounts from his experience why Issan thrived in this environment: "When he used to say he wasn't intelligent, or something like that, it wasn't true at all. He was extremely intelligent. But his intelligence, if we were going to define it and admit his difficulty with reading and memory—his intelligence was expressive, sensitive to situations, a field intelligence, aware of what was happening around him, of what people were thinking. He had the right sense of what was appropriate, and what the essence of a situation was. You didn't have to explain things to him. Ideal for the koans, and for understanding the processes of the *sangha,* and other people. He always had a realistic perspective on things, without ornament."

A few weeks later, the last fancy ceremony of the practice period took place, also in the form of question and answer, this time with the abbot. Traditionally, the sense of combat is diminished here: each student asks a question—a real question drawn from their own practice—and is expected to frame it as though they were asking for everyone. In that zendo, the abbot sat in the front of the hall, the assembly sat on the sides, and the questioner, who asked from the back of the room, gave their effort full voice. With Zen's healthy disregard for niceties, almost anything could be brought into the dialogue, so when it occurred, nearly two hours into the ceremony, that a student shouted: "There's a fire back here!" everyone assumed it was the good beginning to his question. It was instead a genuine cry of alarm.

Baker-roshi, facing the questioner, first saw that he was right. Baker unfolded his legs, fairly leapt off the shrine, and hurried to the back of the zendo, trailed by stiff-legged members of the fire crew. Within seconds the fire blazed wildly in the zendo entryway, blocking egress. Stunned and unbelieving students roused themselves from solid sitting positions on the floor, and with their best robes fluttering, stumbled out the side door. The fire found its way into propane lines that ran below the zendo, and only a most orderly exit by the group prevented fatalities. The zendo had become a blow-torch. People watched helplessly as window after window in the structure blew out.

Everyone raced to disrobe and to get into fire-fighting clothes, but the zendo—with its drums, bells, and twelve-hundred-year-old Gandharan Buddha statue—was quickly engulfed by huge, furling sheets of flame. Students fought the conflagration with bucket brigades drawn from the creek, because the portable power pump had been sent to town for repairs just the day before. The battle lasted into the evening. When the flames were finally doused, the zendo, library, and most of the dry food storage had been burned. The kitchen itself was saved, as were the neighboring guest rooms, but in the night disheartenment hung in the air as thick as the foul smell of scorched food. Zen students had protected Tassajara from a monumental forest fire in the fall, and they'd rendered harmless the rumbling creek, swollen with runoff from denuded hills during the winter, only to lose a crucial building to an inexplicable fire in the spring.

In the morning though, everyone assembled, cleared and swept and rearranged the dining room, and finished the ceremony. Within a few days, Baker-roshi left for San Francisco to commence fund-raising for rebuilding. Issan remained at Tassajara as the head monk. The monastery, which depended on stability and tranquillity, now had neither. Construction crews began booming back and forth across the grounds with heavy equipment and truckloads of lumber. People tried gamely to work out new logistics for practicing, new schedules, new routes. Baker-roshi: "It was an intense, crazy atmosphere—it wasn't so much a matter of making decisions; things just happened. The decisions were pretty obvious, how we had to do it. But the atmosphere that made it work— Issan supplied a large percentage of that. He had such a loving way of working with people, presenting things, making people feel good about it and willing to just try."

Issan stayed on at Tassajara another year. He was head monk through the summer, then head of the meditation hall for the fall and spring practice periods. Because no one else had figured out how the forms of rituals, meals, and ceremonies would be in the new zendo, Issan did much of it on his own, intuitively. Later, Baker-roshi and Issan worked out the details together. A good part of the decorum at Tassajara derives from his work in those disruptive days.

Issan moved back to San Francisco in 1980. After a brief stint as the maître d' at Zen Center's most spectacular foray into public commerce, Greens Restaurant, he became the director of the City Center and all its associated properties—an unlikely assignment. Baker-roshi's aides told him they thought Issan would never be able to handle the job—logistics, budgeting, meetings, and endless administrative complications seemed not his strongest areas. Baker-roshi: "When I first asked him to be the director of the building, he told me he couldn't do it. Many people at Zen Center said he couldn't do it, that he didn't have the skills, couldn't remember anything, he just didn't have any organizational skills. But I just knew that his presence would make the building so much nicer for people, and I think that when he was the director, the building was the best it's ever been: warm, open, taken care of—a good, communal, loving, family feeling there. Issan always had a perspective that made things work. He let people come and stay in a way that supported the natural integrity of the place. When I asked him to do it, he far surpassed my expectations. He had a genius for it."

Sometimes it took a genius. As spiritual centers seem to do, Zen Center attracted its share of disturbed people. A woman working in the front office one day opened the door and found herself confronted with a large, loud, confused, scary man, who walked past her, lay down on the floor, and announced repeatedly that Jesus had sent him. The distraught young woman called Issan, who came from his room a few doors away. Issan sat on the floor with the man, held his hand, and interviewed him about Jesus. Issan soon told the man that Jesus had just told him (Issan) the man needed something to eat and drink and that they were preparing it just now. Calmed, the man dozed off. After arrangements for a shelter had been made, Issan woke the man and said that Jesus had told him about a special place they should go, where he'd be well cared for, and off they went.

Perhaps because of his own long years of derangement, Issan related better than anyone to people who saw things in altered ways. But as director, he also faced problems to which there were no answers. In the winter of 1979, thieves murdered a Zen student named Chris Pirsig, son of the well-known author Robert Pirsig. Chris, a shy, sometimes spacey young man—the kind that made the Zen community nervous—had already brought out Issan's empathetic instincts. He'd made sure Chris had access to the benefits of Zen Center life and that he fulfilled his responsibilities as well. The police turned up no clues in Chris's brutal killing, so at Baker-roshi's urging, Issan and, later, actor Peter Coyote (neighborhood resident and Zen practitioner) took up the trail.

Coyote: "Chris and I had been roommates at Tassajara, the first time I'd gone there for a summer period. Chris and I shared a tent, because Marilyn and I weren't married and they wouldn't let us stay together. I had known Chris and liked him, and of course, I had known his father's book and I was quite shocked that he died.

"I think it was the day after the murder, I came out on Haight Street and Issan was walking around looking around for witnesses. I didn't have much to do, I joined him. We started walking up and down the street, and we had sort of like a hard-cop, soft-cop act. He was this priest, and soft, and I was sort of like this long-haired doper. Somehow, between the two of us, we seemed to do pretty well, putting people at ease, getting them to talk. One old man told us that he had seen two boys on the street that night, and he described them, and he happened to know whose apartment they'd come out of. They were like porn models, gay porn models for some guy—an older man who lived on the street. I guess he had pictures and audiotapes of young boys.

"So Issan and I figured the place to find them would be the Tenderloin. We went down to the Tenderloin, and I think we were gone about three days, running around, running around, meeting people. We went from connection to connection. We talked to the man who took the photos, and he just knew the first names of the kids. That was a start. We went from hotel to hotel, and it was obvious that we weren't cops. Finally we tracked these two guys down that were the models. They were really scared to death—they'd never seen a man murdered before, and they were freaked out. One of them was a parole violator from Ohio.

"We contacted the detective who was handling the case and told him we had two guys that would talk, but they needed to get a fix on their parole. The cops arranged it, and these kids came forward, and they described it. They basically gave us Chris's last moments, you know. They did tell us the story, they saw the whole thing. We found the kids, we got them to the police, we got the first description of the murderers. Well, they never found the guys, but Bob Pirsig was gratified by this. . . ."

Despite troubles, the first three years of the 1980s were a kind of halcyon age for the Zen Center. The businesses it had started were thriving, making themselves felt in the Bay Area economy, with four million dollars a year in cash flowing through them. People thronged the meditation halls daily and packed themselves in to overflowing for Baker-roshi's Sunday lectures at Green Gulch. Baker had engineered Zen Center's expansion carefully and thoroughly. He also issued invitations to people he considered seminal thinkers—movers of culture, pivotal players in the politics of city and state—to come to Zen Center and meet with one another.

At best, Baker-roshi was recognized as a "magnificent orchestrator of events." The young Baker had worked for the University of California in arranging conferences and was responsible for the first Poetry Conference at Berkeley in 1965. A year later, he organized the national symposium on LSD—the one Issan's friend Yves had attended and heard about meditation, the one that in some way was responsible for Issan's introduction to Zen.

In the early 1980s Governor Jerry Brown met Gregory Bateson in Baker-roshi's living room, a meeting that led to Bateson's appointment as a regent of the university. Daniel Ellsberg advised the abbot about travel to Russia. "New Age" pundits—from philosopher William Irwin Thompson to Esalen founder Michael Murphy, from *Whole Earth Catalogue*-er and Merry Prankster Stewart Brand to astronaut Rusty Schweickart—all rumbled into Zen Center monthly to attend the meetings Baker-roshi called the Invisible College.

This loose association of individuals met to see what ideas about politics, economics, science, philosophy, and education would emerge if they did, and to identify a governance and inner Bay Area culture. Very few Zen students participated in these conferences. If Issan appeared at the Invisible College at all, it would have been as Baker-roshi's assistant or, more likely, as a cook and meal-server.

Artists joined the parade of luminaries. Visiting Baker-roshi and Zen Center over the years were painters David Hockney, Hayden Stubbing, Mayumi Oda, Mike Dixon, and Edward Avedisian; sculptors Isamu Noguchi and J. B. Blunk; musicians Linda Ronstadt, Herbie Hancock, Paul Winter, Lou Harrison, Jim Carroll, and Earl McGrath, manager of Rolling Stone Records; from the film realm André Gregory, Bob Rafelson, and Peter Coyote.

Poets were probably most richly represented of all: Robert Duncan, Allen Ginsberg (and father Louis), Anne Waldman, Peter Orlovsky, Diane di Prima (Zen student with Suzuki-roshi), Robert Bly, Michael McClure, Michael Palmer, Joanne Kyger, Gary Snyder, and Philip Whalen (who lived at Zen Center, and practiced as an ordained priest) all came.

Assorted roshis from Japan and Korea, *tulkus* from Tibet, elders from the Southeast Asian countries—virtually all the major teachers of all the sects of Buddhism came to the Zen Center to pay respects to the memory of Suzuki-roshi, to visit with Baker-roshi, and to deliver a lecture to the students. Buddhist scholars and translators also arrived in a steady stream to teach, confer with one another, and to absorb the atmosphere of authentic practice. The City Center functioned as the hub of all the activity, the nerve center, and there Issan ran the show.

At the same time, Issan began to want a way of working with other parts of society, the parts that he had lived in so long, the gutter. He was unable to ignore the homeless kids in San Francisco's Tenderloin district, young addicts, dealers, runaways, and prostitutes. He began talking about a soup kitchen down there, throwing the idea around in conversation, and making preliminary inquiries about town. He and Baker-roshi even went to inspect an abandoned bathhouse as a possible site. His interest later led him to Ruth Brinker. Between them they put together a food-service program for the homeless called Open Hand, which runs in a much-expanded form today.

Even as he rose with the tide of Zen Center's fortunes, Issan escaped some of the snags. Peter Coyote: "There was a kind of high episcopal elegance to Zen Center that always rubbed me the wrong way. There was just a kind of grandeur that often bled over into being judgmental. It's one thing to do things impeccably, and it's another to be judgmental. I'm sort of a fuck-up as a person, and I struggle hard, you know, and my feeling is, you make a mistake, you just go back to your breath, you just go back. We're all on some level fucked up, and so I was put off a little by that.

"But Issan was just so human, and so hip and so wiggy, and obviously nothing in Buddhism was contradictory to everything he was, so how could there be a problem. He seemed to be very comfortable with his practice, very comfortable with himself.

"One way Issan allowed himself to be authentic was that he

described himself as a faggot speed-freak cross-dresser, and at a certain point if you do that, you realize that that definition is a joke. No definition can contain a whole person, but where most people would define themselves as the director of this or that and *hide* the faggot speed-freak cross-dresser, Issan fronted that, so what kind of airs could you put on? He just had this humorous thing, like, you know, 'I'm the worst nightmare your mother could imagine. Here I am.' He was forgiving toward himself, and forgiving toward other people. You really felt that he was not judgmental. Consequently he just gave you a big field to run around in."

At this same time, a new movement bubbled quietly, almost unnoticed in San Francisco's Castro (gay) district. Sexual orientation had never been a reason for excluding anyone from any activity at the San Francisco Zen Center, but several gay men felt less than comfortable with what they perceived as an overwhelmingly "straight" vibe there. An ad appeared in one of the local gay rags calling for an initial meeting of gay Buddhist meditators, and someone posted a copy of the notice on a Zen Center public bulletin board.

A surprisingly large meeting of concerned men coalesced in April 1980, including Issan. He'd already discussed the issue with Baker-roshi and in fact had been present at a meeting Baker held with Robert Aitken-roshi, a Zen teacher from Hawaii. Aitken questioned Baker about how he would make Buddhist practice available to the burgeoning gay and lesbian communities. Baker pointed to Issan: "This is our contribution to the gay community." The meeting turned into a series, held every Tuesday evening at 57 Hartford Street. The group called itself the Gay Buddhist Club and later changed the name to Maitri, the Buddhist word for friendliness. Issan called it the Posture Queens: "At first we'd just sit around and smoke cigarettes and complain about how hard it was to practice and be gay. Gradually, we began to meditate for a while before our discussions, and pretty soon there was a Buddha and incense and flowers."

Issan put Zen Center's facilities at the disposal of the group. He also showed them, with his own integration of homosexuality and Buddhism, that the two were not incompatible, nor was the big, imposing Zen Center all that forbidding. But he encouraged the group to strengthen itself independently. A few members began to sit zazen regularly in the basement of their house on Hartford Street—a space that had been "tamed" years before.

The building at 57 Hartford Street was a single-family house with eight rooms on three upper floors and a basement, handsome but unremarkable on a block of many such houses. It had been the home of the San Francisco Dharmadhatu from 1973 to 1979; that group had used the large, wood-paneled basement as a shrine room, while the resident teacher and students lived upstairs. Chögyam Trungpa, Rinpoche, had visited the center and blessed it with rice and invocations in the traditional Tibetan way. The space had also been blessed by His Holiness the Sixteenth Gyalwa Karmapa on one of his visits to San Francisco. Eventually the Dharmadhatu moved to larger quarters, but one of the residents stayed, delighted to find himself at the geographical center of an explosively developing gay community. This man opened the space to the Maitri group.

The group grew steadily and hosted speakers at their meetings, including Allen Ginsberg, Ram Dass, and Baker-roshi. They bought the Hartford Street property and affiliated, though suspiciously, with the Zen Center. Finally on December 8, 1981, in an early morning ceremony, the group formally inaugurated a zendo in the basement, where the old Tibetan shrine room had been. Issan became the group's "spiritual adviser," and at his urging, other priests from Zen Center began to participate there, leading meditation and giving occasional evening talks.

At this point, Issan was directing Zen Center administratively, directing Hartford Street spiritually, and studying with Baker-roshi. Then suddenly, and with terrific force, the fabric of Zen Center life began to tear, and ultimately it came to tatters.

9

"You Get What You Deserve, Whether You Deserve It or Not."

The scandal that tore apart Zen Center began with an afternoon of sex in early April, 1983; a few hours in a hotel room, between consenting adults very much in love. These adults were married, each to another spouse. Richard Baker-roshi was one of the lovers; he thought of his partner primarily as a member of his social circle. The Zen community however, and later the general public, regarded her as one of his students.

Zen Center's and Baker's troubles began with sex, but soon the problems spread to issues of power, money, and religion. Though the events swirled most furiously around Richard Baker (and in the telling they necessarily have that focus), they affected Issan both obliquely and directly. As director of the City Center, he worked closely with Baker. Issan kept the abbot informed of every significant development in the physical plant of Zen Center, the student body, and the surrounding neighborhood. He also served as Baker-roshi's religious attendant in San Francisco, helping him with ceremonies and scheduling all his practice-related interviews. On any given day, when Baker-roshi came into the Zen Center building, his first stop was to check in with Issan.

As closely as they had worked, Issan and Baker-roshi linked much more tightly during and after 1983. What happened to Baker in that year changed the shape of his life radically, cutting his official relationship with the Zen Center and catapulting him out of the Bay Area. A sincere and unencumbered disciple of Baker's, Issan soon followed.

If the community ripped open suddenly, operative forces had been building for a long time, and had, in fact, put Zen Center in an unprecedented place in the history of Buddhist institutions. Japanese Zen hierarchy watched as the outfit grew from an insignificant splinter group, composed of (untrustworthy) foreigners, into a thriving Zen complex where Americans practiced with freshness and enthusiasm long absent from Japan.

To the dozens of Buddhist groups spread across the United States, and particularly to the ten or so main Zen groups clustered on the East and West coasts, Zen Center seemed a powerful, successful example. No other Zen or American Buddhist group had undergone the loss of a charismatic founder; Zen Center had, and had come through it remarkably well.

Other Buddhist *sanghas* paid attention to Zen Center also because of its economics. The institution had grappled successfully with the problems of supporting a non-income–producing religion in a non-Buddhist society. Buddhism's "right livelihood" meant earning money in a way that didn't hurt others or contribute to their being hurt. The idea behind Zen Center's business was to offer the public, as commerce, things the community already did for itself. Baking bread, serving meals, making clothes, and hosting guests in resort situations all yielded valuable experience that could be turned to producing income. Baker described Zen Center as "the container for a kind of nutrient-rich soup, something that would generate forms for Buddhism in America"—something, therefore, that should be bolstered financially, and made attractive as a place to taste the teachings.

In the years from 1975 to 1983, Zen Center opened the Tassajara Bread Bakery, Greens Restaurant, the Green Gulch Greengrocer, Alaya Stitchery, the Wheelwright Center, Whole Earth Books, Wheelwright Press, and Mountain Gate College, a state-approved seminary. A spurt of real-estate acquisition paralleled the growth of the businesses. By 1983, Zen Center owned the City Center, Tassajara, Green Gulch Farm, the Jamesburg house and surrounding land, several apartment buildings near the City Center, and five Victorian houses—two of them old and valuable as architectural landmarks. It owned or managed property on all four corners of the intersection of Page and Laguna, as well as units up and down both streets, creating a sense of an urban village within the larger city.

The force behind this vinelike development was perfectly clear: Abbot Richard Baker. Baker mobilized people and organizations with uncanny skill to meet Zen Center's needs; he knew instinctively how to blend the arts, celebrity, and media to advance Zen Center's causes, and how, at the same time, to keep himself out of the media. Baker-roshi captained Zen Center's journey to a position of corporate power and complexity, but he insisted he was only following a course charted by Suzuki-roshi, who apparently suggested things to Baker as specific as opening a bakery. Still, not everyone thought well of it. Issan: "When Baker-roshi started doing all these various things—the Neighborhood Foundation, stores, and all this stuff—I thought I've got to get out of here and find someplace to just practice. This guy's weird."

After Suzuki-roshi's death, Baker-roshi did more than influence Zen Center policy, as he had done; he now dictated it. Technically, the abbot and the Board of Directors shared power; practically, if Baker-roshi wanted to do something he felt would develop Zen Center, the board was powerless to stop him. Baker talked convincingly and well, argued when necessary. The bold—some thought rash—experiment of the businesses went forward.

Commercial work issued a juicy challenge to the meditative calm and daily mindfulness stressed so heavily in Suzuki-roshi's style of Zen. As such—as an irritant—business perhaps was valuable, the tradition being that calmness developed in action is superior to calmness born of quiet solitude. Hours at work also gave younger students a way to spend constructive time alongside older students, and a kind of osmosis took place; newer students absorbed the elusive Zen feeling for how things were done, and older students felt invigorated by the brightness and freshness of their juniors. The businesses provided the Zen community with a place to work and get job experience, and they made the Zen Center a lot of money.

A series of cookbooks made Tassajara famous, and local celebrities—Joan Baez, Taj Mahal, Marty Balin, Michael McClure, Margaret Jenkins, Herb Gold, Jerry Brown, and Linda Rondstadt among them—came to renew themselves at the hot springs. The businesses and their very stylish patrons thrust Zen Center into regional and sometimes national prominence, but they also caused thorny problems for the Zen community.

Long hours and low pay obscured for many the religious benefit to be derived from their jobs. Students began to come to the scheduled meditation periods less and less regularly; they often felt tired for weeks on end and became emotionally frayed.

Particularly at Greens, students worked extremely hard. Restaurant pace was faster, more confusing, and more pressured than serving a meal to students, or to a dining room full of guests at Tassajara. Glamour surrounded the work—President Carter, Sammy Davis, Jr., and Michael Jackson were just a few of the famous people who ate at Greens, while flattering reviews appeared everywhere from the *San Francisco Bay Guardian* to *Gourmet* magazine—but it stretched individuals and Zen Center's labor pool to a breaking point.

It was not uncommon for a person to work all day in a Zen Center desk job, go to Greens to serve dinner until well past midnight, sleep in or sleep through meditation the following morning, and return to one or another of the jobs by 9 A.M.

Students snagged themselves on other problems as well. The businesses paid low wages, yet placed the students in a world full of fast cash. Some people skimmed a little money from the register at the bakery now and again, and several of the floor crew at Greens admitted to pocketing tip money that was supposed to be shared. The specter of drugs and drug dealers lurked there too. Waiters overheard deals in process and occasionally witnessed a transaction. While not uncharacteristic of the tonier restaurants in San Francisco, such activity harmed a few students who, by virtue of their heavy work schedule, were cut off from the equilibrating force of meditation and study. Students managed to work and keep meditation practices together only through immense effort. Zen Center business dazzled the public's eye, but did so through a great deal of self-sacrifice and personal difficulty for the Zen Center community.

Baker-roshi immersed himself in the details of every aspect of Zen Center. With a new business venture he would be on the scene every day, asking questions, giving advice, and generally "smudging everything with his big thumbprints," as poet and student Philip Whalen teased. This sort of visitation would continue until the business had its own momentum, at which point Baker would divert his attention to another project.

To shore up the financial base, Baker-roshi traveled across the country regularly to meet with friends, private donors, and foundations. He trained students to help him with fund-raising and took them along on his forays, but donors seemed most interested in the head man, either because they found him charming or because he was the living continuation of Suzuki-roshi's work.

An extremely perceptive person, to students Baker often seemed something of a fussbudget. Zen lives most vividly in details of routine events, however, and Baker's eagle eye helped students focus and sharpen their mindfulness. It required no shift of gears for him to look up from an intellectual or financial conversation at Greens, ask a waiter to inform the kitchen that the soup had a bit too much pepper in it, and to please straighten the corners of the tablecloth at the dessert station on his way in.

Baker-roshi's style of running Zen Center kept him hidden a good deal of the time from all but his most senior two or three students and his assistants. He virtually never worked physically alongside students, and time with him—especially casual time—was extremely rare. He complained about this separation from his students, but never rearranged his priorities to remedy it. Most of his students knew little of how Baker-roshi lived, nor saw him as anything but a presence in the meditation hall.

His work took him to the perimeters of the community, where he interacted with people who could aid or block Zen Center's progress. Expending enormous energy in these endeavors often left his personal relationships with students bankrupt. Baker confessed that "students called me 'their teacher,' and I always referred to them as 'Zen Center students,' as a way to support the institution and as a kind of realistic modesty. But it turned out to be mostly an avoidance of the responsibility I would have felt if I said so many people were my students. I didn't have either the courage or the foolishness to say so many people were my students. But in fact they *were* my students, without my acknowledging it or accepting the true responsibility of the recognition.

"As the institution developed around me, I found myself landlord, mayor, administrator, entrepreneur, and fund-raiser, as well as abbot and teacher. This was too much power for me to have, and many people couldn't handle it over time." Whether Baker found himself in these roles, or systematically or unthinkingly built himself into them, his analysis of his situation and of the community's reaction, is accurate.

The most pernicious effect of Baker's doing many jobs was that it hindered his ability to teach. He delivered lectures regularly, and attended meditation with students as much as his schedule would permit. Necessary and honorable means of teaching Zen, they are not sufficient. Zen masters convey Zen through example. A student watches closely not only how the teacher sits in meditation but how he or she eats, walks, talks, works, rests, and relaxes. In a tradition where precious little instruction is ever given and textual knowledge is considered secondary at best, clues to understanding are dropped and caught in mundane, daily events.

By 1982 and 1983 Baker divided his time so finely between so many places that it seemed to students in any one location as though he lectured less frequently, practiced in the meditation hall less frequently, and saw students in *dokusan* less often. This separation bespoke estrangement on another, invisible level. The bond between Zen student and teacher resonates with the slightest movement on either end; shifts in understanding or commitment pass instantly across it. Very much like lovers who subtly know things about their relationship without knowing how they know, teachers and disciples lock into each other's emotional lives. When Baker-roshi told his students in one Monday night lecture that he needed to attend the meetings he did and associate with his outside friends as much as he did because he got sustenance from them, it sounded like a husband offering excuses to his wife about why he was taking off for the weekend with another woman.

"We were in love—Love, nothing!—We were totally blitzed. Nothing quite like this ever happened to me before. I feel certain the same was true for her." In mid-March of 1983, Baker and his paramour hadn't yet become lovers, "but we were hanging on a cliff by our fingernails."

This dangerous vision of sex was something Baker had contemplated a good deal. In noncelibate styles of Buddhist practice, the matter of sex is highly individual. Baker said the same teacher might sanction sexual activity for one student and proscribe it for another. In a thorough discussion of Buddhist sexuality, Baker did formulate three basic rules for sexual conduct at Zen Center: "Don't hurt anyone, don't deceive anyone consequentially involved, and don't set a bad example for the *sangha*." There were auxiliary rules as well, especially for people who had been around for more than ten years—things like not being sexually involved with a person until they had been at Zen Center for at least six months, and not getting into any liaisons during the first training period at the monastery.

The best way to think of sex, Baker said, was as reproducible: the kind of intimacy generated between lovers could be extended to every person. On the other hand, he cited Huston Smith quoting the Buddha's saying if there were another thing in the world like sex, religion wouldn't stand a chance. As an absorptive state, Baker said finally, as profound and delightful as sex was, he thought it second best to meditation.

Second best or not, Baker-roshi made time for both practices during his term as abbot. His marriage to Virginia—a tall, dark, statuesque beauty—seemed to drift more and more toward a friendship, a productive partnership. Virginia had an extremely close friend in Renee des Tombe, who lived with the Bakers and provided constant companionship for her and their two daughters. Like many middle-aged men (early forties) in such a marriage, Baker-roshi looked outside it. When knowledge of this dawned on the Zen Center community, it stunned most everyone. Ironically scorned for a misguided love affair, Baker-roshi's real crime was that he seemed to have strayed from his deeper love affair with the body of students in the community.

As the affair with his student became public (largely through the efforts of her husband), several other women ventured forward with stories of their affairs with Baker-roshi—relationships that had occurred both before and during his term as abbot. Each subsequent revelation sent a wave of ire and disbelief through the *sangha*. Students charged Baker with hypocrisy. For years he had preached the virtues of fidelity; he'd given a very hard time to students in leaderhip positions for sexual indiscretions, and now, it appeared, he had chosen a very different set of guidelines for his own behavior. One person close to Baker-roshi expressed indignation that she'd had to help cover up not only his dalliances but the painful consequences. That more than one of the women he'd slept with had been or had become his student—one of them his personal assistant—made some in the Zen community doubt his integrity as a teacher.

When the dust settled, it looked as if Baker-roshi had been involved with something like five women connected to Zen Center during his thirteen years as abbot. Baker's lovers—generally beautiful, talented, and independent—were won through his own efforts. The affairs were discrete—one at a time—and discreet. Holding to a limited idea of honesty, he informed Virginia of each affair and carried them out with some form of acceptance on her part.

The *fact* that Baker-roshi philandered was a well-kept secret (at the request of his wife), but the temptations of his position were not. As many as four hundred Marin County and San Francisco listeners would wait and watch as Baker-roshi walked ceremonially into the Green Gulch zendo, offered incense, prostrated himself before the altar, slowly crossed the hall to his raised seat, mounted it, and arranged robes that looked elaborate and gorgeous; he was the star. His brilliant lecturing style, his facility during question periods, his coterie of attendants and senior students all contributed to this image. At six foot two, with elegant gestures, easy East Coast manners, a shaven head, and friendly, intellectual good looks, Baker-roshi exuded charm.

His new lover was different from his others; her extraordinary looks aside, she was more agreeable, less independent. Her husband advised Baker on financial and organizational matters, and found a niche as a kind of personal consultant to the abbot. A forward-thinking entrepreneur and economist, he appealed to Baker-roshi. The two men moved in similar social strata and soon became fast friends.

When Baker told the man that he was falling in love with his wife, his confession alone set off emotional earthquakes—even though, according to Baker, he hadn't yet had sexual relations with the woman. The exact sequence of events may now be buried in a rubble of passionate memories, but what Zen Center students were told a few days later was the following: that their abbot had had an affair with a student, a married woman; that the husband had threatened suicide; that he'd come to Zen Center's senior practice leaders for help; and that Zen Center's Board of Directors was meeting regularly to figure out what to do.

Students knew something was up, but no one was quite sure what. One senior practitioner remembers, "I saw her boots outside Richard's cabin at Tassajara for four hours, two afternoons in a row. Here Richard is only there for a little while, and he wasn't doing any *dokusans,* and he's having what I assumed were these really intense talks with her about her husband. Somehow Richard had convinced him that they were such good friends that he should want to do this: that man ended up feeling bad because he didn't want to offer his wife to Richard. But those guys were so close, I really thought they were the ones about to have an affair.

"In fact later, when someone called me, and said, 'Did you hear what happened?' my first flash was that he and Richard had had an affair, and that she was upset. That was honestly what I thought. The real news hit me like a bolt out of the blue."

Baker and his new lover were torn apart by the maelstrom of scandal; they wouldn't see each other again for nearly ten years.

His shield of invulnerability punctured, Baker-roshi's power, both administrative and religious, deteriorated at an astonishing rate. A number of problems facing the community had reached a critical point, and news of his affair triggered an explosion of complaint.

On April 8, 1983, members of the Board of Directors convened in San Francisco—the first time they had ever done so without Baker's instigation. The news sprang out that Baker-roshi had had sex with a student, that her husband had threatened suicide, and that he remained upset.

At the same moment that Baker-roshi was celebrating Buddha's birthday with his Tassajara students in a meadow overrun with fragrant wildflowers, Zen Center's board, in a cavernous Victorian meeting room, forced passionate emotions into formal procedure. They emerged three hours later feeling shaken, somewhat groundless, but resolved that as a unit of moral authority, they would change the abbot's behavior, consequences regardless. To a member they saw his affair as a critical mistake.

The story even hit the *San Francisco Chronicle*: gossip-columnist Herb Caen began his piece that day saying, "The Abbot of the Zen Center has been making goo-goo eyes at someone else's wife. . . ." At the Tassajara Bakery a note taped to the register instructed students not to discuss the mention of Zen Center in the paper.

A few of Baker's senior students met with him early on, and one reported: "His whole attitude was like 'Okay, I may have made this mistake, but I'm still basically good, right? You still basically trust me, don't you? I mean, look at all these other good things I'm doing.' And of course that was true, he was doing lots of other good things, but his attitude bothered me a lot, and I told him so.

From the point of view of Buddhism, it's usually considered healthier to keep your eye on your faults, and let other people mention your good points.

"Then he went out to Green Gulch, and Virginia talked to him—all night. The next day this cavalier attitude was completely gone."

What had begun as a desire to stop Baker's inappropriate behavior quickly changed to a move to stop him. The board decided to meet directly with Baker-roshi the next night. Everyone wore full-length black robes, and the meeting began with a chanting of the Heart Sutra. "It felt heavy. It felt like a funeral," one board member remembered.

Baker-roshi too wore robes, and came in with his shoulders crooked and tight. He looked grim as he knelt on his heels in the center of the group. Various board members expressed shock at the pain he had caused, the sense of collusion they felt in not having had the courage to speak out to him before, their desire for changed behavior and attitudes—put most bluntly by one woman: "I want you to stop."

For his part, Baker-roshi felt betrayed. He'd appointed most of the sixteen board members himself. He'd shared teaching responsibility with Reb Anderson and Lew Richmond, and he had done a major Dharma transmission ceremony with Reb only three months before, establishing Reb as a lineage holder. Baker-roshi expected if not loyalty, then at least a sympathetic hearing. Instead he found himself in the midst of a palace revolution.

Issan: "When the shit hit the fan at Zen Center—and most of the people who had encouraged me to stay at Zen Center early on, because they were doing it, and saying how wonderful Richard Baker was and all—well, now they were attacking him. That's when I decided to say, 'He's my teacher.' "

Baker: "During that time I was in, what shall I say—not a state of shock exactly, but I was in a state of being stunned, and I couldn't quite believe what was happening, so I was just kind of watching everything. I couldn't quite feel . . . A lot of people went from being unbelievably affectionate, overly affectionate, almost hanging on my every word, to the diametric opposite, saying the weirdest things: that I was a pile of shit, that I was this and that. I was like, what's going on? What's happening to people? At the same time, I was completely in love.

"But Issan was one of the people that all the way through it, my relationship with him just remained exactly the same. If anything, it improved. He was just present, understanding, and we continued as if nothing ever happened. Between Issan and I, the Zen Center 1983 mess didn't happen."

Meditation began at 5:00 A.M. at Zen Center, when the head priest walked into the zendo, trailed by an attendant carrying incense. For the fifteen minutes before five o'clock, a wooden board was struck loudly with a mallet once each minute. After seven minutes, and then five minutes later, the striker performed a rapid series of hits known as a roll-down. The roll-downs signaled how much time was left. The knocks could be heard clearly throughout the three floors of the Zen Center and into the neighborhood, where local kids called Zen Center the woodpecker building.

In dim, fragrant silence the head priest performed three slow prostrations. Having rearranged slippery robes, he or she then circumambulated the room with hands held palm to palm in the traditional Oriental greeting pose. As the head priest passed, each student responded by raising their hands in the same pose. This required mindfulness, since in the Soto tradition most students sit facing a wall. A person listened for footsteps—bare feet on wooden floor—or waited for the sound and smell of perfumed robes.

When Baker-roshi was in town, he usually performed this "morning greeting" and then either sat in meditation himself or went to his quarters to receive students in *dokusan*. When he was out of town, or when, as had become more and more the case, he'd been up working late, or talking with guests, Reb Anderson did the morning greeting. In either instance, Issan functioned as the attendant, carrying incense and managing the list of students who wished an interview.

As Baker-roshi trod into the zendo on April 11, the air was charged. Word of the affair had spread from the board to senior students to the practicing membership like lightning. Zen students take refuge in simple upright meditation, especially in turbulent times, and the zendo was packed. This time, however, no one could leave their distress at the door; its very source had just walked in and was now making bows. Some outraged students declined to return Baker-roshi's gesture as he walked his rounds. Others sat and stewed in confused emotions. His mere presence in the meditation hall troubled many.

If the emotions ran mixed about his attendance at zazen, they were fiercely clear about Baker's doing the morning service. During the half-hour of chanting and prostrations, the head priest directly faced the altar and made many offerings on behalf of the entire group. At least one student objected so pointedly to Baker's performing the service that he deferred, and Reb led the ceremony.

During the next few days, realizing that simply coming to zazen made matters worse, Baker-roshi stopped, and began to practice in his house next door. Once or twice he ventured over to Zen Center to greet students, to shake hands and ask forgiveness, or just to receive them in an informal setting, but the sensation of his being awkwardly unwelcome grew, and he soon sequestered himself in his house. The board asked him not to lecture, and the couple he was to wed that weekend requested that he not perform their ceremony.

Things turned cold and lonely for Baker-roshi. After days of continuous, painful discussions, Virginia, Renee, and children departed and took up residence at the Green Gulch house. Baker wandered around the high-ceilinged rooms of his Victorian house. He ate poorly—soup from cans, bowls of cold cereal. Dust gathered, mail piled up, laundry accumulated. He remained under a kind of self-imposed house arrest.

Issan had declared himself Baker's student. Period. No further discussion was necessary or particularly welcome. He had trouble enough running the building.

Like boxers unsure of an opponent's power, Baker and the board circled each other all summer, without much direct connection. Baker traveled to Switzerland and Austria for conferences he'd previously agreed to attend. He spoke with the Dalai Lama there and came away from the conversation encouraged to continue his work as a Buddhist teacher.

Baker then went to southern France for a month's retreat with Thich Nhat Hanh—a Vietnamese Zen master and peace activist who seemed to move him in a way no one had done since Suzuki-roshi. Thich Nhat Hanh wrote a letter to the Zen Center community:

> . . . in this quiet place we have tried to look and see the situation in the light of Buddha's teaching. To me, Zen-tatsu Richard Baker-roshi has undergone a profound change during this period of re-introspection. He is now like a new person. . . . He seems to have found peace for himself after a long period being deeply affected by what happened. Virginia Baker whom I invited over for the last ten days also witnessed this transformation in him. . . .
>
> Zentatsu Richard Baker has a tremendous capacity of becoming one of the most illustrious Buddhist leaders of our time, if only all of us could correctly help and support him. To me, he embodies very much the future of Buddhism in the West with his creative intelligence

and his aliveness. I am positive that Zentatsu is now
worth our trust and I completely invest my trust in him.

But Thich Nhat Hanh's letter came last in a series of three
heavy letters to the students at the Zen Center. The letters arrived
within a month of one another. Robert Aitken-roshi—American-
born Zen master, trained in Japan, and leading groups in Hawaii
and Australia—wrote first with a detailed account of his August
visit to the Zen Center. The second was a handwritten letter from
Baker-roshi himself:

> I am continually aware of how much and painfully I miss
> all of you. I also continually find myself flooded with
> pain and remorse in all that I have done to cause all of
> this.
> I realize that I have betrayed my best friend and our
> relationship, that I have caused him and his wife much
> suffering, and that I have seriously disrupted and harmed
> their marriage and family life. And I have caused Virginia
> and my own family incalculable suffering too.
> And also I realize that I have betrayed and let you
> down as students by not being mindful enough of your
> needs and by not being available enough for the next
> step in practice and teaching during the last few years.
> And when I think of the extraordinary effort and
> intelligence all of you have put into making Zen Center
> such a wonderful place to practice and such a wonderful
> place of refuge and help to so many people, I am
> ashamed of my unmindful, imperious and busy manner
> which often prevented me from hearing your heartfelt
> concerns and criticisms over the years. . . .
> To this day I remain overwhelmed and humiliated by
> the irresponsibility and insensitivity of my actions that
> have so seriously threatened the existence of our won-
> derful Zen Center and cast such a shadow over the hope
> and trust that Suzuki-roshi placed in me.

Although I have been out of touch with Zen Center
recently in many ways, still since 1971 and especially the
last 5 or 6 years I have been able to go on because I felt I
was answering a request and need of Zen Center and the
larger society, but now that does not seem to be the
case, a main source of my effort is gone.

Yet I am still ready to go on if you want me to and if
you will help and support me. I feel and think I can do it
with your help.

Continuing Suzuki-roshi's lineage and teaching is my
only fundamental goal and the only goal I can give my
full energy and commitment to.

I am sorry that I have somehow allowed the size and
work of Zen Center to obscure my great joy in practicing with you.

Now that it is clear that the administration of Zen
Center goes on quite well without me, I look forward to
a calmer, more continuous and mindful time at Zen
Center.

I hope you can accept my deep regret, remorse, and
apologies for what I have done and that together we can
find a way to continue Suzuki-roshi's lineage.

Sincerely,
Zentatsu,
9.27.83

This confession and apology did not have the desired effect
when it arrived in early October. Perhaps, as one student put it,
the letter tried to make a whole egg out of an omelette. Or
perhaps the community was feeling the influence of Aitken-roshi's
letter, in which Aitken listed three steps Baker-roshi could take if
he and the community decided to work together again: (1) work
service "shoulder to shoulder with the students in the upkeep of
the temple and grounds"; (2) psychotherapy; and (3) study with
other teachers. Though Aitken took pains to clarify how traditional

his first and third suggestions were in the history of Zen, even for deeply realized and experienced teachers, and how personally valuable therapy had been in his own work as a roshi, his letter conveyed a feeling to Zen Center students that as things stood, Baker-roshi was inadequate to the job of abbot. Little rancor, if any, sullied Aitken-roshi's letter with regard to Baker-roshi, or with regard to senior students at the Zen Center, whom he judged as yet unready to assume teaching responsibility. Nonetheless, his letter dramatically affected the way people thought about Baker-roshi and reconciliation with him. Subtle vilification crept into the discussions, so that when Baker-roshi's letter arrived, it was little publicized and not sincerely believed.

Throughout this whole mess, Issan laid rather low. He did his best to manage the affairs of the City Center, which proved no easy task. Alienation and unhappiness caused more than a few Zen students to move out of the building, and for the first time in anyone's memory, the residence was less than full.

Baker returned from France and resumed living in his house adjacent to the Zen Center. He demonstrated a much more vigorous spirit than he had before his trip, meeting with students and friends, formulating a spectrum of plans, reading, writing, and painting. He began holding classes to study Zen koans, and there were soon two groups of eight to fifteen people each, meeting with him weekly in the city and another group at Green Gulch. Though the community as a whole remained suspicious, these students could not resist a chance to discuss the Dharma in an intimate, informal situation with Baker-roshi. In fact, the number of students who in one way or another supported Baker-roshi began to swell. None of this group could overlook his troubles or spend energy in defending him, but given this teacher, his mistakes, shortcomings, even his character flaws, was it worth it to study with him? They thought yes.

This distinct minority found it increasingly difficult to maintain friendly ties with Baker's most ardent detractors. Friends who came down on different sides of the political line with regard to Baker-roshi might not have much to talk about. People recognized this depressing trend and did their best to counteract it, but polarization set in. In one corner sat the board and most of the community; in the other corner, Baker-roshi and an odd assortment of students who for varied reasons chose to side with him. Issan's ability to be firmly *for* Baker-roshi and yet not *against* anyone else—a nonprejudicial friendliness, rare at the time—made his presence invaluable. An alarming number of students turned away from the whole conflict, likening it to an ugly marriage on the rocks: don't like him, don't like her.

Zen Center board meetings began to get virulent, particularly as Baker and the board negotiated how to proceed. One board member, in slow, emphatic tones, declared, "Richard Baker is a venomous snake." Another said, almost casually, "He's a liar," and yet another said, "I don't want him to have the dignity of retiring. I want him to have to resign." The vehemence of the meetings sharpened polarization in the community. The pushing got harder, and just as with boys who have escalated insults to the verge of a fist-fight, a circle of observers closed around the combatants, increasing the pressure.

Donors began to pull rank, demanding of the board this or that action with regard to Baker-roshi. One donor demanded an audit "to determine to what extent Zen Center's funds may have been misappropriated."

The public that associated with Zen Center through its commerce also seemed to take time out to watch the fight. Zen Center's businesses functioned from May to December, but barely. Income fell from expectations by hundreds of thousands of dollars, and Zen Center's administration felt lucky to keep the doors to the businesses open at all. In past financial crises, Baker had pulled

Zen Center through with fund-raising magic. He was in no position to work it this time, even were he willing. As one student put it, "It had been a great juggling act, but take away the juggler, and all the balls come falling down."

The aggrieved husband joined the circle of hooting observers and began to make things really tough. He talked of the large sums of money he wanted back, and of pending lawsuits. Some days later, in a stunning surprise, Baker-roshi resigned.

Dear Zen Center Students and Friends,
I have waited all these months trying to decide what to do because I did not know what to do to fulfill the vow I made to Suzuki-roshi to continue and to develop a place for his teaching which would endure.

Now I see that my role as Abbot and leader is more damaging to the Sangha and to individuals than any help I may add by staying. And I see even more that the present situation and any effort I make in it is damaging to the teaching and this is completely unacceptable to me.

I want to do what is best for Zen Center and the lineage and the teaching. And I want to do whatever I can to lessen, to end the deep suffering and pain many persons feel. So it is with deep regret and shame before Suzuki-roshi and you, that I resign as Abbot and Chief Priest of the San Francisco Zen Center.

I resign with the trust and hope in your wisdom, in the strength of your future, and in the compassion and intelligence of each of you and of all of you working together.

Please heal and help me to heal the wounds I have opened and please end and help me to end the suffering I have caused. I know you can work together to make Zen Center the wonderful place to practice and place to share your lives that I know it can be.

Thank you for being patient with me all these months
while I absorbed the truth and teaching of this situation.
And thank you for being patient with me all these years.

Sincerely,

Zentatsu Baker

December 20, 1983

During "all these months," Issan had worked quietly at what
he thought of as his job: running the building, supporting his
teacher, maintaining the peace. Baker: "I saw no reason why he
should stop. This building deserved to be taken care of, and he
was doing it, and all the political stuff going on around him wasn't
so important.

"He understood very well that his supporting me as a teacher,
and as his teacher, helped me survive what happened at Zen
Center. I think he was clearly trying to help me. It wasn't just him
asking me to help him. He clearly knew he was helping me in
what he was doing, because the teacher is really the relationship
itself, and he so beautifully supported my relationship with him,
and his with me. It was unerring and unfailing. I feel deeply
grateful to Issan for helping me continue as a practicing Buddhist
and a teacher. If anything, he helped me more than I helped him."

10

Santa Fe

When Baker-roshi realized he couldn't stay at Zen Center, he relocated to Santa Fe and started a small group there. This left his San Francisco students—no small number of them—without a teacher, and without a hospitable place to practice and hear his talks. Baker called his Santa Fe outfit the Dharma Sangha, and his San Francisco group Dharma Sangha West. The West Coast group acquired property in which to establish a meditation hall and lecture space: a huge, three-story structure atop a two-story rock atop Potrero Hill, formerly the Rudolph Schaeffer School of Design on Mariposa Street.

Just at this time, Issan found himself pushed and pulled by conflicting emotions. He'd been elected to a newly constituted Board of Directors in Zen Center's first election. At the same time, he was having an ugly tussle with the administration over what amounted to a health-care issue. Finally, he'd been asked by Baker to take care of the new Dharma Sangha West space on Mariposa Street.

Baker: "He had gotten disillusioned about being in the Zen Center building—he was getting nowhere by being there. When I started Mariposa, he made clear that he wanted to help, and I asked him if he wanted to be the director. When he decided to do it, he had no money, I had no money, Mariposa Street had no money, and Issan needed a hearing aid, or to get his fixed. Zen Center, after all those years of his working free, told him that they couldn't afford, or wouldn't give him a hearing aid, because he was leaving.

"I remember that that really kind of sealed it for him. He felt it was such a little thing, and he lived there for years, devoting all this time and at no salary, or a very meager stipend. Just at the point when people were starting to pay themselves very substantial salaries, they wouldn't help him with his hearing aid. That kind of clinched it for him. He kept relations with people, but I don't think he ever felt again that he belonged at San Francisco Zen Center."

Paul Rosenblum, another member of the new board, recalls the period: "After forcing Baker-roshi to resign, the board itself resigned and was reconstituted through an election. There were people on the new board who were very sympathetic to Baker-roshi, but still, Issan and I were on the short end of a lot of eleven-to-two votes. Kind of an awkward time.

"He'd been living at Zen Center and had a relationship with these people on the board, including people who were adamantly opposed to Baker-roshi. I think the ones who were most extremely opposed, Issan stopped having a relationship with them—it was too difficult. People felt like, 'How can I be civil to you if you're supporting Adolf Hitler and I'm a Jew?' When people felt that strongly, it was difficult to have a relationship.

"There were a lot of people who were clearly opposed to Baker-roshi but who had an ability to be open, and I think what Issan wanted to do was to keep the lines of communication open. He was starting another temple, and he wanted to continue a relationship to Zen Center. The practical level was just that he was kind and open and nice to people, and so he's going to be that way."

Issan worked hard at his tangential tasks, but had a rough time of it. Paul Rosenblum: "Starting a new place required a lot of energy, but he went on the Board of Directors and stayed on through his one-year term. We both stayed out our terms, wanting to find some way Baker-roshi could possibly be still involved with Zen Center. It was very clear that Issan was committed to having Baker-roshi as his teacher. He said it explicitly. He said, 'Baker-roshi is my teacher.'

"Issan didn't see Zen practice as excluding somebody. He developed the theme in his practice of 'settling in closeness.' He could never exclude somebody, because his practice was so inclusive—particularly if that somebody was his teacher.

"Then things got unpleasant around Baker-roshi's move—what was his, what was Zen Center's. Issan's attitude was like, 'Oh, the kids. They're just squabbling now, but they don't really mean that. It's just the kids.' We were in touch with Baker-roshi during this time, and it was a time of unbelievable pain for him. We felt the need to be more of a support to him. Our feeling was to be generous—he was clearly suffering, and he was our teacher—and not to talk about whether he should pay five hundred dollars more or less for this or that. Issan used to get angry sometimes, but it was more frustration than hatred. It frustrated him—'We shouldn't be doing this!'

"It was painful to be at the meetings, but one of the things that made it possible for both of us was that we were both there. Sometimes, if it was about money or something complicated, he would say to me, 'Do you know what they're talking about? How should I vote? Does it matter if you do the insurance this way or that way?' But the negativity there made it essential that there were two of us.

"The other thing that made it possible in the face of those attacks was that we were doing something positive, setting up Mariposa Street. You didn't feel like all you were doing was pushing the river.

"I think emotionally for Issan that was a very difficult time. It also involved a big loss of financial security for him."

Difficult though it may have been, for the first time Issan ran his own Zen show. He was still spiritual adviser to the Hartford Street group, and now at Mariposa he ruled his own turf. The aplomb with which he did it set his future Zen course. Baker: "At Mariposa, as soon as I made him director of the practice as well— with his giving lectures—he began attracting students right away. It was clear that his gift as a teacher—not just as the director of a building, but as a *teacher*—was profound. I felt I should start the process—we talked about it—of really making him a teacher and acknowledging him as a teacher. We began the process at that time, which he understood would require him to go to Santa Fe at some point. It was clear that the time was ripe to do it, and he proved that in the way he immediately and naturally took charge at Mariposa."

Baker here is describing the Dharma Transmission ceremony. Such a ceremony affirms the essential and subtle attitudes that embody the teachings and the lineage, and marks that the disciple has inherited the teacher's mind. The disciple becomes a fully qualified teacher in his own right. Though Issan's osmotic absorption of Baker-roshi's teaching had been going on for many years, preparations for the transmission ceremony itself meant months more close study with Baker-roshi. The ceremony itself would require days. As a first step, Issan began to do the requisite calligraphy, and even though he was stretched by his conflicting responsibilities, he accomplished a good portion of it.

The crew Issan attracted to Mariposa Street included the usual suspects. Along with refugees from Zen Center's diaspora came wanderers from society's fringe generally: displaced, disoriented, or just misunderstood, such people might spend a night or more getting their bearings while Issan puttered around the oversize building. In particular, Issan's friend and lover James came around more often.

Issan had now tried for years to weave James into Zen Center's pattern and had bent rules to accommodate him. James had been known to show up at Zen Center's door any hour, hungry, out of money, nowhere to stay. Issan usually just stashed the young man quietly in his own room, let him rest, and brought him food. Eventually, James was able to live at Zen Center for weeks and then months at a time, following the schedule; he even passed extended time at Tassajara. A solid meditator and generally cheerful person, James still had the habit of suddenly disappearing—turning up missing for something he'd been scheduled to do. Hours or days later, he'd heave back into view, usually manic, often on roller-skates, loaded on drugs, and Issan would have to put him out.

At Mariposa Street, with no local administration above him, Issan was able to devote more time to James and more openly. Intensifying their relationship, however, "solved" nothing. James came and went as unpredictably as ever. He once roller-skated the entire 160 miles from San Francisco to Jamesburg.

While Issan tolerated James's erratic behavior more easily than other Mariposa Street residents, he had their feelings to consider, and he found himself in a familiar bind: wanting to take care of James, loving him, understanding his situation from the inside, but being forced to exclude him. The rule arose that if James was clearheaded and on reasonable behavior, he was welcome; if not, not. James, of course, played as close to this boundary as possible, and it wore on Issan.

This psychoemotional strain aside, keeping Mariposa Street afloat was tough. There was no backer money, and none in sight. A temple this size required a vigorous body of generous practitioners. Zen Center's festering political fevers decimated the number of Zen practioners in San Francisco, and weakened even something as amorphous as the "Zen spirit." Dharma Sangha West never attained momentum. After a few false starts, the group sold the building, and Issan left to join Baker-roshi.

Baker had landed nimbly on his feet in Santa Fe. He lived in a comfortable split-level adobe-and-timber house, with a zendo in a separate building on the property. His house was elegantly appointed with the art, furniture, and enormous library he'd accumulated before and during his Zen Center years. The zendo sat at one end of an open courtyard a few yards away, lit and ventilated with a large skylight. In the center of the courtyard stood a small stupa built in 1976 under the auspices of H. H. Dudjom Rinpoche and blessed by several powerful lamas since. The zendo compound also included rooms attached to the courtyard. Some of Baker-roshi's faithful students lived in the house with him, and some occupied the rooms by the zendo.

The band of Zen students who'd departed San Francisco with Baker had come to Santa Fe with the idea of studying with him intensively, in fairly close quarters, but they were having no easy time of it. Baker tried to parlay the success of Greens Restaurant into a new local culinary venture. This project—the Desert Cafe—hit more obstacles, took more time, and required more of his attention than either he or his students had bargained for. What it boiled down to was that Baker-roshi wasn't around much.

Issan, though, took up residence agreeably, and without the denomination of a particular position, he began doing his usual thing. Baker: "He was there about a year. We basically just lived together. He worked for a while at the restaurant. . . . We didn't have a really regular schedule. We met sometimes, sometimes with Philip Whalen.

"When he lived at Santa Fe, the garden bloomed, the place looked good, everything was shining, the flowers and the bushes were tended. He just did it. No one asked him, he just did it. He was a kind of—as a real bodhisattva is—a kind of housewife. The bodhisattva is ultimately a kind of housewife, just takes care of things. Spiritual housewife."

Philip Whalen, also a resident of the Dharma Sangha, was working on his Dharma transmission ceremony with Baker-roshi too. Sometimes they all met together, as Baker mentions; other times each heir-designee met with Baker separately.

Baker: "When we began actively studying texts together and doing teachings, Issan would say to me, 'You know, I'm not smart, I'm stupid, I can't remember anything. I can't read. I read something, and I don't know one minute later what it is.' Things like that, he used to say to me, and he usually blamed it on the drugs. Maybe the drugs did destroy some ability to hold connections. When we talked about concepts or practices that were tied together or that made sense primarily through linked verbal information, he'd hear it and kind of look blankly at me, and the next day we'd meet again, and he'd say, 'I don't remember anything we talked about.'

"But I found that if I could frame these things or feel these things more in images, and in concepts that weren't verbally linked but were, shall we say, proprioceptively linked—that is, if we talked in such a way that as I talked about it with him, I went at a pace and in a way that I could feel it in my body and his body, then the next day he had it.

"In this way, he helped me too, because I learned even more clearly that if he was going to get it, I had to feel it physically. If I did feel it physically, then he got it. He couldn't necessarily reproduce it conceptually, but I knew he knew and understood.

"The most far-out teachings, when we started doing transmission, he immediately understood their practicality and application. It was from that touchstone that he understood one thing after another. If he tried to understand intellectually, or tried to make sense of it, or was intimidated by it, or intimidated that he didn't understand, then he could get overwhelmed. But he understood one thing after another, like taking care of a kitchen, then making the bed. One thing follows from another."

Before and during his time in Santa Fe, Issan took reasonably good care of his health. He'd been tested for the HIV virus several times and had turned out negative each time. Such sexual encounters as he'd had—from his account, they were very few and mostly with James—had been "safe." But on a quick visit to San Francisco in the winter of 1985, Issan and his lover neglected to protect themselves.

Back in Santa Fe, he underwent a battery of medical tests as part of a general checkup. Blood samples were taken. "They told me over the telephone, almost as an afterthought. . . . They talked to me about everything else, and then at the end they said, 'Oh, by the way, your HIV test came back positive.' I said, 'Oh, I'm HIV positive?' and they said, 'That's right,' and hung up. That was it. I felt kind of shortchanged."

Baker: "He had an AIDS test. I encouraged him to—he kept kind of coughing, and was sick—and I thought at least he should check for AIDS. He had the first test, and it came back positive. Then he did it a second time. We didn't get too worried the first time—it was like, maybe it was a false positive. Then I remember I came home and he was there and he said, 'Well, it's positive a second time.' I looked at him—we were standing in the living room—and he looked at me, we didn't say much. Then he said, 'Well why shouldn't I have it? It's been my life. It's sort of appropriate. Why should I be spared?' "

While enduring this tough personal news at home, Issan also heard distressing reports from the Hartford Street group. The emphasis on meditation there seemed to be slight. One man who sat regularly described the house as "a collection of gay men living together in the middle of the Castro district who keep a pet zendo in the basement." The late afternoon zazen period often had a dozen or more people sitting, but the morning periods, starting at 5:00 A.M., were seriously underattended. Few people came from outside, and house residents grumbled at having to rise at this unsociable hour to light candles and incense, to open doors, ring bells, and chant.

The core Hartford Street group preserved its main functions: board meetings, occasional half-day sittings, and Tuesday "Maitri Evenings," which featured an open dinner and guest speaker. A rotation of priests from San Francisco Zen Center continued to lead periods of meditation and to participate in administration of the fledgling community. But lacking the nourishment of strong daily sitting practice, the Hartford Street group and many of its individual members grew weak in terms of purpose. Squabbles flared at meetings. Accusations of shirked responsibility flew back and forth, little quarrels grew into grudges and mucked the functioning of the house.

In fact an ambiguous sense of community existed, at best. The residents felt themselves bonded by being simultaneously two different kinds of minority: gay and spiritually inclined. But in mundane truth they lived privately in separate rooms, they had separate, marked sections of the refrigerator, and they worked at house jobs independent of one another. They'd become a small community linked by their commitment to meditation, and that commitment languished.

The group soon decided that their floundering was the result of being leaderless. They made contact with Issan and Baker-roshi in Santa Fe to see what it would take to get Issan back to San Francisco. Issan's Dharma transmission work with Baker-roshi could continue at a remove and over time, so the matter seemed primarily fiscal: Issan would need plane fare, room, board, and a monthly stipend. Word went out to the extended sitting group around Hartford Street, and the necessary funds were arranged.

Baker: "When he was in Santa Fe, Hartford Street wanted him

to come back, but they wanted him to come back in a kind of loose way. Maybe they'd pay him, maybe they wouldn't, maybe it would be zen—but they just wanted him *back*. We discussed this a lot, and I would say there was a transition at this point. In the earlier discussions, we'd been very much a partnership, and although he was supplying the ingredients, telling me what was happening, he generally took my advice.

"At this point, we had the same kind of conversation—should they support him or not support him—and I was making the same kind of suggestions, thinking through the implications—but at this point, he took the responsibility on his own, very clearly. It wasn't so much coming from me anymore, even as a partner. We'd discuss it, he'd use me as an adviser, but *he* was saying, 'If I go back, they have to support me, it has to be a Zen place, and they have to take this on. I will not go back until they tell me they have enough money.' It was exactly right. It came from him, and it was another stage in his taking responsibility and knowing exactly what to do."

A little less than a year after he left San Francisco, Issan came back, this time as teacher-in-residence at Hartford Street Zen Center.

11

Opening the Door

The first change Issan brought to Hartford Street was that he made sure someone was in the zendo every morning—himself. He got up at 4:00 A.M., made coffee, and dressed carefully in his robes. Starting at five, he sat both forty-minute periods of zazen and led the daily twenty-minute morning service. He then did temple cleaning and cooked breakfast. He let it be known that as teacher-in-residence, he regarded 57 Hartford Street primarily as a Zen center.

At an early meeting with house residents, Issan heard questions about how things were changing. Would they be allowed to have a drink in the evening? What if someone wanted to smoke pot now and then? What kinds of plans did he have in mind? Issan's response was that they were asking the wrong questions. The only thing he felt each person should seriously ask himself was whether or not they wanted to practice Zen there. According to Issan, what went on at Zen places was meditation and mindful daily living. Those who shared this view were more than welcome to stay, but men living in the house for social reasons or because it was convenient to the main Castro Street drag were encouraged to think about moving. Issan tried to steer a course between Zen's stricter forms and his own open, casual feeling.

Very soon after he took up residence in San Francisco, the

Hartford Street group put on a big spaghetti fund-raiser. The idea behind the dinner was to create an identifiable membership for the temple and to raise from that group funds for ongoing temple maintenance. Both purposes were fulfilled admirably; from outright contributions and pledges, Hartford Street was assured of $1,200 per month in membership dues. This was, in the words of the then-director, "Not bad for a little operation where nobody came to sit."

From my journal:

18 December 1989, Palm Springs; vacation

We flew on a tiny thirty-seat prop job, with an L.A. stewardess who kept up a stream of what looked like seductive conversation with the pilots, as well as delivering a steady stream of beverages that LOOKED LIKE BOURBONS to them.

We talked on the flight about famous San Francisco whores of the 1950s: Jivey, an American Indian beauty; Desirée, a blonde starlet headed for Hollywood but held back by her gangster boyfriend, George Raft.

These folks lived with Issan briefly, at the Wently Hotel on Van Ness. To hear him tell it, they all had monumental drug habits. What did they use? Anything. Whatever was around. Where are they now? Dead. Most everyone we discussed was now dead.

Very rough descent. Issan and I must have had the same thought at the same time, because he turned to me and asked if I thought "this was the big one"? I admitted it crossed my mind.

"God, what a relief that would be. Then I wouldn't have to go through all that sickness and suffering. . . ." Finally we landed amid brown and pink mountains at sunset, and were the last ones off the plane.

After minor hassling at Dollar Cars (mostly Issan's playing with the mind of the short, squarish, straight-arrow agent) we acquired a big silver Corsica four-door sedan. Issan kept asking if the car were big enough, fabulous enough. "I like big," he said. "I told them I wanted a *big* American car."

Five minutes later, we pulled into Hacienda En Sueno, a little complex of apartments around two heated pools. Issan pushed through the gate into the private interior world created by tall, carefully trimmed hedges and called, "Hello, he-lo-oo, I'm home." Walker greeted us and let us into our rooms. Walker is thirty-five, slim, enthusiastic in a cowboy way. "He does all the work," Issan confided.

The minute we arrived, Issan's spirits began to soar. He *loves* playing house, and the setup here is convenient. The kitchen is clean, airy, and well organized. The bathroom and living room feel clean without being sterile, comfortable without being run-down; 1960s queenie furniture, and good paintings on the walls. Magazines and brochures lying here and there clue you to the Palm Springs gay scene, but there are no big pictures of naked men posted anywhere. "This isn't one of those seedy gay places," Issan said. "This is high class."

We got back in the car and followed Walker's directions to an upscale supermarket. Cart in hand, we went down every aisle in the store. Issan got happier and happier as we went, and when he realized he'd forgotten whipped cream, he actually trotted toward the dairy case to get it.

His costume began to attract some serious attention from the well-heeled Palm Springs shoppers. He wore a Japanese cloth tied around his bald shiny head. A tattered, lovingly repaired, blue denim *hippari* [jacket] was tied above a black turtleneck, black linen pants, black socks, and little black Chinese kung-fu shoes. I watched person after person regard him with suspicion. When they got a look at how happy he was, though, a quick smile would play over their faces. They seemed halfway between indulging his strangeness and being infected by his delight. We bought $95 worth of groceries, including a big bottle of Tanqueray gin and two six-packs of good beer. . . .

At five P.M. Issan fixed himself a martini, and I poured a beer.

"You want a cocktail?" he asked.

"Well, I just drank a beer."

"That's not a cocktail. That's just having a beer."

"I'm about to have another one."

"Oh. Then that's definitely a cocktail."

The plan was to dress and drink awhile, then talk for the tape recorder, take a walk, and go out to dinner. This we did. We didn't really have a formal beginning to the interview. I noticed that he was telling extraordinary stories about being a "bad Chicago queen" so I turned the machine on and set it between us.

When we went out, it had suddenly gotten cold—in the low forties. Issan, as ever, dressed very deliberately: silk long underwear, turtleneck, sweater, *hippari,* Japanese print head-rag, Guatemalan poncho, and a white wool scarf. I'd never seen anything like it. Around his neck, beads, and over his shoulder, the little black cloth priest-bag he refers to as his purse.

On our two-block walk, I noticed how inexhaustibly curious he is.

"What kind of place do you think *this* is? Let's go in through those hedges and look. . . . Do you think these are private houses or what? Let's go look. . . . Think this one here is another gay place? Let's cross over and look."

"Issan, I never met anyone as nosy as you."

"How are you going to know what's going on if you don't look?"

In 1987, Issan absorbed himself completely in his new San Francisco life. Driving home one night with an old Zen friend, they paused at the last crest of Castro Street before its drop into the Eureka Valley. Issan surveyed the panorama of the Castro district that lay below and said, "There they are. Those are my boys down there."

During his first year back, he blew a huge breath of fresh air into the Zen community on Hartford Street, instituting a vigorous schedule of meditation, classes, open meals, community events, lectures, and meditation instruction. When you called Hartford Street, Issan answered the phone. If you dropped by, he would sooner or later bustle past, cleaning something, rearranging furniture, or making plans with two or three people simultaneously.

Issan's impressive burst of energy had several sources. For one thing, he was simply glad to be back in San Francisco, out of Santa Fe, where he'd had to endure the dry and sometimes extreme climate.

Pride also seemed to give him a boost. With Issan's nurturance over the years, the Gay Buddhist Club had incorporated itself as a Zen center, bought property, and kept up a regular schedule of meditation. They'd grown mature enough to recognize their need for a teacher and had pulled things together to import one.

If the delight of seeing a little project blossom into a big, successful one was operative from below, Issan was also thriving with approval from above. Suzuki-roshi had originally envisioned the San Francisco Zen Center as a place where students might train for a limited period of time. His express hope was that teachers would train there, and then scatter "like seeds in the wind," carrying with them the practice and understanding of Zen. But in the twelve years between Suzuki-roshi's death and Baker-roshi's expulsion, virtually no one had scattered. People had been stationed variously for brief, experimental teaching stints, but no sustained foray had been made. The Hartford Street group's request for Issan marked the first genuinely American step toward fulfilling Suzuki-roshi's vision.

When Baker-roshi let Issan go—even though Issan's formal training and transmissions were incomplete—he was tacitly acknowledging Issan as an authentic, independent Zen teacher, and Issan knew it. He always remained deferential to Baker and spoke of him only in terms of gratitude. At the same time, Issan insinuated himself into every aspect of Hartford Street life and marked the proceedings there with his highly personal approach.

Issan also made the larger gay community his business. He ate in local restaurants, patronized the shops, drank in the bars, and danced in the clubs. He forged links with other gay-oriented spiritual groups in town and was soon being called upon to participate in interfaith conferences and Gay Men's Spiritual Retreats. Articles about him appeared in the *Bay Area Reporter*, *The Advocate*, and *The Sentinel,* local gay newspapers. With his shaven head, unique mode of dress, and overflowing humor, Issan quickly became a well-known figure in the Castro district. If Harvey Milk had been the "Mayor of Castro Street" some years earlier, Issan Dorsey was now certainly one of the parish priests. As much as he enjoyed cutting a stylish swath in the gay community, Issan was sobered by it. He took the overall temperature of his surroundings and announced his finding: "The gay community is fucked!"

One reason for this judgment was that he was being called on to perform a constant stream of funerals: "These kids are dying all around me." AIDS not only killed gay men each day who had been vital and active, it threw a terrible dampening scare into men in the community who had so far survived. Do I have it? Am I HIV positive? Does he have it? Should I be tested? Who'll know if I decide to go ahead with the test? How will the knowledge be used if I turn out positive? Questions that have since come under intense public scrutiny were, in 1987, just dawning in the minds of San Francisco's gay population. As a result, uncertainty, confusion, paranoia, frustration, and outright anger plagued the community.

18 December 1989, Palm Springs; vacation, continued

We tooled out into the night to find Gloria's. This restaurant, another gay place, is run by an old and locally famous lesbian. Issan told me it was just like going into a gay bar of the 1950s in San Francisco. Same ambience, same feeling. We walked through the bar into a dimly lit dining room. As far as I could see the clientele was exclusively male—mostly older men, though there was a range. No one could peg Issan's look, but they were intrigued. Before sitting down, he undressed rather ritually.

First the "purse," slung over the back of the tall leather chair. Then fold the scarf, fold the head-rag. Slip out of and carefully, carefully, fold the poncho. Poncho on the high-backed chair, wrinkles smoothed out, then the scarf and head-rag. Sit down, and then into the purse for cigarettes, lighter, pills, and Chapstick. Arrange it, and rearrange it all, then slowly smoke. Instant ritual. The martini glass placed down as in tea ceremony, or like a stick of incense in a bed of ash before a ceremony.

I ask if the slow motions are a reaction to years of shooting speed. "No. I was busy then, doing a lot of stuff, but I never got frantic or rushed about it. In fact, I used to shoot speed and lie down. Just lie there and groove my head."

The towel on the pool lounge chair is laid out and smoothed as carefully as the robes, as deliberately as every sheet and blanket layer in a bed he's making. And the objects are all arranged in a design, always. Ten bottles of pills in the bathroom cluster neatly, precisely, behind the spacious array of toiletries. Salt, pepper, and hot sauce sit just so on the kitchen counter beside the gin and vermouth. The clothing hangs neatly spaced in the closet.

Moving through his world, I don't feel that order has been imposed rigidly, or in a clumsy attempt to make sense of things. He seems perfectly willing to go with your arrangement if you have one, or to let things shift as they do. Issan seems instead to be in love with the things around him, and to arrange them out of affection. He told me once about cleaning. "You don't clean to make things clean, so much. You clean even if it's not a mess. You just go around and make things look like somebody paid attention to them."

It didn't take Issan long to observe that while the newspapers ran series of articles on possible AIDS cures, AIDS doctors, AIDS researchers, their quarrels with one another, AIDS funding and government policy—on the street level, the gutter level, the level on which Issan himself had spent most of his life—the care was very flimsy indeed. Following the money trail or the media trail led to research, prevention, and politics. Once a person infected with AIDS passed into the latter stages of the disease, no one really wanted to hear much about him or her, unless, of course, they were famous.

To Issan, though, it was obvious that a great many people fell through the nets of social and medical care and ended up fatally ill, unable to tend to themselves, and lacking an adequate support system. He thought of these people as functionally homeless. From his own years on the streets, Issan developed a natural sympathy for the underclasses; it appeared to him that no matter how well intentioned a grant may have been—from the government, or from a richly endowed AIDS organization—money was slow in trickling down to the street. This problem was compounded by the fact that he saw the disease as just beginning to manifest. Things were not going to get better, he predicted, they were going to get rapidly worse, and anyone who even pretended to have their eyes open would have to pitch in and do *something*.

During the same trip to San Francisco on which he became infected with HIV, Issan had another crucial encounter, this one of a nonsexual nature. He paid a visit to a bright young man named Penn Andrews, someone who'd practiced and worked at the San Francisco Zen Center for years. Now sick with AIDS, Penn was living with two men who seemed to have simply taken him in. They'd put a room at his disposal, and as Penn became weaker, they provided meals and care. The quality of the attention—daily, casual, mundane—and the nature of the environment—in a home, among friends—impressed Issan.

On first moving to Hartford Street, Issan had no intentions of social or political action. He understood his "mission" simply to be the Zen-practicing community. He arrived in San Francisco a sought-after Zen teacher, a person confirmed by the ancient Buddhist lineage, who lived vigorously and cheerfully with an HIV infection.

Discussions with temple residents, particularly with a man named David Sunseri, often touched on the AIDS epidemic and what an appropriate gesture from the Zen group might be. Sunseri had long been involved with the Shanti Project, one of San Francisco's earliest responses to illness and death from AIDS. He had undergone the comprehensive Shanti training in caring for sick and dying people.

David had also worked in a "Shanti house"—a building purchased by the Shanti Foundation to provide rooms for men with AIDS. In these houses, men lived in separate rooms, had individual care-providers, and had little contact with one another or with the larger community. The idea had been to get gay men sick with AIDS off the street and into a place where they could be cared for until they became terminally ill. This the Shanti houses accomplished, but little more. The Shanti houses had no enduring residents, no care-providers with continuity. No one actually *lived* in the houses. Still, against the horrible horizon of steadily mounting AIDS deaths, the Shanti houses were a brave response.

David Sunseri and Issan tossed around the notion of starting such a house, but neither could see exactly how to do it, or what the steps might be. Both men were sympathetic to the idea. But the exigencies of simply getting the Zen temple going and keeping it funded, meant the Shanti house project stayed at the conceptual stage.

Another model of hospice care soon presented itself to Issan. Coming Home Hospice, located a few short blocks from the Hartford Street temple, housed another old Zen student named Colin. Colin had practiced both at the San Francisco Zen Center and at Hartford Street, and had been one of the early regulars in the new group. Issan made a point of visiting Colin nearly every day. His natural inquisitiveness led him into rooms adjacent to Colin's, and pretty soon he was visiting one or another of several people at Coming Home Hospice.

At the beginning of 1987, members of San Francisco's gay community bore the pain of an AIDS death mostly in private. Sick men spent the last weeks and days of their lives being cared for primarily by a lover or by whichever friends could extend time and psychic energy. Although death from AIDS was a massive, widespread phenomenon, the actual event took place in isolated nooks. The exception to this was at Coming Home Hospice.

Coming Home, started by the Visiting Nurses and Hospice organization, recognized the glaring need for a response to AIDS illness from the nursing and social-work professions. Accordingly, the hospice was patterned on a standard medical and hospital model. Beds and rooms were provided; the physical situation remained constant, but the staff came and went, and administration was accomplished from a distance. So far, no one had thought to place AIDS hospice work into a domestic situation, into a residence where people carried out the variegated tasks of daily life.

Though he was living in a geographical center of the AIDS epidemic, and feeling an intense need to provide care, Issan contented himself with visiting other facilities—until one of his own students became ill. In November 1987, J. D. Kobezak moved into the Hartford Street Zen Center to die. He had been diagnosed with AIDS dementia and peripheral neuropathy, which meant that in addition to having bouts of serious mental disorientation, he was unable to move about under his own power. The doctors predicted he'd live about six months.

Both J. D. and his lover Pierre were practitioners at Hartford Street. When J. D. became ill, Pierre found he was unable to care for him adequately, even though J. D. made use of the social services available to him. A person as sick as J. D. became eligible for MediCal; through a complex arrangement of social-service agencies, SSI and MediCal funds were channeled to J. D. He was also given seven hours of care each day by the Visiting Nurses and

Hospice. Issan's goal was to provide twenty-four-hour care to
J. D., and he filled in around the seven hours with volunteers from
the community.

J. D. became a kind of local star at Hartford Street. Here was
one of the members of the Zen community actually sick with
AIDS, actually dying, actually doing it. Trainees in hospice care
programs came to attend him and glean what wisdom they could.
But J. D. had little to offer. From the beginning of his stay at
Hartford Street, he confounded medical wisdom and thrived. He
did suffer periods of dementia and periods of being stubbornly
uncommunicative, but on the whole he seemed to relish the
attention and care afforded him by the Hartford Street community,
and he gained strength.

With J. D. in a bed in the temple, Issan felt the necessity of
offering hospice care even more piercingly. He began to magnetize
supplies; when someone even peripherally connected to the Zen
community died, the wheelchairs, bedpans, and hospital beds
seemed to end up at 57 Hartford Street. Running hot on the
energy of service, Issan put out feelers to the Visiting Nurses
Association, letting them know he was interested in having a
second person with AIDS move into the temple. He reasoned that
the effort required to provide twenty-four-hour care to one person
could easily be spread to two or three sick people. It seemed to
him this would be equally easy in terms of scheduling, and vastly
more efficient. Within a few months Bernie Ortiz, a small Haitian
man with a huge smile and a soft, high-pitched voice, began living
in another room of the temple.

Not all temple residents found this a charming development.
Some felt the job of a Zen temple, and a Zen teacher, was to
promote Zen; social causes however laudable, were up to the
individual. They had come to practice Zen meditation and were
now being forced to live in a hospice. If not a corruption of the
original bargain they'd struck with the temple, it was at the very

least a turn askew. Other residents responded more viscerally: they simply didn't like the idea of having death, particularly the terrifying shade of AIDS death, cast into their living room.

But Issan was resolute. His entire approach to Zen practice was based in the mundane, the local, the immediate. Like some blind people who develop extraordinary, compensatory powers of hearing, Issan's lifelong aversion to scholastics gave him a finely tuned intuitive understanding of Buddhist teachings.

"The Path is under your feet," he repeated in lecture after lecture. He stressed also "careful attention to the details of daily life." For Issan, creating a hospice was inseparable from Zen practice. It wasn't something extra, another burden to shoulder; it was the simple extension of compassionate awareness. If there was dirt on the floor, you swept it up; if a child was sitting in the middle of a busy street, you grabbed them; if your friends and students were dying, and in need of attention, you took them in. Simple, direct, nonconceptual.

Baker: "He's a very good example of the three forms of compassion. First, you are compassionate with other people's ego, their foibles, and weaknesses. Issan was always completely sympathetic about people's weaknesses, and forgave them. But he forgave them in the context of assuming, and seeing, that their intentions were good. He'd just say, 'Oh, that's what people do,' and he had the feeling that underneath that was like Suzuki-roshi used to say, 'Even a thief steals for his mother.' Issan always had that, that at the root, people's motivations were good.

"The second form is to be compassionate for the stuff of a person, the physicality of a person. In that sense, if they're hungry, you give them food. If they need a bed, you give them a bed. It means to be compassionate to the *skandhas* and the four elements. He was very immediately compassionate to people not worrying about who they were. He'd just take care of them.

"The third form is to be compassionate for the unseen, for the way in which a person is already a Buddha or has the history of a Buddha but just hasn't connected the dots.

"You could almost say that those three kinds of compassion are central to his genius as a teacher, a presence, a friend, a buddy, and a person who really took the teachings and just immediately understood their practicality and application."

Even as Issan gathered equipment, tied together networks of social workers and nurses, assembled boards of directors and advisory boards, corralled old, trusted Zen Center friends into positions of fund-raiser, medical director, and so on, even as he worked indefatigably to give birth to a hospice and to publicize it, he also tried to deconstruct the notion. He mistrusted presumptions of loftiness, any feeling that a hospice was something "special" or virtuous: "We're just taking care of people with AIDS. We're not legally working as a hospice. We don't ask for the legal considerations that you ask for when you are a hospice. We're just *saying* we are a hospice. Actually, what we are doing is renting rooms to people who need twenty-four hour care, and who are in the last six months of their lives."

But residents of the temple thought differently, and one by one they moved out—or, in the words of one embittered man, "were engineered out"—until in January of 1988, only Issan and David Sunseri and the two patients remained. If Issan's resolve wavered at all here, a tragic death focused his feelings immeasurably. James's brother David—one of the young boys taken in by the Family and a very dear, old friend of Issan's—was found dead on a bench in San Francisco's Civic Center. David, like James, had become something of a street urchin, hustling, getting by any way he could. One night as he slept on a public bench in the Civic Center, he'd been set on fire by hoodlums. San Francisco General Hospital had saved his life and discharged him, but just a few days later he expired anyway. Citizens were so inured to the homeless plight by this time that David apparently had lain dead on the sidewalk near Civic Center for as long as a day before anyone noticed.

Hurt personally and ashamed of a milieu that could let such a thing happen, Issan now made several moves crucial to the development of what he had begun to call the Maitri Hospice. He asked his longtime Zen friend Steve Allen to move into Hartford Street to become director of the hospice. Issan and David Sunseri were burning out. Both men were strong in networking and interpersonal relations; faced with budget summaries, grant proposals, coding, fund-raising, and an endless complexity of logistics, they'd begun to buckle. Issan thought that Steve, with many years as the San Francisco Zen Center's treasurer behind him, would remain unfazed by overdue loans and balloon payments. After wrestling with the proposal for several weeks, Steve and his wife Angelique agreed.

Next, Issan began to negotiate with Visiting Nurses and Hospice (VNH) through their administrator, Jeanne Parker-Martin. As Issan saw it, VNH was providing hours of attendant care to J. D. and Bernie as if they were living in separate parts of the city. He proposed a plan to VNH in which Hartford Street would get the same number of attendant hours for J.D. and Bernie—seven hours a day for each—but they would schedule the hours to avoid overlap. Two attendants at the same time for only two patients seemed wasteful. Why not rearrange it to have fourteen hours of coverage? VNH went along with this plan, since it worked to their benefit as well, extending the care they could provide with the same number of person-hours.

Aiming for twenty-four-hour care, Issan realized he would have to have several more hospice residents to warrant the requisite attendant hours. Despite the shrinking population of Zen students and a certain amount of rancorous internal criticism for his whole hospice endeavor, Issan walked next door one day in mid-1988, and asked to buy the house adjacent to the temple. He was told it was not for sale. Issan went on to explain what he was doing at 57 Hartford and why he should also have 61 Hartford for his purposes. A few weeks later, the owners changed their minds and called Issan. Now they wanted to sell.

With no significant resources at his disposal and none in sight, he told the owners he would buy the house anyway. "I went to one of these real-estate places and did whatever it is you're supposed to do. I told them we were going to buy it and we put a thousand dollars down. Just a sign that we had entered into negotiations. Then we had to have a big hassle over what the down payment was. Actually it wasn't much of a hassle, because I couldn't come up with a down payment."

In a timely twist of fate (or karma, as Buddhists would more likely say), one of the Zen students doing overnight attendant shifts with J. D. inherited a large sum of money. He offered to buy the house outright, and lease it to the hospice with an option to buy. The deal was done, and almost immediately the flurry of cleaning and refurbishing that had taken place when Issan moved in to 57 Hartford began again next door.

Baker: "Steve came, and within a few months my role lessened a lot, as it should. From then on I was like a sounding board, rather than a real active part of the decision making. Issan would call me up, and mostly I just listened. Up until this point, everything Issan did, we discussed together—whether he should have a shot of whiskey before going to bed, I mean, at that level. We discussed the effect on people, he liked to do it, should he do it, should he have a sexual life, what kind of sexual life, and so on. But there were various points where he took charge: being at Hartford Street, having Steve as his partner, and developing the hospice with Steve. Then my role became more and more discussing teaching things with him."

As if in physical reenactment of his spiritual understanding, Issan started knocking down walls between the two buildings, and swirling the functions each would serve: a large chunk of dining-room wall was torn out to provide an internal door between the houses; the backyard garden was extended to ramble across two plots; food preparations for the two houses were moved to one kitchen, with the other kitchen relegated to cleanup; offices and nonpatient rooms were scattered between the two buildings. Technically, the Zen temple was in one building and the hospice was next door, but the traffic patterns and osmotic exchanges between the two made them functionally indistinguishable.

In short order, Issan attracted a fresh group of Hartford Street Zen Center residents. Some drifted back, returning from flights away from the 1983 San Francisco Zen Center mess. Some people, already meditating regularly in the zendo, simply moved into the vacant rooms. Others, volunteers at Maitri and relatives of patients there, found themselves drawn by the unique atmosphere in the buildings and the curious Zen style. They tried out the practices and were soon fully engaged in the Hartford Street Maitri community.

November 4, 1988

It's two P.M. and Issan is out of it. Or so he says. His Eminence Jamgon Kongtrul Rinpoche, one of the senior teachers of Tibetan Buddhism, is due any minute and Issan—dressed in a scoop-neck ribbed T-shirt, white *juban,* and black *rakusu*—is wondering aloud how he will get through the day.

Last night he had one of his more unusual experiences as a Zen priest and hospice worker. He'd gotten a call in the afternoon that a friend of his, a man he'd counseled for nearly three years, was dying of AIDS. "I went to see him. I crawled into bed with him and just held him for about half an hour. I left at four. Before I left, I told him, 'You know, I'm not going to see you again this time. And it's all right.' I heard that he died at five. They called me at eight, and I went back over. I wore my robes and took my bell. I sat with him and chanted and rang my little bell. Then about nine, his other friends came over and the thing turned into a kind of wake. Somebody brought tequila, someone else brought gin . . . there was pot, beer, I don't really remember. . . . So I sat and drank with them, and then went back in and chanted some more and rang the bell, and cried, and went back out and drank some more, and cried, and it just went on like that all night. I have no idea what time I got home, but it was late. . . . Then I had to get up at four this morning to lead zazen. I can't believe how out of it I feel. . . ."

A blue limousine and red Jeep Blazer pull up outside 57 Hartford Street and Issan slides around the house in his sandals shouting, "They're here, they're here. . . ." Jamgon Kongtrul and entourage greet Issan and entourage outside the Hartford Street Zen Center, then all proceed inside for a tour: the usual inspection of the building, polite murmurings, a stop in the meditation hall to offer incense, which His Eminence, though Tibetan, does in a Zen style. His Eminence is pleased to learn that his teacher, H. H. Karmapa, had blessed the space, as did another famous Tibetan teacher, Chögyam Trungpa, Rinpoche.

Issan tells Jamgon Kontrul that he wants this Zen Center to reflect the needs of the surrounding community and that he is determined to open a hospice. To that end, he simply began providing care for members of the Zen community who were dying of AIDS. At this point, he has two such men living in the temple; Issan has managed to lease the building next door to expand his project.

His Eminence climbs to the second floor to look in on J. D. (Bernie is at the doctor's office). He talks with J. D. a little, gives him some Tibetan medicine, and has his monks give him some supplemental pills.

Members of Hartford Street would like His Eminence to have tea with them. Jamgon Kongtrul, on the other hand, seems determined to visit Coming Home Hospice. Issan has arranged for His Eminence's visit there and suggests they go together. Attendants scatter for the cars, but His Eminence, learning the destination is only four or five blocks away, decides to walk. He and Issan set out surrounded by monks, attendants, and interested parties—a soft parade.

The route to Coming Home Hospice goes directly through the showiest part of the Castro district. It's the first sunny day after a week of cold gray ones, and the boys are out in force. We pass a number of rather affectionate male couples, several bars that seem to spill onto the sidewalk, an astonishing array of shops, telephone poles, and fences crammed with garish posters. The monks are intrigued, and they gawk. They are in turn gawked at. There is no hint of malice or threat in this land of high costume art; just curiosity. His Eminence and Issan walk on, absorbed in conversation. Issan apologizes if he should seem spaced out—he recounts his last night's adventure, complete with detailed list of intoxicating factors. Jamgon Kongtrul seems amused.

Finally we reach Coming Home Hospice, where admittance is strictly monitored. Issan and His Eminence are allowed in; the rest of the group is told to wait outside. This does not sit well with His Eminence's attendants, who eventually gain entry. Only His Eminence and Issan are allowed upstairs, though, to the residents' rooms. Issan later said of the visit, "Usually the way it works is that they take me around to a room, tell me I can go in, and introduce me to the person. That's kind of what we did this time, except I had His Eminence with me.

"I usually hold people and kiss them, get right in there—you know my style. He stood back and watched while I did my thing, then he came over and held their hands and put his hand on their foreheads. Everybody seemed to like him. I tried to introduce him, but one time I completely forgot his name. I said, 'This is His Eminence. . . .' Then I had to turn to him and say 'Your Eminence, what is your name again?' Even so, I could never pronounce it very well.

"I guess we went into about ten rooms. We finally went into the Memorial Room, where they have the list of names of everyone who has died there. He picked up the book and was reading through it. . . . He looked shocked. He asked me, kind of like he couldn't believe it, 'All these died—here?'

"After that we went back downstairs. At some point I realized that he wasn't behind me anymore. From the bottom of the stairs I looked back and saw him. He was on the top stair, perched there, with his heels on the floor and his toes out over the stairs. He was rocking back and forth teetering; it made me kind of nervous. Then I looked up further and saw his eyes. They were completely rolled back—you could only see the whites. He was swaying, and I finally noticed that he was chanting. After about thirty seconds or so, he came downstairs."

12

Death at the Door

One foundation of Buddhist understanding is the principle of change: everything changes. A logical corollary states that "All conditioned existence is subject to decay." The biggest building, the most skillfully diversified corporation, the toughest team, the most ruthless empire—all come down eventually. An established and solid-looking Buddhist group will, if it adheres to ancient recommendations, foster in its members an awareness of its own transience. Maitri Hospice never had a problem maintaining this awareness.

Hospice business wasn't a thriving concern. The demand for it was there, clearly. AIDS and other diseases supplied an endless stream of customers. But most of these "customers" were impoverished. Work at Maitri Hospice was constant, but most people there did it for reasons other than financial well-being. The intentions of the founders, too, had little to do with a bottom line. They aimed at something much more like a "top line"—a line that would measure motivation, societal efficacy, tenderness. Maitri's fiduciary health was thus shaky at best.

The financial plan was clear, simple, and guaranteed to lose money. A person—Joe, say—becomes sick with AIDS. Unable to work or to find work, he applies for MediCal (state funding) and SSI (federal funding.) With an AIDS diagnosis, Joe would eventually be given six hundred dollars a month and a certain number of hours of attendant care. When he reaches a six-month-or-less prognosis, he lists his name with Maitri. By this time, Joe has quite likely burned many of his bridges and worn out or alienated those in his support system. He is dispirited and feels there is nothing to live for. One of the last decisions Joe makes is to enter a hospice. He puts his name on the Maitri waiting list.

When Maitri has an opening, they admit Joe, and they make the following deal: Joe pays five hundred dollars a month to Maitri and pools his attendant hours with the hours of the other patients in the hospice.

In return, he receives room, board, and twenty-four-hour care from a highly trained team of doctors, nurses, nurses' aides, and social workers. Joe lives in a homelike environment and eats his meals communally as long as he feels comfortable doing so. He is never completely isolated, though his privacy is respected. His family and friends are welcome to visit. He is surrounded by the meditative atmosphere of the temple, and though this atmosphere is not always serene, it is at least dedicated to being mindful and self-aware. Joe need not be Buddhist, nor does he have to subscribe to any particular set of beliefs.

When he dies, Joe's body is handled carefully. If he did happen to be Buddhist, friends and temple staff come and meditate in the presence of his body. If he desired a Buddhist service in the temple, it is performed. If he wanted to go anonymously, be cremated, and have his ashes scattered in the ocean or from the highest local mountain, that too is arranged. In short, from the time he checks in until he checks out, Joe is thoroughly and attentively monitored. For five hundred dollars a month.

Given these working arrangements, there is no mystery as to how the hospice might run aground on rocks of financial ruin. It stayed afloat largely by begging, as Steve Allen described it, staving off a succession of crises with donations from individuals and an occasional private foundation grant.

22 March 1990
On an airplane to Ojai, for a conference called
"The Encounter with Death":

Issan said, "I can't remember what I did last time we did one of these retreats."

"You didn't do much," Steve replied.

"I know I didn't go to the morning sittings. Did I make it for brunch?"

"I think you did. Brunch is at ten-thirty, and it seems to me you were getting up around eight-thirty then, which would have given you time—"

"I had to take my meds."

"—to take your meds, right, and go to brunch."

"I have no idea though, what I'm going to say for my talk. That's why *you're* going to give my talk," he said, turning to me, laughing.

Steve said, "You don't have any idea what you're going to talk about beforehand, do you?"

"Well, seems like I didn't have any idea last time, and I did okay."

"Yeah."

"In fact, I seem to recall that we went overtime with it."

"That's right. You'll do fine."

Issan lapsed into silence again. Steven went back to reading, and I sat holding a leaking pen over my notebook.

"I have these periods, though," Issan said abruptly, "where I can't think. It's hard to put things together. . . ." He waved his hands in front of him, painting a picture of little birds in the air, scattering, refusing to be herded.

"Don't think, then," said Steve. "Just go up there and put your mouth in motion."

Issan opened and closed his mouth several times in quick succession, a ghastly pantomine of chattering dentures.

24 March 90; at his sister Carolyn's house in Ojai,
still on the way to the conference

A document sat on the dining room table, something to do with the sale of the family house, the Big House.

"Look at all those handwritings," Issan said, rummaging in his bag for his glasses. He found the case and very slowly opened it and extracted his pince-nez. He unfolded the earpieces one at a time and used both hands to put them on. He bent down and scrutinized the blue paper, ran his finger down his siblings' signatures, all in blue ink.

"They all look exactly the same," he said. He dug into his bag again and pulled out a felt-tip marker, rounded, broad, and black. His signature bore no resemblance to the eight below it, those written in neat, obedient Spencerian script. Issan's hand looked primitive: the letters were clear, distinct, and almost childish. An irregularity informed them, though, that no child could have produced. He wrote slowly, pushing the letters into the page very firmly, as if they might run away.

From the hypothetical case of AIDS patient Joe, explanations emerge for Maitri's "failure" in its mission: people got there and lived. Patients, by definition, were supposed to come to a hospice to die. But often, basking in steady, warm care, these patients thrived. J. D. lived two years longer than his doctors thought possible. Men did die at Maitri; they died often, and each death was a heartbreak for the staff. But an extraordinary number of the deaths were preceded by a stunning blossoming of life-force.

The overriding thrust of hospice work, though, is toward death. Dissolution. Buddha's teaching on impermanence was hammered home week after week for the staff, and the lesson came not just from having a thin financial lifeline, but from the daily disappearance of companions. Someone like Joe became a regular at the lunch table, a person to fight with for the comics section, someone you wished would hurry up in the bathroom, who told interesting stories or terrible jokes, who had train sets, teddy bears, or pinups decorating his room. Then suddenly Joe stopped coming out of that room.

Then the sphere of interaction shifted to Joe's quarters, to the infallibly personal and often private world of his room. As staff, you now fetched things back and forth: tea, food, medicine, flowers, messages, bedpans, discards, garbage. You adjusted the blinds, turned down the light, opened a window. You escorted family and friends in and out of the room, and got to know them in the process. You watched Joe grow horribly emaciated, fevered and brilliant. One visit, you noticed Joe wasn't breathing anymore. Maybe you were with him and saw him stop, or maybe someone came to tell you. Quite possibly they woke you up to tell you. Within a few days, Joe was taken out, his room was cleaned, freshened, and then Joe moved in.

24 March 1990, Ojai; from Issan's lecture:

"The encounter with death begins at birth, not when we are actually sick and dying. Baker-roshi, my teacher, had me speaking about the fact that it should be our practice to keep in front of us all the time, 'I certainly am going to die. I certainly am going to die.' When I was listening to his lectures, I always said, 'Oh I understand that. I know that.' Because I had been close to death many times in my life. Also, I had already begun some minimal work with people with AIDS. This is before living at Hartford Street Zen Center. In my mind, I felt I understood what that meant: 'I certainly am going to die.'

"But lo and behold, when I had my HIV test in Santa Fe, and it was positive, the relationship [*chuckling*] with 'I certainly am going to die' changed. Radically. And then all along the way. You know the first time I became sick. . . .

"After I went through those initial changes and came back to San Francisco, I felt quite healthy and had a lot of energy. I was helping to establish more the practice place at Hartford Street Zen Center, giving classes and lectures, and thinking about how we might involve ourselves with the AIDS epidemic. We made a lot of great changes at Hartford Street then, and it took a lot of energy.

"In my lecture book here, I see that in the last lecture I gave at Santa Fe, I discussed the Five Fears. I must have discussed them because they're written down here: Fear of Loss of Livelihood, Fear of Loss of Reputation, Fear of Unusual States of Mind, Fear of Death, and Fear of Speaking Before an Assembly. Probably I'm experiencing all five of these fears at this point, right now. Except Loss of Reputation—it's too late for that.

"I had been given permission, actually instructed by Baker-roshi, to speak about my reactions and feelings about AIDS. I read in the *Santa Fe Recorder* a short article that I thought was appropriate: 'There is a sign on the wall at the New Mexico AIDS Service, Santa Fe Office, that illustrates the feeling of the men and women who work for the fledgling organization dealing with AIDS patients, their family and loved ones. It is of paramount concern: "One must live as if it would be forever, and as if one might die each moment," the sign read. "Always, both at once." '

"It's too bad that it took such an epidemic for us to begin to think this way. We have not only the opportunity, but the responsibility to spend time with people who are dying. Probably my great-grandmother had her whole family with her when she died. But my grandmother died in an old-age home.

"Baker-roshi said, 'The most basic meditation for realizing impermanence must be, of course, "I certainly am going to die." It's something we could meditate on, keep in front of us all the time. Not with sadness, but just . . .

"Somewhere along the way we came to think it was unfortunate to be sick, and to get old, and to die. If sickness, old age, and death are unfortunate, then certainly, so is birth."

Living in an AIDS hospice, according to Steve Allen, is like watching the decline of Western civilization in your living room: "The entire medical system is at a loss. They don't understand AIDS really, and doctors are very frustrated about that. They don't know what to do. Insurance companies know they can't ever cover the AIDS crisis. The social system is in breakdown; they can't possibly cope with an epidemic of these proportions. There is nothing in place to take care of these people, not to mention who it is that gets sick with AIDS and whether our social system would want to take care of them in the first place.

"That's one level. Other institutions in our society can't handle it either. Families come apart over this issue. Relatives often go into denial about AIDS—that their son, brother, father, daughter, whatever, has it. They can't let that information in.

"Churches are split about it. You see it all the time in the papers, mostly because it's been related to homosexuality, and as you know, churches are in an uproar over that. So that's another level.

"Then there is the whole issue of who it is dying in an AIDS hospice. For the most part, we are dealing with young men, so when you watch them die, it's particularly painful because it's as though you're watching the death of youth altogether. Many of these men are handsome, young, smart; some of them are extremely talented people. When you watch them die, it's like watching the death of physical beauty, or the death of intellectual agility, or artistic talent. It seems like it's all coming to an end right before your eyes."

What then made it work for the Maitri staff? How is it that they opened their home to terribly sick people, tended them through their deaths, and were willing to do it again? The answer must lie in the pith teachings of Buddhism and in the style with which the Hartford Street Zen Center put those teachings into practice.

Traditionally, Zen people do and don't take the Buddha at his word. At the end of more than forty years of walking through India giving teachings, the historical Buddha said, in effect, "Don't do what I say just because I say it. See if I'm right; test it for yourself." *That* particular teaching always appealed to Zen students, long considered the most stubborn and irascible of the Buddhist flock. The pervasive nature of change is not allowed to remain a convenient intellectual understanding in Zen. It must be cooked and tasted and found personally nourishing before being accepted as worthy teaching. The usual caldron is meditation practice; the meal is daily life.

One fruit of Zen meditation is direct, personal knowledge that while unmoving, one's body is in constant flux. A complementary knowledge of mind reveals that thoughts, which are neither encouraged nor suppressed, nonetheless arise, abide, and fade constantly. Hours on a meditation cushion soak a practitioner with impermanence in an undeniable way. The idea of change doesn't tend to sneak up on Zen practitioners; sickness and death are regarded as straightforward extensions of the shiftings observed in a meditation period.

But Buddhist meditators have no secret spell by which they avoid suffering when a loved one becomes ill or dies. Quite the contrary: a refined awareness of body and mind often allows emotions to pierce even more deeply. However, Buddhists try not to cave in to the feeling that illness and death are occasions for panic, something unfair or unacceptable. Richard Levine, medical director of Maitri Hospice and a Buddhist priest himself, says that as a result of the AIDS epidemic and in a heightened way in the hospice, "pain and suffering and death are once more reclaimed as part of human experience."

24 March 1990, Ojai, continued

Issan reads from his notes, quoting Baker-roshi: " 'How do we get rid of the idea that somehow an exception is going to be made for us? It means to withdraw your primary energy from your plans. Unglue your energy-glue from your plans. To know you certainly are going to die is ultimate nonpossession. To know it and meditate on it. You don't even possess your life. So if you really know for certain you are going to die, today or tomorrow, you are in the middle of dying right now. It won't be so difficult to take your energy out of your plans. Your plans are important, but not as the primary value in your life. The primary value in the structure of Buddhist practice should be residing in your breath-mind. If you can do that, it simplifies life a whole lot. To reside in your breath-mind.'

"So don't think that there's some secret plan you've got to fulfill ahead of time to die right now. I was talking with my friend Alan on the phone. He was at Rocky Mountain Dharma Center, maybe a few weeks before he died. We were old friends, and we were talking to each other, and I knew he was sick. They said, 'He's sick, and he's going to die.' In my mind I'm thinking, 'It can't be true, he was just here a year ago, and he was healthy as a horse.' But he sounded kind of sick, and he said, 'I feel very good about dying. I've done everything I had to do, and I'm going to die.'

"And I said, 'Well, I can't die, because I have these kids I have to ordain [*laughing*], and there's a lay ordination coming up, and a priest ordination, and a Mountain Seat Ceremony coming up.' And he said, 'It's true, you can't die yet. [*laughing*] But I can.' And in fact he did. He died! [*laughter*]

"To keep in front of you 'I certainly am going to die' all the time. We forget. Because even now, if I have quite a few healthy days in a row, my whole attitude changes, until all of a sudden I get another little *ckkch*! [*makes a jabbing motion*] saying, 'Hey, you certainly *are* going to die.'"

To sustain a meditation habit, it becomes necessary to accept whatever shows up in meditation as part of the practice, and not as an enemy to be subdued, or as a savior to be supplicated. Zen tradition eschews distinctions of good and bad. Appreciation is the point, not discrimination or evaluation, therefore a Buddhist meditator can afford to start with what actually is, with whatever physical and mental state they have, rather than with an ideal, or fantastic state.

This willingness to relate to everything characterized the inception of Maitri Hospice, and each subsequent day there. Issan and Steve Allen never had a formal plan for it. Watching it develop was more like being a spectator at a surfing contest than at a building site. Steve: "We have always dealt with whatever came to the door. We started the hospice because death came to the door. . . .

"You can deal with a complex, changing situation because you don't have to control it; you don't have to force it into an ideal pattern. You can actually allow it to be whatever it is, and allow yourself to adapt to what it becomes. Because this is the way we proceed, we have to respond to the immediacy of the situation, and therefore we have to be very practical. . . .

"We have created an environment that allows anxiety to be present. Rather than hiding from it or trying to avoid it, we actually created it as part of how to take care of the present moment. Because it *is* a part of the present moment. We will not escape the anxiety. We will not escape the fears that we have. Our function is to allow all that to be present and to settle with it, to allow ourselves to enter into that part of ourselves we are trying to avoid."

The usual assumption about a religious group's involvement in altruistic projects is that compassion is the motivating factor. But for Zen people compassion doesn't mean what it usually does— feeling sorry for a being of lesser station. Many Buddhist teachers have described compassion as the ability to react freely and accurately in any situation. Being nice or feeling sorry for someone may be called for, but so may being fierce or unyielding. When sweetness is applied indiscriminately, it is seen as "idiot compassion."

24 March 1990, Ojai, Issan's lecture, continued:

"Anyhow, when I started giving this talk, I told you I don't give talks anymore, and I am thinking of this as a discussion group with you all. So we can get to know each other better. I wanted to present something first, that maybe you could tune in to a little bit. If you wanted to ask me some questions, please do. If you want to say something, please do."

Question: [*inaudible; about compassion*]

Issan: "I think what I said was that the definition of compassion that I like is: endless dimensions of this moment. Endless dimensions of this moment. I've been thinking more and more of this word *compassion*. Almost the way I've begun to think about it is, like if you begin to discuss it, already you've missed it. It's more a question of *being* compassion.

"Yesterday Steve talked about Avalokiteshvara Bodhisattva, the bodhisattva that looks down and hears the cries of the world. Kanzeon is an aspect of Avalokiteshvara. They are the same. They are the same, but there is a little difference, right? I might just be making this up—but it's a nice way to say something. Kuan Yin, Kanzeon is a very feminine aspect of Avalokiteshvara. Kanzeon deeply penetrates the sounds of the world. It means Kanzeon *is* the sounds of the world. So there is no separation. So ultimate dimensions of this moment is . . . I think there is no other way I can explain it, really. But I'd like you to think about it, a lot. Why don't you say what that brings to your mind."

Question: "What that does is make me think I can't be compassionate with other beings while I'm considering them other."

Issan: "Exactly. You got it. [*laughing*] Little by little, if we can have a taste—not an understanding, but a taste—of the indivisibility of all beings, this is what we mean. Something else?"

Question: "With all the movements that you are going through, you are more aware of, you know, dying than most of us are. Do you find that there is a curiosity toward death? A kind of excitement, almost, looking forward to it?"

Issan: "I do. I find it fascinating, and curiosity is there too. Also fear. It's interesting to own that and not to think, 'I'm a Buddhist priest, I've been sitting for twenty years, when death comes, I'm just going to slide right out of there.' [*laughing*] You know, I don't know if I'm going to go out kicking and screaming [*laughing*]. Most people who die at our house die pretty well, don't they? I'm encouraged for myself. As I see people get very sick—young people getting very sick—and see how well they do it, it makes me feel bad that I complain and groan so much over my little loss of energy, and anxiety attacks and sicknesses that I received from the medicines. I do that and then I see these young kids doing it so well. . . ."

Question: "Do you think that they receive a final teaching at that moment, to go through that final act peacefully?"

Issan: "It's not like you have much choice. But a final teaching—where does a final teaching come from?"

Question: "From within yourself."

Issan: "Uh-huh, so I don't think you can talk a lot about death. [*laughing*] I mean, I'm not dead, I don't think. But our relationship to the concept . . . I think it's different as we get sicker. It's easier.

"I have what's called severe disabling ARC. It's not AIDS, because I haven't had one of the opportunistic diseases yet that means that you have AIDS. People who have had the opportunistic diseases and have had AIDS—and this may just be my vision of it—but it seems that they are dealing better with their sickness than I am. Sort of like being in limbo. I'd be glad to be out of here. We are talking about 'The Encounter With Death' as if we knew what we are talking about. [*laughing*]"

The inner reason that the Maitri staff continued performing the dour chores of a hospice is simply that they liked it.

Steve Allen: *Maitri* is a Sanskrit term that literally means 'friendliness,' but when we were thinking of a name and its function with what we were doing, we chose to emphasize the *joy* of friendliness. We use the term with that sense of joy, the joy that arises when we come together to do something to support each other, to take care of each other, our individual lives together and our wider body of society."

At its core the hospice most clearly resembled a family. From his role as the eldest son in a large family, Issan went on to recreate a family setting for himself and his friends many times throughout his life. In the navy, he and Mack drew an entourage around them. During his performing years, either on the road or in a town for an extended stint, "I always had my kids around me"—loose, fast, drug-addicted perhaps, "bad" certainly, but still a set of fringe siblings. The commune of the early Haight was explicitly called the Family, and whenever Issan was given administrative or religious autonomy within Zen Center, he manifested a "family."

With Maitri Hospice, Issan took advantage of the fractured San Francisco Zen Center *sangha* and reined his closest friends in to his project, and by that route, for some, back to formal Zen practice altogether. Three senior Zen priests from the Zen Center moved into Issan's temple to shore up the meditation practice and to help with temple and hospice duties; several more participated in administrative, medical, and advisory capacities. Dr. Richard Levine: "I would say it is my practice, yes. One can't separate . . . Zen places a great emphasis on bringing the mind of meditation into one's daily life activities, and this kind of work is a great opportunity, a wonderful vehicle for that. The issue of community, of doing that with other people who are like-minded is another matter, and Maitri Hospice has provided me with a situation where I can work and practice with people I've practiced with for many years. This is a particularly delightful situation in which to do that."

Having gathered a clan around him, Issan at last began to make significant connections to his blood family. "They are very nice people, but they have no idea what I did. Or what I'm doing, to tell you the truth. My oldest sister Phyllis broke the ice. She was married in a Catholic ceremony to some man. Then she wanted to get married again, so she called me up and asked me to come to Santa Barbara to marry her to her new husband. But this is also her way of saying to the rest of my family, 'I acknowledge the fact that my brother is a priest, a practicing priest, and he can do this.' After, I told her I had cut the ceremony and left a lot of the Buddhist stuff out, because I didn't want to freak anybody out. She said 'No, you should have left it in, that's the reason I asked you to come.' So now since then I've married two other sisters, and I did the full Buddhist ceremony. It was all their second marriages, and they were all married Catholic the first time. The second time, from me, they took vows and precepts."

Issan finally assumed his place as an honorable family member, prodigal older brother. With a gathering and swelling energy, he began to bind together strands in his life. He wrought a warm home for the terminally ill out of Zen's icy style. He created a solid practice center for practitioners who'd misstepped or lost their way, and he managed to make the practices seem indispensible to one another. Then on November 4, 1989, with a crowd overflowing the commingled buildings, Baker-roshi installed Issan as the abbot of the Hartford Street Zen Center, and renamed the temple Issan-ji, One Mountain Temple. When Issan climbed the Mountain Seat to become abbot, he stood at the external pinnacle of his Zen life. In good, traditional Zen style, he immediately stepped off into space.

24 March 1990, Ojai, Issan's lecture continued

"I don't think we ever really know until we get there. A little while ago, I began having these anxiety attacks. I call them that because I don't know what else to call them. I had never experienced anything like it, and that seemed like a good word for it. I didn't have the energy to do anything, but I couldn't not do anything. I couldn't put on the TV and distract myself. I couldn't read, I couldn't sleep, I couldn't lie down, so I just started walking. An anxiety attack . . . why are we talking about anxiety attack . . . ?"

Question: "Not knowing till we get there . . ."

Issan: "What I keep doing in my mind, when I have these anxiety attacks, small ones, I keep trying to back up and do it all over again. You know: 'Ooops I slipped, I better go back.' [*laughing*] But you can't do it, you know what I mean? Or sometimes I look out the window and I see people running, laughing, having a good time and acting in a way that I can't do right now. But we have to own these things.

"At first I used to think, 'You're a good Buddhist priest, you've been sitting for twenty years. You shouldn't have to be going through all this.' [*laughing*] But *because* I'm a Buddhist priest, I have to own everything. Including my fears and anxiety attacks.

"I think most people aren't lucky enough to live in these insights until the impact of death. . . . There's an idea of time, 'We don't have time.' We don't have time to take care of each other, it's time-consuming to spend time with someone who's dying, and take care of them. Particularly with AIDS, and cancer I think, because it's slow. There is a lot of caregiving to be done."

If Issan did his share of caregiving, he wasn't shy about letting the world know it. He went to conferences like the Ojai event (which was his last public teaching), and he did an interview with Frank Browning of National Public Radio for a piece on the gay community's response to AIDS. Articles about him sprouted up in most Buddhist publications and, of course, in the gay papers. A local Buddhist writer named Katy Butler featured Issan in a *New Yorker* magazine "Talk of the Town" piece. But Issan himself worried, "I've got two real problems: Hartford Street Zen Center and James."

Issan felt Maitri Hospice had its own life; he thought it had enough backing and interest and reason to exist now, so that he could pull back. But he didn't exactly see how to *develop* the zendo. And while James seemed to be getting a little better all the time, Issan conceded that the improvements were noticeable only to him. "James is crazy, stuck somewhere around seven years old emotionally in a thirty-five-year-old body. People talk to me about codependence, but if it weren't for me, I know he'd be dead, just like his brother. Meanwhile he's sitting every day and trying. He sat all the way through the two-day sitting. He was the only one in the zendo the whole time. Sat there like a rock."

As a Zen teacher, Issan had run only half the gauntlet of Buddhist ceremonies. He'd taken the ordinations, gone through Dharma transmission, and climbed the Mountain Seat. Now he faced a full calendar of them again from the other side of the table—this time as preceptor, transmitter, abbot. But Issan's energy was wearing thin. Run down from birthing a hospice, he suffered a tough winter in 1989; the days found him often laid up in bed. Still, he agreed to give a monk's ordination to three of his students. One of them, a sturdily built, square-jawed man named Paul Higley, also suffered from AIDS. Issan darkly remarked one day from his sickbed—a day on which Higley was also direly ill in the hospital—that there would definitely be an ordination in February, provided anyone lived long enough to make it.

The temperature in San Francisco on February 24, 1990, was the highest for that date in recorded history, and it caught people by surprise. Almost everyone in the large crowd of family and friends looked hot and uncomfortable; as they crowded into the basement shrine room, they sweltered.

In his first ceremony as abbot, Issan wore more complicated robes than he'd worn before, and he carried a long, white horse-hair whisk. He moved slowly and deliberately through the opening purifications. Even so, as he swung the whisk in the ritual way, it grazed the altar and extinguished the candle with a soft popping sound. Had it been intentional, it would have seemed a deft gesture. Issan's face registered the surprise of a child who's just discovered that dropping his favorite toy breaks it. Half a second later, it all seemed funny. Issan remarked, as the candle was relit, that he'd "never carried one of these things before."

The ceremony was a long, elaborated procedure. David Bullock,

Angelique Farrow, and Paul Higley came in wearing grey kimonos. They had their heads washed and shaved; they received two sets of new robes, new bowing cloths, bowls, vows, names, and lineage papers. Little verses describing each item were chanted, and three bows to the floor followed each presentation. It seemed they were forever bowing—more and more awkwardly as they donned the new, confining garments.

The high point of the event was the tonsure—the ritual cutting of the last hair. Issan stood behind Bullock, senior of the three, holding the shaving implements. He announced: "This last hair is called the *shura*. Only a Buddha can cut it. Now I will cut it. Do you allow me to cut it?"

"Yes, I do" came the clear reply. Issan bent forward, razor in hand, then stopped. "Where is it?" he asked his attendant. Grinning sheepishly, he said to the crowd, "I should have brought my glasses for this part." They were fetched and he continued.

The tension broken by Issan's levity remounted as he approached Paul Higley's large, blocky skull. Question and reply sounded forcefully, and the sight of one terminally ill man shaving the head of another in the most ancient of all Buddhist ceremonies reduced a good section of the audience to tears.

As the afternoon went on, Issan tired badly. His spirit remained bright, his tenderness toward the ordainees radiated throughout the room, but he grew pale, and it became difficult to hear him. By the time the procession assembled upstairs for photos, Issan was peaked, trembling with fatigue. He revived briefly with the sociability of the reception, but had to have the front door closed, despite the very warm afternoon air, because the draft chilled him.

25 March 1990, Ojai Conference

Next morning, the ridge was socked in with heavy fog. Someone had started a fire in the little pit, and Issan sat on a stone bench nearby, sipping coffee and waiting for his sublingual pill to dissolve. Retreatants and staff sat with him, mostly a silent group, warming themselves and enjoying the fragrant, crackling flames. When his pill dissolved, Issan began to chat quietly with whoever greeted him or sat next to him. After a bit he stood up, dusted himself off, and headed for the Portolet. "Once for the coffee, and once for the vitamin C," he whispered as he passed.

"Sounds complicated," I said.

"It gets more complicated than this."

When he got back, two women approached; one of them had a brother dying of AIDS, and he'd asked her to find out the Buddhist position on "self-euthanasia," "morphine-drip," or "shunt," as it was variously called. Issan reiterated his position: "I don't want to hear about all that 'clear-mind-no-drugs' talk. I don't even want to hear it. That's not the mind we're talking about. The mind we're talking about when we say 'clear mind' isn't affected by a little morphine."

Joking him, I said, "Issan, seems like you've been on a kind of 'slow-drip' yourself for about thirty years."

"Yeah, well it's time to get it *turned up*."

13

The Greatest Teacher

When something is dying, that is when it is the greatest teacher. —Shunryu Suzuki-roshi

11 May 1990

Issan, back from three days of vacation in Sonoma, called to say he'd enjoyed getting away, enjoyed spending time with Mickey, but that he'd felt so bad most of the time he couldn't really say he'd had a good time. It seems to have been exclusively his back this trip, by which he means, I assume, the continuing ache in his shoulders. He said it made him so crazy one night that he took an Ativan. "That cleared my head up some, and it seemed to help the back too." He only took one of these, though. For pain, he's been given something called Vicodin. I asked him what it was and he gave me another name for it, pronouncing each syllable distinctly: *hy-dro-cor-done,* making it sound like an Italian gangster relative of his. "It's supposed to have codeine in it or something, but it doesn't feel like codeine. And now the good doctor wants me to come in to Ward 86 on Tuesday to do a whole *lot* of tests."

Ward 86 at San Francisco General is the AIDS ward, one of the front lines in the field battle against the disease.

"What kind of tests?"

"Everything—they're going to test for pneumocystis, they're

going to do blood tests, a test for my lymph gland. I've been running a hundred and two temperature the last few nights."

"A hundred two? You're kidding!"

"No."

"You don't sound sick now."

"Now I feel fine—it's in the evening it starts coming on."

I called Dr. Rick Levine's beeper number, though I'd meant to resist using that. When he called back, Rick said that just between us, he *was* worried about Issan. There had been lab abnormalities, and Rick thought Issan just might have lymphoma.

"Jesus, what does that mean?"

"That means an official AIDS diagnosis, a lot of chemotherapy, and a generally poor prognosis."

We'd both expected something like this for a long time, but the words going back and forth in the air shocked us both into a pause.

"I've told him there's a bridge two hundred yards or so down the road, and god knows what's on the other side, but we'll worry about it when we get there. There's nothing we can do till Tuesday anyway."

15 May 1990

I let myself in to 57 Hartford through the unlocked door, walked by the class being held in the living room, and went up to Issan's room. He lay quietly on top of his bed, in pajamas. The room was extremely warm and dim. I gave him roses from our garden, and he delighted in them as he went for a vase and water. When my eyes adjusted to the room, I saw several other flower arrangements, maybe four in all, dotting his dresser table, and shelves.

He said I'd come at the right time—he was fading, as usual, in the evening. When I asked more about how he'd been feeling, he pulled off his pajama top, stood a foot from me, turned around, and gave me a tour of his back. Pain seems to have crept back down into his hips and legs and low back, though he knew of plenty of places that ached and pulled across his shoulders as well. He turned around, stood to my right, and grabbed my neck with both hands;

"and last night my neck just locked up. Just locked up, I could barely turn it at all." He said he'd taken two Vicodin and that they had dulled the pain but left him too stoned. "You know, nodding. Out of it. Like an opiate."

He lay facedown on the bed, and we began to work. (I'd made a living for three years as a bodyworker, and was now putting that training at his service. It also gave me a good way to keep an eye on him.) His body was noticeably frailer. There was less of him, and he was much more sensitive to pain. "I'm probably going to take an Ativan after you leave. For sleeping."

"Ativan? Rick said it was okay?"

"Yeah, every once in a while, as long as I don't get too strung back out on them."

He'd just come through a nasty withdrawal from Ativan. He'd been taking a sleeping pill, a muscle relaxant, and this Valium-like drug Ativan, in addition to AZT. His doctor had warned him that these drugs could be addictive, and addictive in a slimy way. Apparently they played with your moods, so that when you quit taking them, you felt dysphoria. Issan told me he'd heard stories of people who'd taken a year to get over addiction to drugs in the Valium family. "You don't ever get high from these things. You don't really notice them working at all. They just smooth everything out for you. Like if I were to take one right now, everything would be smoothed out. I'd be like, fine, no problem."

"So, harder to kick than other drugs? Harder than heroin?"

"Oh yes, much harder."

"Speed?"

"Speed's not so hard." Issan fell quiet for a while, then said, "To tell you the truth, I can't ever remember feeling this bad before."

"Do you think that's because you never felt this bad, or because you can't remember?" He lifted his head slowly from a twisted, facedown position on his bed, slowly rotated his neck, and rested back down again, other side of his face up. "Probably I can't remember."

When I told him he looked skinnier, particularly in his legs, he said he was just not getting his appetite back. "For two weeks there, I didn't eat much at all. Just a little cheese and applesauce, and farina. Now I'm starting to eat food again. This thing has almost been a month now—how long do you think it can go on? I hope not too much longer."

Impatience with his discomfort surfaced again and again throughout the hour. He seemed completely tired of being at loose ends mentally and physically.

"I haven't been in the zendo very much recently, but the other day, when I did go, it just made my back worse. So I'm not going to do it anymore. It's too hard."

I suggested that his limbs were shifting around to accommodate a weight loss. He agreed but went on to say that it could also be the AZT, which was why his doctor had taken him off it.

"Off AZT? For how long?"

"For good. Since last Thursday—he's going to see if I can get this DDI. It's one of the new drugs."

"Government approved and all?"

"Approved, but new. They have to monitor everything very closely. I'll know more about it all tomorrow, when I go to the hospital."

I let the news settle in a minute, that he'd finished a twenty-three-year meditation habit and had just quit taking a life-prolonging drug.

I mentioned that I was planning a trip to Ojai this weekend and hoped to interview his sister Carolyn. He said I could probably see her, and two others easily, and that if I went to Santa Barbara, I could see another four siblings. "In fact, my brother was just here today. David—he's forty-eight or forty-nine, nice man. He's deputy sheriff there. He's been a cop since he was twenty-one. He was up here for a corrections meeting or something, and he came by to visit. I think he's worried about my health generally."

"Does he know your situation?"

"Yeah, I told him everything. Told him I'm going to the hospital tomorrow to have a biopsy for my, uh, lymphoma. We went to lunch where we could talk kind of privately, then we came back here and sat in the backyard. I introduced him to everyone. He's a good man. I've only sort of seen him at family functions—weddings, funerals."

He was silent for a few minutes. "Actually, I'm not supposed to say *lymphoma*. My doctor says it's premature to say that. I think, though, he thinks I have it. I don't know, I guess I'll just do the next thing."

"What's lymphoma supposed to be like?"

"I don't know. Jim had it. Lots of radiation therapy, chemo-therapy. . . . He's better now."

"You going to do all that stuff?"

"Whatever my doctor says."

I worked pretty carefully on his neck and skull.

"You know, I was surprised. I never really gave my brother a chance to be such a nice man before. I never let him get to know me."

17 May 1990

The tests at General went well—they'd only taken a couple of hours, and Steve Allen had stayed with him through every step. The lymph biopsy had not been pleasant—they stuck a needle under his arm to get what they needed—but it wasn't nearly as painful as having blood drawn.

Rick Levine, who'd ordered the tests and who was also present for them, ended up having to take blood from Issan's groin. "They tried for a while in my arms, but they couldn't get any. Then the doctor came by and said, 'Don't worry. I'll get it from the groin.' "

"The groin? What do you mean exactly, the groin?"

"You know, your crotch—on your leg at the top up by your balls. I guess there are two or three big things running through there. They can't *see* anything, but they feel around for the artery. They say they can feel it—then they just go in there with a big needle. They drew a *lot* of blood."

"Rick did this?"

"Yeah, he did this part, and it really hurt."

Issan has been given to complaint about a wide range of topics over the years, but he's been no sissy about bodily pain. I've never heard him complain about the dentist, about burns or cuts he sustained in the kitchen, or about the bruises he got in the course of his relationship with James. He's been very macho in enduring the sizzling pain that can come up during Zen meditation. He's bounced through a lot of physically extreme situations and come out cheerful, but I think the constancy of his current pain, and the duration, are beginning to wear him down: "This thing going on so long is making me kind of crazy."

It also seems this pain is more threatening to him, because it may be associated with a terminal illness. It's not something he can tell himself will be over soon, so he can get back out there. He doesn't believe it anymore. Rather than doing a lap or two in a well-tended pool of pain, he's swimming in a rough sea of it, and can't sight the shore.

18 May 1990

Next morning, rather early, Rick Levine called. He sounded tentative and said, "Shall I come right to the point, or shall we do some morning chitchat?"

"Right to the point."

"Okay, Issan has AIDS, officially. Before this, he had severe disabling ARC, but now his tests show he has lymphoma."

After a bit, I said, "Isn't that what Jim had and recovered from?"

"Jim, and Katagiri-roshi, and Suzuki-roshi, if I'm not mistaken. But Issan's got a special kind. It's called AIDS-related lymphoma; it's somewhat more aggressive, and it's more refractory to treatment."

"You've told Issan."

"Last night. I called him and we talked a while—how are you? up, down, this that—then I said I'd like to come by and talk to him about a couple of things, so I think that gave him a little idea. I went over with Frances; she stayed downstairs while I went up to talk to him. He was sitting with Jamvold and Steve Allen on either side of him."

"Watching TV?"

"Exactly. He was in his chair, one guy was in the other chair, and one was sitting on the bed. We talked about things for a few minutes, then I said, almost casually, 'Issan, you have lymphoma.' 'Oh, I have lumphoma,' he said, with nary a hitch in the conversation. 'What does that mean?' and so on."

"Well, what does it mean, Rick?"

"In terms of a prognosis, it's not good. It means he'll be going into the hospital, starting tomorrow morning at 8:30. He'll go first to Ward 86, which is an outpatient ward, and from there, he'll be admitted."

"How long is he going to be there?"

"That depends. Five days at least. First, he'll be staged for lymphoma. 'Staged' means he'll have a series of tests to determine how far the disease has progressed."

"Blood test?"

"Blood, bone, lumbar insertion. . . ."

"That's a spinal tap, right? Isn't that supposed to be really painful?"

"Not if it's done right. That part shouldn't hurt. But starting probably on Monday, he'll be hydrated in anticipation of chemotherapy. We'll have to supersaturate him with fluids, because kidneys for one don't function well with chemotherapy unless they're being constantly flushed. It's heavy; he'll be pretty miserable. He doesn't need to know that now, by the way."

"Sure." In the background, I could hear Rick's beeper go off.

"That's Issan calling now."

20 May 1990

Issan called late in the afternoon and left a message on the machine. I didn't reach him till about ten at night. I said I'd heard from Rick and asked how he was doing. He said he'd taken an Ativan and that the only thing hurting him was his "damn back." He wasn't worried about the spinal tap so much, but Rick had told him the bone biopsy would be a bitch. "I guess there's just a certain amount of pain you can't get out of. They have to find out"—here he yawned enormously—"how to proceed."

He wasn't sure how he was going to fare with all of it, but he sounded relaxed, even relieved to finally be engaging his disease. We covered a lot of the same ground Rick had sketched out, but Issan filled in a number of gruesome details. To hydrate him for chemotherapy, he said, almost bragging about it, they would have to "run a line in." He repeated it several times: "They'll have to run a line in me." I said I'd imagined that's how they'd do it—with an IV.

"No, no," he said. "They can't use my veins. The veins in my arms are shot. You know that thing Paul had to have in the middle of his chest? That's where they'll run a line in me. My arms couldn't take it; they want to run in too much stuff for *that*. Then they have to go in my head too."

"What do you mean, 'go in your head'?"

"Drill in there and find out if my central nervous system has the lymphoma. They go in there and wash it out. They have to put the chemo in there separately, I think. I'm not sure; seems like the head is a whole different trip."

"Well, are you okay with all this?"

"The only thing bothering me now is my fucking back, to tell you the truth. It's kind of taking a front seat at the moment. But I don't know, I don't really have anything to compare it with. I'm planning to count a lot."

"What, count your breath?"

"Yeah."

"Issan, listen. You know I'm going down to Ojai this weekend and I'll see your sisters and probably your brother. Do you want me to say anything?"

"Yeah. Tell them. That would be good."

We gabbed a bit more, then realizing that neither of us had packed for our journeys the next day, we wound down. He said, "I'm glad you're seeing my family. I like them better all the time. And give my love to anyone down there who looks like they need it."

"I will, and I can assure you that everyone down there will be sending you their love."

"That's good. I can use all I can get."

Collect call from Issan this morning. "I'm sorry to call this way, but they tell me to call out of here, I have to dial 07. I do it and this is what happens. I haven't figured out how to put it on my tab yet. Excuse me a second."

In the background I could hear a steady triple beep. Then it stopped. "This machine that's hydrating me doesn't like it if I move my left arm in certain ways."

"How are you feeling?"

"Not too bad, actually. I have a headache, but that's about it, and I'm taking some pills for that. People are amazed—I mean after what I've gone through here. It's been pretty hairy."

"I bet."

"The spinal tap people said that would hurt, but it didn't; and the bone biopsy, Dr. Levine told me, would hurt a lot, but it didn't. All I felt was pressure, really. Then I had a CAT scan too. The people here are good at what they do. I have two central line implants now."

"What's that, the thing that goes in your chest?"

"Two of them, yeah. I have one that goes, that takes stuff in, and one that takes stuff out."

"How long do you have to wear those?"

"Till I'm done, in October. Then I get a little vacation."

"Done with what?"

"The *chemo.* I had that too last night, you know."

"I heard you might. How long are you in there?"

"One more day I think. They want to do another scan, an MRI, to see if this pain in my back is from the lymphoma."

I told him a bit about visiting his sisters and brother. He said his brother David had called and told him how much he'd enjoyed our visit. "He said you were a nice man."

"Well, that's good to hear. I wasn't sure. It was kind of heavy talking to your sisters, though."

"Why?"

"Well, I had to tell them. You know, about you being in the hospital and having lymphoma and all."

"They didn't know?"

"Huh-uh."

(In fact, it had been awful to tell them. I'd debated how to do it driving to the meeting, and had decided to clear the air of bad news first. But when we met, amid the noise of our surroundings and the fluster of new introductions, it just hadn't come up. After we'd finished a formal interview and were saying good-bye, they asked how Tommy was. I told them what I knew. They were visibly struck by the news, and they fell silent. The thought haunted me that I'd ripped them off in some way since I'd told them at the end of our interview rather than at the beginning. We felt like friends by this point, so it was especially tough for them to bear news of their big brother dying from AIDS.

Once we were talking about it, though, I told them he definitely *was* on the way out, and I urged them to visit him soon. By way of mollification, I tried to give them a sense of his importance in San Francisco's Buddhist and gay communities—what he'd accomplished in a life largely invisible to them. Perhaps this talk just filled an uncomfortable space, but they seemed to like hearing it, and they cheered up a little.)

"Well, my sister is sick too, you know," Issan said. "Did she tell you?"

"No."

"Yeah. She's had about four inches taken out of her colon. She thinks she's going to die pretty soon, or anyway, that she's not going to live a *long* time."

"I had no idea." A clicking came on the line.

"Do you want to talk more now," I asked, "or hang up?"

"No more now."

"Would you like a little visit?"

"Yeah. I haven't seen you in a while. A short visit would be nice."

26 May 1990

Issan was on the phone when I walked into his hospital room.

"No, no, I'm okay. Okay. Yeah. Tomorrow. Okay. Yeah. I love you too. David Schneider just walked in, I have to hang up now. Okay. 'Bye."

Turning to me: "That was James. He's freaking out."

"He must be."

Issan stood up from the bedside chair he'd been in and shuffled toward me. We hugged. He'd lost weight and he had a funny red-orange tinge to him; I also noticed a slight but rapid trembling in his face and hands. I wasn't sure at first if it was just my perception—not being able to focus—or him. But nothing else in the room was doing it.

"You look fine, fine," I said.

"Yeah. Today's the first day I've been feeling pretty good."

"Hey, I didn't feel those implants. Do you have them in now?"

"You don't want to see them?" he said, untying his blue bathrobe. "Do you?"

"Yeah, show me."

"Untuck my shirt in back so I can."

He pulled up his shirt and displayed two plastic tubes which dangled from the left side of his chest, like remnants of an Indian initiation rite. He patted down the tape that fixed them to his breastbone. "This one puts stuff in, this one takes stuff out."

"Sit down," he said, pointing to the chair he'd been in. "I sit over here, in this. This is the A-1 chair. I should take this one home. It's a perfect TV chair." He eased into a big, red-leather hospital chair.

I looked around the room. A Japanese scroll hung on one wall, and one of Issan's Buddha pictures hung on another. In front of the window on the sill, someone had set up a little altar: Buddha statue, flowers, candle and incense. Though none of it was lit, it was surprising to see it at all, given all the warnings on the door about "oxygen in use, no flames or toys. . . ." A clock, a box of tissues, a glass of water, and some medicines sat orderly on his bedside table, around another flower arrangement. It looked like Issan's room anywhere. It felt more like being in Issan's room than being in a hospital room. Gold, late-afternoon sunlight filtered in through the window.

"This is nice in here."

"Yeah, I even have a view of the Golden Gate Bridge from my bed."

I clambered up to look and true enough, you could see a small red stretch of bridge. Big gray clouds floated past it.

"So how are you doing?"

"Actually, I'm okay. Once or twice I've waked up with some negativity happening. But mostly I'm okay. Today I feel nothing so much as just sad. This social worker kid was in here talking with me this morning. From New York, only been here three weeks. He'd read about me somewhere, he knew all about me."

"Maybe Katy's piece in *The New Yorker?*"

"Many places," he said, waving his hand down. "In the gay papers there, I'm not sure. Maybe they syndicated something from the *B.A.R.* or the *Advocate*. Anyway, we're talking and he says, 'After all this work you've done taking care of people, helping them die, don't you feel kind of strange being in bed now yourself?' I said, 'Yes I do,' to him, and I just started to cry."

The trembling in Issan's face increased. He grew flushed and his eyes got shiny, but he talked through it. "I've been feeling this way all day. It's just kind of pervaded everything today."

"I see."

"It's kind of nice, though, you know? It's not like having the anxiety or confusion. This is fine. It's kind of touching or something. So how did you like talking to my family?"

I said everyone had praised his dad.

"My father was a fine man." Issan pushed up from his chair and began to rummage through the closets and drawers of his room. "I never really knew him until it was too late."

"What are you looking for?"

"A handkerchief."

"Here. There's tissue everywhere here."

"I like a handkerchief. I don't like not having one in the pocket of my robe." He found one and showed it to me, then he opened it and blew his nose. "This was my father's. . . . Not too late, really. Last couple years I actually got to know my father pretty well."

Issan sat back down. "I have a lot to do now, you know, to take care of myself."

"Like what?"

"I have to clean these out every other day or so," he said, fiddling with the lines running into his chest. "And I have to shoot myself up with medicine a couple times a week."

"You have to shoot up?"

"Yeah," he said, miming the act. He put an imaginary hypodermic into his thigh, slammed in the medicine with his thumb, pulled the works out like a wine cork, then opened his palm, as if to say, "See how simple?"

"That's incredible, Issan. All your life you shoot up. Now you *have* to shoot up."

"I know it. I actually prefer to have somebody else do it. They trained me, and Michael learned how to do it too."

Right then, Michael Jamvold knocked on the door and came in. A minute later, Steve Allen came in. Then another knock and a male nurse came in. In no time the room had gone from calm and quiet to jammed and active. Issan sat in his chair and watched. He seemed at ease with the tidal flow of population.

Jamvold engaged the nurse in a small argument about the temperature at which Issan's medicine should be stored once he left the hospital. The nurse calmly tore the foil cover off a big pill, gave it to Issan, and told him to put it under his tongue. Even with mouth full, Issan too began to grill the nurse, a tall man with thick glasses, as to why he hadn't had certain medications today, when were they going to start, how much was he going to have, how often . . . The nurse seemed not to mind the badgering, and answered everyone's questions as best he could before leaving. Steve Allen also left, so Jamvold and Issan disputed each other awhile:

"God, she's so pretty, that other nurse of yours."

"Who?"

"Your main nurse, the really pretty one. She looks like—"

"*She's* not my main nurse!"

"Yes, she is. She's your head nurse. She'll be on your case constantly for the next seven months."

"I thought she was going away."

"Only for two months."

"Well that's not seven months, then, is it?"

I broke in, but pretty soon they were at it again, sniping about which glands had been affected by the lymphoma and which hadn't. Jamvold seemed to enjoy wielding what knowledge he had. He knew he didn't have much, though, and he was proved wrong often enough so he didn't take himself terribly seriously. He also maintained a good sense of humor. Issan seemed to relish the bickering; first exercise in a week.

The upshot of the argument was that so far only one gland, the one under Issan's right arm, had been affected. MRI tomorrow might show whether the adrenals had been affected too. If they were, it could help to explain Issan's back pains, since the adrenals sit right above the kidneys.

Jamvold scooped up various things from around the room and asked Issan if there were anything more he could do. He hugged Issan, and kissed him and left. Issan seemed proud: "He's been here every day. Steve too. One comes in the morning, and one in the afternoon and evening."

"So you're always attended."

"Uh-huh. I've got the best care in the world. Tell you what you could do is rub my back a minute, if you would. Look there—do I have holes or anything where they did the bone biopsy? I'm sore there."

Again he lifted his shirt and turned around. Two little red spots, one above each hip. "Here?" I said, pressing them.

"Oooh. Yeah."

"There are teeny red dots, one each place, and a couple of Band-Aids right in the middle."

"What are *they* for?"

"Your spinal tap, I imagine."

"Oh yeah that's right. I forgot. Rub up here, would you? I'm getting kind of stiff."

We stood side by side in the middle of his room, with me working the area around his neck and shoulders. I did one side, then went around and stood on the other side. "You know, Issan, you look pretty damn good."

"Yeah, I know. I've lost weight; everybody tells me how good I look. I always look good when I'm sick."

I got ready to go, and Issan said in a conspiratorial tone, "I got one of those doctors to fix up the morphine situation."

"What do you mean?"

"See, at first they just had me down for this pizzly little dose." He put his thumb and forefinger together to show how insufficient it'd been. He sounded genuinely insulted. "I mean *nothing*. Then at the same time they were giving me this other stuff, which knocked me out totally and made me feel shitty and hung-over. . . . So I talked to them about it. . . ."

2 June 1990

Steve and Mike were just rousing themselves, though it was early afternoon; they'd been up most of the night before.

Issan had gone back to Ward 86 of General on Wednesday for a scheduled appointment with one of the doctors monitoring his study. His blood counts had been worrisome: 600 white cells (normal is 3,900), and 0 in several other categories. The doctors had said to watch him carefully for fevers, the idea being that his defenses were extremely low, almost nonexistent.

Back at the house he'd eaten well, which encouraged everyone, but within an hour of dinner, he'd begun to feel bad and his temperature started to climb. "102 was the magic number," Michael said. "They were definitely to have him in the hospital if it got that high, but they didn't wait. When he showed a temperature of 101.4, they took off."

According to Michael, Issan got pretty scared. He'd begun to breathe in rapid shallow gasps, and was unable to follow Michael and Steve's advice about slowing it down until he'd been readmitted to the hospital and given antibiotics.

Word from Hartford Street is that he's to have no visitors, though Michael, who's rising to this occasion with something like administrative skill, said he considers immediate family to include me and my fiancée and we will therefore be allowed short viists.

Sunday, 9, June 1990

Issan didn't have much chance to get settled this week. Wednesday dragged him back to Ward 86 for a diagnostic spinal tap and other blood pleasantries. He was in all afternoon, a solid four hours.

The big commotion of the early week was that James was permitted to visit Issan at home, despite the restraining order. He'd tried several times to see Issan but had been thwarted, not so much by the Hartford Street directors as by Issan's own unwillingness to receive visitors. Finally it worked out from both sides for James to have dinner: he was allowed one hour and was confined to Issan's room.

During these few days, Jamvold kept me posted about Issan's blood counts. He seemed to relish telling me this or that component of the blood at a particular level: "Yours and mine are at X; Issan's is way down at Y."

Thursday, Issan was back at General getting a transfusion, and Michael suggested I go down to the hospital with him to collect Issan and bring him home. (Vigilant as Michael and Steve are protecting Issan from too much socializing, they also seemed concerned that he does see and hear enough from friends.) Michael thought Issan would be feeling pretty strong with all the new blood: "He's just going to be *lying* there all day."

"You're going to love this nurse," Michael said as we strode through General's fluorescent-lit halls. "She's really cute." She turned out to be short and dark, with huge eyes and a ready smile, Thai or Filipino. She brushed past us, said a quick hi to Michael, and walked to the machine beside Issan's bed. A bag of dark red blood hung on the metal racks of the machine, tubes running from it and joining other tubes to the control panels, all feeding eventually into Issan's chest. The machine beeped softly like an alarm clock, with the opening notes to Beethoven's Fifth Symphony: *beep beep beep booooop, beep beep beep booooop . . .*

A tall Mexican or American Indian man with black hair and black-framed glasses bent to the machine. He pressed buttons and jiggled connections. The nurse joined him and the machine quieted down.

Issan, who lay in bed dapperly dressed in a black turtleneck, rolled his head on the pillow to watch the mechanics, then looked across the room to us. His look chilled me; it was the look a football player on a stretcher gives to the TV camera as he's being carried to the locker room, a flat countenance that barely rises above a mass of pain.

The nurses backed away from the machine, and our group went over to greet Issan. The machine began to beep. The male nurse came back, smiling and clucking, and pushed some buttons. Someone said it'd been beeping for the past hour. The pretty nurse returned, too, squeezing through the crowd we made around Issan's bed. She fussed with the tubes in his chest, but before she'd even squeezed back out, the beeping began again.

We visitors backed out to give the medics room to work. Issan's bed this time was one of four, in a ward divided floor-to-ceiling by a sliding plastic curtain. Another man, very sick-looking, shared Issan's half of the room. I couldn't see the far half, but a big color TV blasted both halves with Oprah Winfrey's show.

The male nurse asked Issan, "Do you have any veins?"

Issan shook his head no. "*Every*body has veins, silly," the guy said. "Maybe we'll see if we can find some in your arm." Issan gave him a sweet, doubting look and said nothing.

"He has veins," I whispered. "They've just all been used up."

Pam Jackson said, "I know. He was trying to tell the man on the cool."

They sat Issan up in bed and went to get something with which to tie him off. The beeping abruptly stopped. After trying and failing to find another way into Issan, the nurses decided that if he just sat up and held his position, that might do the trick.

We filed back into the room and stood around the bed. There wasn't much to say; Pam had been there for hours. The blood had run smoothly into Issan for the first four and a half hours, then stalled the last hour. Though literally he was being filled, Issan looked drained. He hadn't been able to rest, and now would have to sit, propped up by his arms to just the right angle, to keep the demented Beethoven alarm quiet.

"Has Dr. N. been in to see you?" Michael asked.

Issan shook his head no.

"He hasn't?"

Again just the shake of the head. "Frances has been. She's looked in four or five times."

"She's so great."

Issan was silent another minute, then said, "She's great and everything, but it's also her job."

Pam—tall, statuesque, copper-colored, with high cheekbones and an hourglass figure—took her leave. She and Issan had gone out to hear music together regularly when she lived at Zen Center. They'd dated, really, and had a kind of love affair. She was one of the few women Issan outright adored. Their good-bye was prolonged and tough somehow, but gingerly done, in respect of the machine.

"Ha-ha," the male nurse said to the man in the other bed. "Nobody loves *you*!"

"Fuck you!" the guy said back, laughing. They watched Oprah Winfrey together, commenting about how stupid the show was.

13 June 1990

Issan's room at Hartford Street. He picked up a little yellow Post-it from his desk and read it to me: " 'Mind arises on breath. Field of Breath. Field not cows.' "

"These are notes from a phone call I had with Baker-roshi yesterday. Mind arises on the breath. Then see it as a field, a field of breath." Here he shook his hands outward, to extend space. "See it as a field. Pay attention to the field, not the cows in it. He told me this, you know, to help with the anxiety attacks."

"He called?"

"Yeah. He called from Brussels or somewhere, I don't know. He's thinking about me."

19 June 1990

Issan said, "I sat a half-period of zazen yesterday."

"You did? How'd it feel?"

"It felt good. I sat the second half, then I stood for service. I'm pretty low energy, though."

"You didn't lead it?"

"No, I couldn't do the bows. It's just that I can't get down and back up that fast. I really am very low-energy these days. My energy is just not so good."

Hearing this, I suddenly felt that the exhausting rounds of chemotherapy and the whole drug approach were useless. It seemed there was something much more basic, something Issan called "his energy," that would determine how long he lived. When he said his energy was low, I heard it as his life-force. I heard, "I don't have long. I'm worn out."

11 July 1990

I found him sitting up on his bed looking as pale as the walls behind him. He blended in with his undershirt. It'd been another hard night; he hadn't slept until sometime after 4:00 A.M., then for only a few hours. He blamed his medicines for this restlessness.

I noticed reddish-brown marks of dried blood on his undershirt. A couple streaky lines ran from his chest to the V of the shirt neck, right above where his new "line" was.

"What's that Issan, on your shirt? Is that blood?"

He looked down and pulled the T-shirt away from his body, so he could see. He said nothing, then pulled the shirt off, over his head, and I saw a little archipelago of scabs, a couple inches long, below the tape holding the new needle in his chest. Under the clear tape as well, several red hairlines of blood had been trapped. It looked like veining in a crystal or amber, and it seemed to correspond to the marks on his shirt.

"This is just an abrasion," he said, jamming his chin down toward his chest, pointing to his scabs.

"Has it been bleeding?"

"I don't know. I haven't noticed it. I guess so. Maybe." He looked down at it again. "It's just a little abrasion." He said this quickly, dismissing the subject. Then about ten minutes later he said, "That stuff on my shirt wasn't blood. It's what they used to flush my line. I don't remember the name of it. Some purple stuff."

We had a small argument about the scabs and whether *they* were blood. I then thought maybe he was being sensitive because of his HIV-contaminated blood. I said, "It's blood, I'm sure, but I'm not worried about it or anything." And I immediately felt stupid and exposed. Maybe he hadn't been referring to contamination. I looked over my hands: the usual nicks and cuts that come from playing ball with an eleven-year-old, and gardening with roses. When I did bodywork professionally, I'd been very careful about such things, but I'd forgotten all about it with Issan. I made a mental note to watch what parts I touched him with, friend or no. HIV hadn't proved mutable to good intentions, friendship, companionship, or love. In fact the virus had fed on these connections.

12 July 1990

A call to square arrangements for a Friday visit. Jamvold answers and tells me Issan has been freaked out because his neutriphil count is low. He says Issan worries terribly about such things and thereby gives himself fits. Apparently he's even called the hospital, or his doctor, to get up-to-the-minute counts. "He's going to be the worst patient we ever had," says Michael, "far and away the worst." Then he hands the phone to Issan.

13 July 1990

"Well, what should I do?" He asks this every time, even though we do the same preparation each time.

"Issan, you know you're getting a little skinny through here." He watches my hands as I indicate the upper lateral areas of my own chest.

"I know it. That's where I'm getting skinny. Through here, and also all along here." He rotates on the bed, and lies back and runs his hands down his hamstrings. "All of this is gone. And also my ass. My ass is *gone.*" He says this so ruefully, I can't help laughing.

"Your ass isn't gone."

"Yeah. It is. It's gone."

19 July 1990

"Did you hear the news about Tommy-roshi?" Ken Ireland asks.

"Who? Baker-roshi?"

"No. We've been trying to figure out what to call him. See, Baker-roshi did a little ceremony, a private one, with Issan yesterday, and now Issan is a roshi. We're trying to figure it out. We're all supposed to call him roshi now, but Issan-roshi doesn't quite work. I don't know—Dorsey-roshi? The latest thing we decided on is Tommy-roshi."

Richard Baker: "I acknowledged Issan as a roshi and asked him to be called roshi shortly before he died. I want to be very clear that I didn't do it as some sort of nice thing to do because he was dying, or that it was an honorary thing. It was none of those things. I completely feel as though he is and should be Issan-roshi, or Dorsey-roshi, or whatever. If he did continue to live, he would have been a great teacher and recognized spontaneously by others. Being a roshi is not just a matter of being recognized by your teacher as a roshi, but also being spontaneously recognized by others—peers, other teachers and students, even though they don't know what a roshi is. That would have occurred for Issan if he'd lived. I did it because that was what was true, and should be done. He was magnetic, magnanimous and luminous.

"Before Steve knew about it, Issan talked to me and asked me whether I would do the transmission teachings that I had done with Issan, with Steve. I'd never really taught Issan how to teach the teachings; he'd received them, but how to teach them— normally you don't—there's a ten-year incubation period before you do a transmission after you've received a transmission. But whether he could have done it or not, Issan didn't feel strong enough. The agreement was that I would do the teachings. He very specifically asked me and confirmed it with me that I would do this—it was very important to him, and it was the way he wanted it done.

"If Issan died without a disciple, his name would have disappeared from the lineage. From that point of view, even though it looked like I might have to do most of the teachings, Steve's being Issan's disciple puts Issan in the lineage. But also, he *felt* like he was Issan's disciple.

"It became clear to me over the time they were together that Steve *was* really learning a great deal from Issan, and that Steve was now Issan's disciple as much as he was mine. When Steve came to study with me, I concluded that in effect the transmission had occurred between Issan and Steve. Really, Steve is Issan's disciple."

12 August 1990

The past ten days have been difficult for Issan. He's had little energy, he hasn't rested or eaten well, and he's lost weight. Steve Allen associates this downturn with news about having to have radiation—

or more accurately, with the notion that the chemo wasn't working completely. Steve says Issan's aptitude for treatment was rooted in the chemo and its unpleasantries actually doing him some good. That idea helped him endure. News of having to have radiation seems to have broken his spirit.

Issan's color had gone from pale to a strange purple-red, the color of a hybrid rose too long in the vase. He walked down stairs like a cripple; he'd lean his body back, thrust a leg forward, and tilt down toward it till it hit the stair. With each thudding step he grimaced. At the bottom, I saw the grimace was on his face more or less constantly—a ghoulish smile caused by weight loss. Skin drawn tighter across his bones pulled the formerly round face into a visage of dark hollows.

30 August 1990

The doctors suggested he undergo a galium tracer, so Issan drank the prescribed fluid and went back a couple days later for tests. Ken Ireland told me that when Issan went under the machine, it was clear the cancer had "gone crazy." It had gone into his bones and bone marrow, and as his doctor put it, it was just a matter of time until it attacked a major organ. Dr. Kardin had put forth his information to an assembled group of Issan, Steve, Michael, and Rick Levine. Kardin had apparently said he thought Issan had about a month to live. Questioned about scheduling a ceremony in which Issan must participate, he'd said they should do it in the "next couple of days."

1 September 1990
Descending the Mountain Seat

The ceremony took place almost exactly at its scheduled time—very unusual for a Buddhist event. Many people had arrived early, though, and they assembled quickly, filling the dark, polished-wood zendo.

Steve Allen led in the procession; Issan followed, on the arms of Richard Baker-roshi and Michael Jamvold. A current of shock ran through the assembly; tears formed in many eyes. Issan moved extremely slowly and deliberately. Each step took his whole attention. He looked translucent and thin, like a fish drawn from an underground river. His face, from thinness or from pain, was pulled into a sad grin. At first, I thought he had been crying.

Steve wore the brown robe of a lineage holder, and Baker-roshi displayed an incredibly bright red-orange *rakusu*. Issan had come downstairs in a simply-patterned blue and white Japanese bathrobe, with a brown *rakusu* over it. He looked terrible and beautiful at the same time.

Just inside the zendo a great deal of stage-whispering took place. There had been no time to rehearse or to work out ceremonial details. Issan whispered very loudly; so then did Baker-roshi. At the shrine for Suzuki-roshi, Baker-roshi gave Issan a stick of incense. Issan touched it to his forehead in the traditional offering gesture, then passed it to Jamvold, who took it to the altar, thus saving Issan the steps.

Before the main shrine, there were two wooden chairs, one larger than the other. The higher seat was the abbot's chair, and the lower, smaller chair was for the departing abbot. As Steve did three prostrations to the main altar, Issan headed for the lower chair. When Steve finished, Issan started to sit down and make his speech, but he was interrupted by more loud whispering, mostly from Michael and Steve, who wanted him to sit in the abbot's chair first.

"You want me to warm it up for you a little, huh?" Issan said smiling. "Okay." He sat in the big chair, and while Steve adjusted himself and his robes in the lower chair, Issan casually asked him, as if they were just a couple of guys getting settled at the ball game, "Where'd we get these nice chairs?"

When everyone was still, Issan began to smile. He made careful eye contact with each person in the audience. After he finished, he spoke slowly, in a harsh, weak voice: "As you know, I've asked my best friend, Steve, to sit in this seat. It could be a pretty difficult job. But hopefully, as has been the case so far, with the help of all of you, it won't be too hard."

With that, he abruptly stood up and crossed in front of Steve's chair. Steve stood up too, moved slightly aside, and helped Issan reseat himself, this time in the lower chair. Then Steve unfurled his bowing cloth and made three prostrations to Issan. As Steve approached the abbot's seat, he paused and turned to Issan. "Only for you would I sit here," he said.

"You're the only one I would ask to do it," Issan replied. Steve then "climbed the Mountain Seat." Once settled, he looked over at Issan, and Issan extended his hand. Steve took it and, a moment later, kissed it.

The discreet clicking of cameras that began when the procession entered the zendo now became a rattle. Each positioning and repositioning of the two men occasioned a flurry of shutters.

"Lot of clicking going on in here," Issan said.

Steve then made some very short remarks, starting with the traditional admission of being unready for the job. He asked for everyone's help in carrying on Issan's work, and he promised to do all he could himself. He closed with a spontaneous poem:

> Sitting on this seat
> is like being in a tornado
> in the eye of a hurricane.

Tears were flowing very freely in the zendo now. Two streams ran down Baker-roshi's cheeks. Handkerchiefs and tissues came out of robe sleeves to dab at eyes and noses, and a lot of sniffling and throat-clearing accompanied Steve's short speech.

David Sunseri, speaking on behalf of the Maitri/Hartford Street Zen Center staff, accepted and welcomed Steve, and vowed to support him. Bernie Ortiz then spoke for the hospice residents, but instead of addressing Steve, he spoke directly to Issan. In his soft, high-pitched Caribbean lilt, he thanked Issan for all his work and compassion for people with AIDS, and he assured him how much it had been appreciated. Zen Center abbot, Reb Anderson, also made a short statement about the power of the transmission taking place.

Bells rang to signal the departing procession. Baker-roshi tried to guide Issan out of the zendo, but Issan whispered, "I want to bow to the Buddha." Baker-roshi stepped back as Issan made a slow standing bow, probably his last. He said to Issan, "Now you do a bow to each side," so Issan made slow bows to the east and west sides of the hall, and again smiled and looked long and hard at everyone present. He shuffled out of the zendo sort of spastically—first slowly, then quickly, as if his legs were only working in fits and working unpredictably when they did.

No one moved until the procession had reached the top of the stairs, a scant twenty minutes after it had come down. Issan repaired to his room, where Michael Jamvold guarded him fiercely from visitors for more than an hour, while the bittersweet reception, with its line of well-wishers for Steve, worked itself to completion below.

2 September 1990

This night I went by Issan's with Melissa, who'd flown in a day ahead of schedule. Issan greeted her warmly and congratulated us both on our marriage. He looked about the same.

While we were chatting lightly with him, Steve let himself into the room to administer Issan's Roxanol (morphine) dose. He pulled the barrel part of a needle works out of a cup on Issan's bedside table. The cup held a dozen other such barrels.

"You want orange juice this time?" Steve asked. "Or Coke?"

"Might as well use the Coke, since it's here," Issan said.

Steve located the Coke and poured some in a glass. He drew a barrel full of it and then looked over his shoulder at Melissa and me. I kept wondering when he was going to put the needle part on.

"Are you ready?" he asked, and Issan nodded. "Okay, open up."

Issan opened his mouth, and Steve shot a barrelful of morphine-rich Coke in. He reloaded the barrel with more Coca-Cola and shot that in. Then he shot in a load of water, and then handed Issan a glass of water. Issan took a very small sip.

After a few seconds, Issan began to belch horribly. It seemed his stomach was in spasm, and I felt sure he would soon vomit, but he didn't. Steve explained that the morphine was very bitter and had to be cut with something, then washed down. Issan's stomach spasms didn't seem to bother either one of them. "It's the water makes me do this," Issan said. Within a matter of minutes he began to fade in and out, and we said good-bye.

3 September 1990, Labor Day

Soon I found a spot to massage that made him feel better. He lay down, and we worked together for nearly forty minutes. He was so thin, and frail and his voice sounded so weak that I felt I was working on a ninety-year-old man. I moved him around as I would a baby, when I needed to reposition him. Steve had gone out of the room. The only sounds as we worked were the wind rattling the windows in their frames and Issan's constant labored gasping.

When we finished, he became extraordinarily demanding about the exact placement of things in his room. The lid on the lotion must click shut; the pillow here, the flannel blanket folded so and placed there; the window up a touch; the blanket unfolded, hem-side down; the chair lined up there, with those. Each instruction was issued in his faint, grating voice. Issan always insisted on an order, and a specific arrangement of his possessions, but it seemed now that the details were a lifeline of some kind; a bridge, or a focus on the phenomenal world.

"I'm sorry it's so confusing," he said after a particularly unclear directive about how a cover should be placed over his knees.

Before nodding out altogether, he walked very haltingly to the bathroom to pee, then walked back. He sat in the chair in front of his TV, and for a brief second his body seemed totally relaxed. He rested against the back of the chair as he always had done, and suddenly he looked bigger, more robust and healthier. Then his eyes drooped shut, and his mouth fell open. His breath came irregularly. He popped open his eyes and asked for water, which I gave him in a glass and held it for him as he drank.

He faded out again and his hands began to tremble, and his feet and legs kicked a little, as if on their own. I knelt there with water glass in hand and watched. He sat this way for a minute or ninety seconds; then he opened his eyes and said, "See what my hands do now?"

At quarter after nine, Michael told Issan it was time for his morphine, and asked him if he wanted it squirted in with orange juice, Coke, 7-Up, or what. Issan made no response. Michael put his face a few inches away from Issan's and said clearly and firmly, "Issan, do you want it with ginger ale?"

"Ginger ale would be good."

Michael loaded a barrel and shot it in Issan's open mouth. "You want another?" Michael asked, refilling the barrel with ginger ale.

After a few seconds, Issan opened his eyes and said, "You mean plain?"

"Yeah."

"Isn't that what I've been having all along?"

"Yeah, the same. You want it?"

Issan was quiet a minute, and then with a look of real anger on his face, which had reddened, he said, "I don't know why I can't have a double. I don't know why they are scared of making my body comfortable." He paused. "It doesn't really help, you know."

"What," I asked. "The morphine doesn't?"

"It doesn't help at all. It doesn't make me feel any better." He practically snarled this, with his upper lip drawn back over his teeth. He then accepted a barrelful of plain ginger ale and lapsed back in his chair. Suddenly he said, "I wish I had someone to advise me."

Michael asked, "About the medicines?"

"About all of it."

"Well, you have Rick."

"I know. But he cut me back." Having said this (which in fact was untrue), Issan faded out.

He resisted suggestions that he lie down. "I've been lying down all day. And for days and days." The last of a saline solution finally ran into Issan, so Michael unhooked the bag and flushed his line. Issan mumbled about another procedure Michael should do, but Dr. Mike, as we called him, had done all that was necessary, and ignored Issan's garbled, spacy conversation.

His speech is much worse now, probably partly from having what

Philip calls "a skinful of hop." Issan only hints at some words, and others you catch by inflection. At the same time his communication is very dense, pared down and potent.

I walked behind Issan, to rub his shoulders a little, and his head fell back onto my chest. Steve came back into the room, and after a bit Issan popped awake and said, "What's happening?" No one said anything, so Issan repeated his question, "What's happening?"

Finally I said, "Well I'm rubbing your shoulders."

"I know *that*," he snapped. "Tell me something I don't know." But he made little or no response to any of the attempts at conversation pitched at him. I came around in front of him and squatted down. "Does your shoulder feel any better?"

"No." He seemed to be getting more and more irritable. "My neck does though."

After a silence, he said, "I must be getting tired and cranky."

Steve came over. "Let's do the bedtime procedures, okay?" Issan nodded, then positioned Steve so he could best grab him. As Steve lifted him out of his chair, a terrible grimace came over Issan's face, and he groaned in pain. He stayed upright, though, and seemed determined to walk to the bathroom. He shuffled in inch-at-a-time steps, clutching at whatever he could for support—a shoulder, chair back, desk corner, doorknob. He took Steve's hand for a while, and mine for a few steps, but he seemed to want to do it on his own.

In the hall, I said, " 'Bye, Issan. I'll see you tomorrow." He stopped and turned toward me slowly, and by small degrees. He turned his whole body like a pole. We hugged and he whispered, "I'm sorry to act like such an old man, but I can't help it."

7 September 1990

Yesterday as he ushered me in, Michael J. said, "Tell him you're here. Go up and talk right in his ear."

Issan was resting on his bed, which I saw for the first time to be a hospital bed. The part that supports the head was tilted up, and Issan sat propped with his butt in the V of the bed. His head was lying to the right, and his eyes were closed. He breathed loudly and steadily through his mouth.

I announced myself into his ear and took his hand. He opened his eyes for a flash and squeezed my hand, and mumbled something through a parched-sounding throat. Steve was in the room, and Michael and Rick Levine sat on the bed with Issan. There was little to do but watch him breathe, hold his hand, or massage his feet.

Gradually more and more visitors filtered into the room. By 6:00 P.M.—an hour and a half after I arrived—fifteen or sixteen people stood and sat absolutely silently as the sound of Issan's gasping filled the air. This condition of attention persisted for a solid twenty-five minutes. Occasionally a blind would flap, a floorboard would squeak, or another person would come in the door. But other than that, the gathering felt like a period of meditation from nine years earlier, 1981, when this same crowd could be found each afternoon, dressed in black robes, in the Zen Center meditation hall for a silent forty minutes.

Eventually Issan had to pee. Steve and Rick deduced this from a series of grunts and half-formed words. "Just a second, Issan," Rick said, laughing. "You got company." Issan opened his eyes for a second and took in the scene, but he made no effort to engage anyone. We all cleared out. Half an hour later, the room began to fill again with visitors.

It went on like that all evening. At one point Rick cleared the room, not so that Issan could relieve himself but because it was time to remove the line from Issan's chest, for good. "Because he made me promise he would die without any lines in him, and I felt I should honor that now," said Rick. I stayed about five hours, alternating silent visits in Issan's room listening to him breathe, with talky times downstairs with old friends.

At 1:00 A.M. Rick Levine called to say that Issan had died just past midnight. Apparently he'd gone very peacefully. According to Steve Allen, he'd had one bad half-hour, from 11:30 to midnight. Steve said, "His breathing became very heavy, very intense, and he started kicking his legs and flailing about with his arms. I grabbed his arms, and held them, and held him. He was breathing very hard. It was very intense. It was like watching someone in labor—just like labor.

"Then somehow he pushed through it. It was a tremendous effort, you could see it. He made this intense grimace, he screwed up his face terribly. And then he got very calm.

"All during the heavy half-hour, there was a kind of peacefulness in his body, despite everything. But just about midnight, he got totally clam and peaceful. His breathing got very calm and smooth. Michael walked in then, and no more than twenty seconds later, Issan just stopped breathing."

Issan died then, at 12:05 A.M. on September 6, 1990. He was surrounded by friends—Steve had been literally in the bed with him for seven hours—and the other temple residents came into the room and practiced meditation immediately after he died.

Later Michael washed Issan with herbs and prepared his body for viewing. He cleaned Issan's room and the entire upstairs. When Melissa and I arrived early the next morning, Issan lay on his bed in a beautiful white linen kimono, over which he wore his brown *rakusu*. His head was wrapped in a white silk scarf; this was removed later in the day, so I assume it was there to help keep his mouth closed. He held beads in his hands; an orange scarf, tied in an elaborate knot, kept his feet side by side. His room was cool and peaceful, and it was easy to meditate there.

The Zen tradition is not to move the body, if possible, for three days, and to keep a constant environment of meditation in the room. A continuous stream of visitors began to arrive midmorning.

The earliest date that could be arranged with the Neptune Society for the cremation was Sunday, September 9, at 7:00 P.M. They agreed to send a driver to the house at 6:15. The Society had specified that no more than ten people could attend the cremation (they'd been talked up from four). With nine house residents and Kobun Chino-roshi performing the ceremony, it looked like a full house, but I went along anyway, thinking that the Neptune Society might not count too closely.

At 5:45 P.M. Steve conducted a service in Issan's room. We chanted the Heart Sutra, and the names of the lineage ancestors, and dedicated the merit to Issan's smooth passage and to the continuation of his work at Hartford Street. Each person offered a stick of incense.

When the ceremony was complete, the Neptune driver, a quiet, efficient young man, went to get a gurney from his truck. Since I was practically the only person not dressed in encumbering robes, I helped him. He showed me which levers to push to raise or lower the gurney, and how to collapse it altogether. We carried it upstairs, wheeled it next to Issan's bed, and raised it to match the height of the bed.

At this point, Kobun Chino walked into the room. He surveyed the proceedings and immediately started to chant the Heart Sutra again, in a deep, loud and oddly penetrating voice. Without saying a word, he took control of the situation: when there was work he could help do, he did it; when nothing more could be done, he continued to chant forcefully, and he rang the bells on the tatami mats in Issan's room. His chanting and ringing imparted a sense of sacredness to the rather gritty work of packing up Issan.

Three or four of us lifted Issan from his bed across to the gurney. I ended up with his legs. "People used to pay good money to see these legs," he'd told me once at Tassajara as he paraded around the bathhouse. Lifting him, my hand slipped under his kimono, onto his leg. It felt quite cold.

Steve removed Issan's *rakusu,* and then the man from Neptune covered his body with a plastic bag. Next we wrapped him in a white sheet and covered that with a red velvet drape of sorts. Chino-roshi helped with all this, chanting and chanting as he worked. The body was finally cinched to the gurney with two belts, one across the chest and one midthigh.

Since I had learned the gurney levers, I helped the Neptune man wheel Issan to the top of the stairs. Here we collapsed the gurney, so it became a low stretcher with wheels, and we bumped it down to the first floor, a stair at a time.

At the foot, we had to stand the gurney upright to negotiate the tight turn around the newel-post lamp. I was on the low end, and when the Neptune man lifted his end, I saw to my horror that Issan's head was flopping wildly forward. I caught the head and pushed it back, then grabbed the velvet and the sheet to hold it in place.

Soon the gurney was level again, at waist height. It was a simple matter to roll it out to the truck, load it in, and secure it with bungee cords. Kobun Chino continued to lead the chanting as we gathered around the truck, and he concluded it shortly after the tailgate went up. Kobun then went back inside and got salt, which he placed in mounds to the left and right of the front door and back door. He left specific instructions as to how the living room should be prepared to receive Issan's ashes, and what should be done in terms of cleaning Issan's room.

The driver drew maps of the crematorium's location for everyone and wrote directions down as well. We all drove in separate cars. Half an hour later we congregated on a dead-end street in a nameless industrial district of Emeryville. The Neptune Society turned out to be in the middle of a series of large warehouses, indistinguishable from one another. Other than the address, the building bore no markings.

Inside, it looked much like any other warehouse. To the left, pallets of precut and flattened cardboard boxes stood, stacked to the ceiling, a good thirty feet up. Just in front was an open space, bordered on the far wall by a four-by-eight-foot American flag pinned across it, with ten greasy-yellow chairs below. To the right, up a gently inclined ramp, two large ovens roared. They looked quite modern: a great variety of pipes and rods and cords ran to and from them, and computer monitors overhead read out a grid of mostly unintelligible figures. The floor on both levels was concrete.

When Kobun Chino arrived, he again took thorough control of the situation. We set up a makeshift altar according to his directions: on a big octagonal wooden table that seemed to be part of the Neptune Society's furniture, we set a Buddha statue, flowers, incense and a photograph of Issan. We put Issan's body just behind it. Chino-roshi disappeared for a moment, then reappeared wearing full priest robes, purple. He began to chant again, and the last ceremony was on.

The people from the Neptune Society left us alone. The ovens roared so loudly that I could barely hear anything. I couldn't hear my own chanting, but I could easily distinguish Kobun Chino's astonishing voice. With a glance, or a raised eyebrow, he directed events. At one point he positioned Steve directly in front of the shrine, while he went behind it and behind Issan's body. He uncovered Issan's head to the level of the sheet wrapping and had us turn the body 180 degrees. He and Steve then faced each other across the shrine and Issan's body. Steve followed Chino-roshi's lead as he described several huge circles in the darkening air with a fistful of incense sticks. They looked like mystic railroad signalmen conducting a funeral in hell.

Finally we wheeled the body up the ramp, past the glassed-in shabby office, past the controls and monitors, back around to the oven opening. Chino-roshi passed around incense sticks until each person had one; the shrine flower arrangement was cannibalized till everyone had a flower too. The man from Neptune cranked the gurney up to the proper height and opened the oven door. Inside, it looked like a shelf in a pizza oven. The oven roar increased, and so did our chanting. We threw our flowers on Issan's shroud. When Steve got to the control buttons, the Neptune man quickly pushed the gurney forward. It slammed into the oven, and Issan's body rolled straight in, headfirst. We all hurled our incense sticks in after him, and just before the man closed the door, Issan's body burst into white-yellow flames. Some people were crying and Kobun Chino walked over to embrace one resident who, though not crying, was shaking rather violently. He herded the group back down to the makeshift shrine and concluded the ceremony. On the way past the oven controls, I noticed the temperature was at 714 degrees and climbing.

Steve and Michael had planned to wait for the ashes, but Chino-roshi insisted that since we had all come together, we should all also leave. They could come back a couple of hours later.

After two hours, Steve and Michael did return. Steve said the flames had consumed most of the body by then, but the oven man opened the door so they could look in. Steve could see only the bones of the pelvis and the spine intact; most everything else had gone. "I guess in the area of the organs"—here Steve motioned to his own guts— "and in the heart area, things were still burning. Because when I looked in, I could see those bones, but in the area of the organs and the heart, two distinct flames were shooting up. They were beautiful. White columns of flame." Steve drew his hand away from his own body, as if he were pulling flames from it.

"The guy reached in there with a kind of rake and started to pull the bones toward us. They disintegrated some as they rolled. He got them to this one part of the oven, then pulled a lever and they rolled down a chute into a tray, which was kind of a tumbler. He tumbled them there a little while to break them down further. Usually, I guess, they tumble them a long time to break them up completely, but we'd told him we didn't want that. For the ceremony later, we need to have a few distinct pieces of bone." Steve indicated an area the size of a thumbnail. "He dropped them into another section and put a fan on them to cool them, then gave them to us in a box.

"They were so white. I picked one up and touched it to my forehead. Then another and another. I couldn't help it; I was just grabbing them and pressing them to my forehead.

"Then he raked up all the ashes and dropped them through the chute, and gave them to us. There they were, right there in a box."

The funeral was held at the San Francisco Zen Center (to accommodate the huge crowd) on Sunday, September 16, 1990. It was, as had been widely expected, an extravagant affair. The Hartford Street crew had worked for several days to prepare food for the reception, and before the ceremony the dining room looked like a cornucopia, with rounds of cheeses, loaves of bread, platters of fruit, hors d'oeuvres, cakes, cookies, spreads, juices, waters, and teas, all bordered with flowers and flowering herbs.

The red front hall had been lined with photographs of Issan, from his earliest Zen Center days up to the day before his death. The Buddha Hall itself had been set up with an unusual orientation, not facing the main shrine but facing a bare wooden table near the center of the east wall, upon which a memorial for Issan would be assembled during the ceremony. The forty tatami mats on the Buddha Hall floor had been covered with black cotton mats.

Just back from the bare table, and facing it, sat three ceremonial chairs, the center one higher than the other two. At right angles to these chairs and close to the table was a fourth ceremonial seat—one Suzuki-roshi had used when he was alive. Finally, between the table and the wall sat one last chair, a very plain one, facing back across the table to the three ceremonial seats. It was not at all clear who would sit where, since there were a number of high-ranking Zen people around. What *was* clear, and what piqued the interest of many in the audience, was that Richard Baker-roshi would be leading the ceremony, in his first visit back to Zen Center since he had been ejected seven years earlier.

When the ceremony began, a crowd thronged the Buddha Hall and spilled out into the front hall and courtyard. By conservative estimates, between three hundred and four hundred people were on hand. The procession of ceremonial principals was also outsize. Instead of the usual four or five people, the rare eight, or the extraordinary twelve, this parade ran to twenty people. Some carried the ritual musical instruments: conch, bells, cymbals, clackers, drum; others carried Issan's Buddhist trappings—monk's robes, bowls, whisk, lineage papers; still others in the procession brought in personal effects. Steve Allen brought in Issan himself, ashes in a silk-wrapped box.

The ungainly procession snaked its way through the crowd, up to the ceremonial table. Here, under Chino-roshi's direction, the objects were arranged on the shrine. The effect of the completed shrine had a mind-stopping effect on most viewers. Among the implements of Issan's Zen life stood two large pictures of him—one from the ceremony a few days before his death, in which he was smiling, bald, and fading—and one from his years as a drag queen, dancing in a long gown and high heels and holding a champagne glass. The shot had been taken as he was in a demicrouch, with fingers extended and eyelids batting. It was utterly glamorous. The idea of the shrine seemed to be to bring present the deceased as much as possible with pictures, writings, and objects; there were a lot of facets of Issan's life to include.

Once everything had been arranged, the ceremony began. Baker-roshi took the central seat. He wore brilliant red satin robes, lined in white satin, and on top of them a gold-thread, brocade priest robe that had belonged to Suzuki-roshi. He also wore a tall cowl of the same brocade. He was flanked by the current Zen Center abbots, Mel Weitsman on his left and Reb Anderson on his right. Chino-roshi took the chair angled to the other three; from there, he substantially directed the proceedings. Steve Allen took the plain chair behind the shrine.

Each of the three principals made an opening statement. These were spoken directly to Issan and were framed in terms of gratitude, appreciation, and outright love. Mel used a startling Zen shout; Reb's remarks sounded like a classic Zen poem, terse and strong. Baker-roshi, by contrast, spoke very gently and sweetly, telling Issan how much he—Baker—had learned from him and how hard it was to believe he was dead. Baker seemed completely without pretense and very vulnerable, weeping through much of the ceremony.

Steve Allen came around front to face the Issan shrine and made his statement. Philip Whalen struggled to his sleeping feet and dragged them across the tatami to read his poems to Issan. After these praises, the traditional memorial offerings—sweet water, food, and sweet tea—were made. The attendants somehow found room on the table for stylized lacquer offering trays, and then Chino-roshi led the principals in a mysterious Japanese chant only they seemed to know; certainly it wasn't on the printed handout sheet.

Kobun Chino's voice mesmerized listeners. A slight man, he speaks in a nearly inaudibly soft voice, but when he chants, he seems to draw on a reserve of air and a resonating capacity of something the size of a bull.

Next Baker-roshi announced that a few people had asked to make statements and that they were now welcome to do so, as was anyone else who wished to address Issan. This is the section of the ceremony that determines whether the participants will be drinking tea in three-quarters of an hour, or in three hours.

The stories and tributes began. They were touching, of course, and funny, some of them, and passionate. Issan was not only admired and appreciated—he was genuinely adored. Themes appeared: Issan had been the first Zen Center person to greet many in the audience, or the first one to make them feel welcome, or the first one to smile at them. Stories were told of his skill in relating to social outcasts and misfits as they banged on the Zen Center doors—told often by the misfits themselves. James came to the funeral scruffy and unkempt and made a pathetic speech to the effect that he had been a special person to Issan and that he hoped now to find a place of acceptance in the Zen community. Mickey read a funny rhyming poem he'd written. A well-known street prophet named Cosmic Lady also spoke in inspired spontaneous verse.

Mrs. Suzuki, weeping and talking in a guttural Japanese (later translated by Kaz Tanahashi) urged Issan to say hello to Suzuki-roshi when he got to the Pure Land.

Finally, Baker-roshi concluded with a poignant eulogy. He said Issan had understood Suzuki-roshi's way more than anyone else. In the Zen Buddhist world, Japanese or American, no higher compliment could be paid.

The ceremony ended with several long group chants, during which time members of the procession and specified dignitaries approached the shrine and offered powdered incense. The procession left as it had come, with musical accompaniment.

Upstairs, Baker-roshi and Chino-roshi embraced warmly. Then Baker shook hands with Mel and Reb. Given the tensions and animosities that plagued these men the previous several years, these handshakes—warm and sincere—were landmarks. Credit for them goes to Issan.

"Something touches me in what we've been talking about, which is compassion, life and death, joy and sorrow, good and bad. These themes are in a poem by a man I like very much, and I just happen to know that that poem is right here in this book. Shall I read it? It's by Thich Nhat Hanh:

Please Call Me By My True Names

*Do not say that I will be gone tomorrow, for even now
    I still return
Look deeply.
I arrive in each fresh moment
to be the bud on a tender spring branch
to be the fledgling wings
still soft and fragile
joyfully chirping in my new nest
to be the green caterpillar on the rose's stem
to be the hidden jewel, ripening within a stone
I still arrive so I can laugh and cry
so I can fear and hope
My birth and death breathes
in rhythm to the heartbeats of all that are alive
I am the mayfly, metamorphosing on the water's surface
I am the bird who arrives with spring in time to catch the
    mayfly.
I am the frog singing happily in the clear autumn pond
And I am the grass snake, drawing near in silence
to feed upon the frog
I am the child in Uganda, all skin and bones
my legs as thin as bamboo sticks
and I am the arms merchant, selling deadly weapons to Uganda
I am the 12-year-old girl, refugee on a small boat
who throws herself into the ocean after being raped by
    a sea pirate
and I am the pirate
my heart not yet capable of seeing and loving
I am a member of the Politburo, with plenty of power
    in my hands*

and I am the man who must pay his debt of blood
to my people, dying slowly in a forced labor camp
My joy opens like spring
Its glow makes flowers bloom in all walks of life
Tears stream out from my eyes
enough to fill the four great oceans.
Please call me by my true names
so I can hear all my laughs and cries at once
so I can see my joy and pain are one
Please call me by my true names
so that I can wake up
and the door of my heart can be left open
the door of compassion

Postscript

A portion of Issan's ashes lie in the back garden of the Hartford Street Zen Center, beneath a large granite boulder. The rock—syrupy-looking with streaks of white, black, and gray—was dragged from Tassajara Creek, trucked up one hundred miles to San Francisco, and winched and wrestled into place. Issan's disciple Steve Allen chose it as a marker on an expedition to Tassajara with others of Issan's close Zen friends. During that trip, a second portion of Issan's ashes were scattered ceremonially from the Hogback, a hillside at Tassajara. Suzuki-roshi's ashes and those of some of his oldest students also lie buried on the Hogback. A third and final portion of Issan's ashes rests with his family in Southern California. These arrangements were all in accordance with Issan's wishes.

Issan's teacher, Zentatsu Richard Baker-roshi, teaches at the Crestone Mountain Zen Center in Colorado. He spends nearly half of every year in Europe, leading *sesshins* at various locations of the Dharmasangha, the organizational name for his students in Europe. His book, *Original Mind: The Practice of Zen in the West,* is to be published by William Morrow in 1994.

Kijun Steve Allen practiced as abbot of Issan-ji, Hartford Street Zen Center, for a year and a week. He then passed the abbotship to Zenshin Philip Whalen and went to Crestone to continue his Zen studies with Baker-roshi. Zenshin Philip Whalen currently presides as abbot.

Issan-ji, the Hartford Street Zen Center, and the Maitri Hospice both continue, as they always have, by the skins of their economic teeth. Letters of interest, inquiry, and support are always welcome and can be addressed to: 57 Hartford Street, San Francisco CA 94114.